CAUSAL MODELS IN PANEL AND EXPERIMENTAL DESIGNS

List of Contributors

Paul D. Allison

Duane F. Alwin

H. M. Blalock, Jr.

Cal Clark

Herbert L. Costner

David F. Greenberg

Lowell L. Hargens

David R. Heise

Karl G. Jöreskog

Ronald C. Kessler

Melvin L. Kohn

Robert L. Linn

J. Miller McPherson

Alden Dykstra Miller

Barbara F. Reskin

Carmi Schooler

Richard D. Shingles

Richard C. Tessler

Susan Welch

Charles E. Werts

David E. Wiley

James A. Wiley

CAUSAL MODELS IN PANEL AND EXPERIMENTAL DESIGNS

Edited by

H. M. Blalock, Jr.

ALDINE
Publishing Company
New York

About the Editor

H. M. Blalock, Jr., is Professor, Department of Sociology, University of Washington, Seattle. Dr. Blalock has authored and/or edited eighteen books and has been a major contributor to numerous academic and professional journals. He was recipient of the 1973 ASA Samuel Stouffer Prize and is a fellow of the American Statistical Association, American Academy of Arts and Sciences, and a member of the National Academy of Sciences. He is Past-President of the American Sociological Association.

Aldine Publishing Company
200 Saw Mill River Road
Hawthorne, New York 10532

Library of Congress Cataloging in Publication Data

Main entry under title:
Causal models in panel and experimental designs

    Bibliography: p.
    Includes index.
    1. Sociology—Methodology—Addresses, essays, lectures. 2. Panel analysis—Addresses, essays, lectures.
3. Sociology—Mathematical models—Addresses, essays, lectures. I. Blalock, Hubert M. II. Title.
HM24.C32   1985   301′.01′8   84-24276
ISBN 0-202-30315-2
ISBN 0-202-30316-0 (pbk.)

Printed in the United States of America
10 9 8 7 6 5 4 3 2 1

Contents

Preface

This book represents a companion volume to the revised edition of *Causal Models in the Social Sciences,* which was originally published in 1971. In thinking about the revision of that volume, I recognized that considerable literature has accumulated in the 13-year interval since this volume was published making it impossible to deal amply with the subject in a single volume. As I examined articles that seemed to hold the most promise of expanding the variety of topics in research methods to the causal modeling approach, I began to see that a substantial number involved design issues. The majority of these fell rather naturally under the heading of panel designs involving repeated measurements; a smaller cluster involved discussions of how our understanding of experimental designs could be improved by paying explicit attention to causal models.

This suggested two major headings under which to group the chapters of the book. I decided to present the five chapters bearing on experimental designs into Part I because the issues with which they deal are somewhat more general than those that deal more specifically with the handling of change data. Although many readers may have more immediate interest in these latter papers, which appear in Part II, it seemed wise to encourage such readers to examine some of these broader issues before plunging specifically into discussions of panel designs.

All of the papers in the volume are concerned with complications that may occur in actual research designs, as contrasted with idealized ones that sometimes become the basis for textbook discussions of design issues. Extraneous factors have a way of intruding into all social research and, of course, measurement errors abound. The trick then is to find ways of modeling these complications in such a fashion that problems do not become intractable because of too many unknown parameters, and yet are sufficiently realistic to provide reasonable approximations to what is actually occurring. Perhaps equally important, by paying explicit attention to such complications and by noting their implications, one becomes sensitized to just how important it is to plan one's research design so as to reduce these complications to a bare minimum. The lesson, here, is that attention given to possible design complications *before* a study is actually conducted is likely to have considerable payoff in terms of reduced ambiguities when one approaches the analysis stage of the research. Often it is extremely difficult to compensate during one's analysis for a poorly conceived design that has failed to permit one to assess the possible distortions produced by factors that have been neglected.

I am indebted to my colleague Herbert L. Costner who, like myself, has been very much concerned about the quality of social research and how we can formulate general principles and strategies that are applicable across a wide variety of disciplines and research designs.

H. M. Blalock, Jr.

I

THE USE OF CAUSAL MODELS IN EXPERIMENTAL AND NONEXPERIMENTAL DESIGNS

Most discussions of causal modeling, or of structural-equation systems, focus primarily either on data analysis or on the theory-construction and theory-testing processes. Questions of research *design* are presumed to have been previously resolved or to be merely tangential to these processes. This seems to suggest, then, that matters relating to one's design can be set aside, or that these design-related issues are primarily matters of relative efficiency with respect to time and cost considerations. A sample or population is merely "given" or determined by questions of convenience and relative cost.

All five Chapters in Part I, as well as the later papers in Part II that deal with longitudinal designs, take design features as being of central importance to one's ultimate causal interpretations of empirical findings. The general thrust of all of them is that it is of considerable importance to construct causal models that relate directly to design features as, for example, the relationships between one's actual manipulations in an experimental setup and the usually unmeasured "independent" variables that these manipulations are intended to affect. This, then, makes it possible to make much more definitive statements about what can go wrong in such experiments, and where the "slippage" takes place and with what consequences. The major thesis, then, is that matters of design are far too important to be relegated to considerations of cost and efficiency. Too many things can go wrong, and we must have systematic ways of pinpointing the implications of each design decision we make.

We are all familiar with idealized experimental designs, exemplified by the full factorial design in which factors or treatments are independently manipulated, and where randomization supposedly assures independence between disturbance terms and all the treatment variables. One then conducts an analysis of variance that makes it possible to separate the "main effects" from each other and from the "interaction effects" and to make a series of F tests for the statistical significance of each of these distinct effects. How simple it all seems!

In the social sciences we are also aware of extensive discussions of what can go wrong in the case of real-life experiments with human subjects. It is often impractical or impossible to randomize subjects to treatments, so that self-selection is likely to occur. We commonly assume that such self-selection only occurs *before* the treatment takes place, or at least that the time that the treatment is administered can be pinned down, so that we can separate out those subjects who entered or exited each treatment group at different times. But what if the treatment is an ongoing one, with subjects entering and exiting at times that cannot be precisely related to the time of treatment? And suppose we can only guess as to the reasons they have moved in or out. What then?

Even when these temporal processes can be specified, numerous uncontrolled events are likely to creep into the picture and become confounded

3

with the manipulations.* Such uncontrolled events, and their interactions, will often be confounded with both main effects and interactions among the manipulated variables. In order to handle such problems one needs to formulate *explicit* models that incorporate these complications in such a way that the implications are specifically spelled out so as to guide not only one's choice of design but also the way that the data are analyzed and interpreted. Often the temptation is to combine a verbal discussion of what can go wrong — and the safeguards that have actually been taken — with a far-too-straightforward data analysis in which these very same defects are conveniently ignored.

Traditional analysis of variance designs and data analyses typically pre-suppose no measurement errors, except possibly for strictly random errors in the dependent variables. Treatment variables are assumed to be error free. Furthermore, there is presumed to be no conceptual slippage between one's manipulations or treatments, on the one hand, and the conceptual variables or the labels that become attached to these manipulations, on the other. In practice, of course, any experimental manipulation of human subjects must inevitably be more complex than desired, with the result that it will be multidimensional even where the investigator chooses to represent it by means of a simple label. Thus, although one may speak as though "frustration level," "ambiguity," or "motivational arousal" have been manipulated, a good deal else may have been manipulated in the bargain. This fact is well known and indeed has resulted in numerous discussions of experimenter bias, "demand characteristics," and the like. However, actual data analyses usually do not allow explicitly for such complications. How can causal modeling approaches assist in this regard?

The tack taken in Part I — and particularly in Chapters 2, 3, and 4 by Blalock, Costner, and Alwin and Tessler, respectively — is to attempt to construct simple prototype causal models that explicitly allow for such complications. To do so requires one to distinguish between the manipula-tions themselves, which may be multidimensional, and the unmeasured conceptual variables that are usually of theoretical interest. One then admits to complications of several sorts, including the possibility that the manipu-lations have effects on the dependent variables that may be considered "direct" or that involve additional theoretical variables that intervene be-tween the manipulation and response, but that may have been neglected by the experimenter. It is also possible, of course, that the manipulated vari-ables, or "treatments," do *not* "take" in the sense that they do not really affect the unmeasured variable that is presumed to cause the response, though it is possible that they may be correlated with other *indicators* of this

---

* See Chap. 9 John Ross and Perry Smith, "Orthodox Experimental Designs," *Methodology in Social Research*, edited by H. M. Blalock and A. B. Blalock. New York: McGraw-Hill, 1968.

unmeasured variable. Or the treatment may not affect the "true" dependent variable but may merely affect one or more of its indicators by some mechanism that bypasses this true dependent variable.

Although the permutations and combinations seem almost endless, it is possible to specify prototype models that may serve as reasonably close approximations to what actually occurs in carefully conducted experiments that still contain relatively small numbers of flaws. The question then becomes that of whether or not such flaws could be detected by means of empirical tests. Given that true values will generally be unknown, it will, of course, be impossible to obtain direct estimates of coefficients that interrelate these unmeasured variables. As discussed in Chapters 2, 3, and 4, however, the multiple-indicator approach may be used, provided that there are not too many unknowns relative to the number of pieces of empirical information. Where the system is overidentified, consistency checks can be made to test the adequacy of the model. Where the assumptions necessary for maximum-likelihood estimation can be justified, one may also make a series of significance tests using LISREL procedures, as well as obtaining estimates of parameters of interest.

As indicated in Chapter 5, which concludes this section, comparable difficulties occur in connection with design issues in nonexperimental research. When one adopts a stratified sampling design, for example, it is implicitly assumed that the listing criteria used in the stratification process involve independent variables such as sex, race, age, or occupation. But what if one stratifies by a *dependent* variable or one that falls somewhere intermediate between the independent and ultimate dependent variables in a recursive system? Just because a list is readily available, or a research design is "efficient" in terms of cost savings, does not necessarily mean that one has not violated important assumptions required by recursive modeling. As noted in Chapter 5, a similar design complication may arise in cross-level analyses in which an aggregating criterion (such as spatial location) appears as a dependent or intervening variable in a recursive setup.

Even though the explicitly used stratifying variables (such as sex or race) may be regarded as stimuli that are analogous to one's manipulations in an experimental design, it does not also follow that these stimuli are simple. Is one talking about a "sex" or "race" effect, or a series of unmeasured experiences that more directly impact upon the dependent variables of interest? If the latter, the causal interrelationships are likely to be both complex and indeterminate. Certain relatively simple prototype models may be useful, nevertheless, in helping one assess the implications of complications of different types. Merely ignoring these complications may be convenient and necessary to preserve one's sense of scientific sanity, but it does not thereby lead one to correct inferences or interpretations.

Part I begins with a chapter by Miller that provides a useful conceptual introduction to the entire volume, forming a bridge between the chapters contained in *Causal Models in the Social Sciences* and those in the present companion volume by showing the relationship between the logic of experimental designs and the strategy of working with reduced forms in a two-stage least-squares analysis. What this and the other chapters in Part I highlight is the important point that the essential features of causal analyses based on experimental and nonexperimental research are identical, although the former may permit one to justify a somewhat simpler set of *a priori* assumptions.

1

Logic of Causal Analysis: From Experimental to Nonexperimental Designs*

Alden Dykstra Miller

In recent years, sociologists have more and more frequently felt compelled to make causal inferences in the course of their research. Unfortunately, the discipline as a whole has not had access to a methodology that would permit such inferences in the general case where there is reciprocal causation and where unmeasured confounding influences abound. Appropriate methods have been known to exist but have seemed to be mysteriously shrouded, available only to those on the frontiers of statistical science. Yet, actually, the necessary analytical apparatus has been available in other disciplines and taught at the advanced undergraduate and beginning graduate levels. The logic can be grasped without extensive training in mathematics or statistics by advanced undergraduate majors in sociology.

It is our purpose here to present a part of this logic[1] in nontechnical terms, assuming only an elementary understanding of what a multiple regression equation is. For convenience, we will begin with an experimental design and describe the logic involved in terms of two-stage least squares, sometimes

---

* Chapter originally published in *Causal Models in the Social Sciences,* 1971.

[1] The identification problem, the problem of showing that it is possible to estimate the coefficients of a model, is discussed quite fully in Fisher (1966) and more simply in Christ (1966: 298–346); Goldberger (1964: 306–318), and Johnston (1963: 240–252).

called generalized classical linear estimation. This particular estimator, or technique for solving for causal effects, is one technique from one major class of techniques that might be used. It may be thought of as differing from other techniques in that major class only in the way in which it responds to sampling error and errors in assumptions (see Fisher, 1966, pp. 52–56; Christ, 1966, pp. 347–494; Johnston, 1963, pp. 231–274; Goldberger, 1964, pp. 288–380; Malinvaud, 1966, pp. 497–613; Wold, 1964, pp. 25–33). The logic will then be extended from experimental to nonexperimental designs. The object of our discussion may be understood as a generally understandable and applicable approach for putting existing theory into interaction with data in order to extend theory.

AN EXPERIMENT CONCERNING A SINGLE MEASURED CAUSE OF PREJUDICE

Consider an imaginary experiment with a heavy debt to Miller and Bugelski (1948). It would be an attempt to discover the effect of frustration on prejudice, if any, and would thus constitute a test of one application of frustration–aggression theory. Subjects are subjected to experiences intended to produce frustration, which in turn is expected to produce prejudice. We might, following Miller and Bugelski, have subjects take an impossibly difficult test and miss bank night at the weekly movie, if we thought such experiences would be appropriately frustrating. We could measure frustration in a questionnaire or interview by tapping the degree to which such goals as maintaining a positive self-image and getting to the movie were experienced as important and blocked. We could measure prejudice by tapping negative attitudes and stereotypes toward minority groups.

How might we proceed? It is usual in an experiment to have an experimental group and a control group, with subjects randomly assigned into one or the other. The two groups are then made to differ on the presumed causal or independent variable and tested to see whether they differ on the caused or dependent variable. We would make the two groups differ in frustration and assess the difference that resulted in prejudice. Sometimes this basic design is elaborated to include measurements on the dependent variable both before and after the experimental and control groups are made to differ on the independent variable. Then we could conceptualize the making of the two groups to differ on the independent variable as a change in the independent variable, a change that occurs systematically only in the experimental group, and conceptualize the effect for which we are looking as a change in the dependent variable, where we are checking to see whether the experimental group changed in a manner different from the manner in which the control group might have changed.

We would have the subjects in our experimental group take the test and miss bank night, while the subjects in the control group would be exempted from such treatment. After checking to see that we had actually produced more frustration in the experimental group than in the control group, we would ascertain the effect of frustration on prejudice, either by simply noting the difference between the experimental and control groups in final prejudice level or by noting any systematic change in prejudice level in the experimental group, where that change was different from any change that took place in the control group.

What is the core idea in the design of such an experiment? What makes it convincing as a test of a causal proposition? It is not the fact of manipulation per se. Consider a rather informal version of the experiment we are describing, where the experimenter relies on the idea of manipulation to make his case. He frustrates whom he chooses and observes that they are prejudiced more than other people. He finds himself open to attack as a second Chanticleer on the ground that he might have chosen to frustrate those who have characteristics that would lead them to be prejudiced anyway or on the ground that he might have tended to frustrate people who were already prejudiced.

Instead of the fact of manipulation per se, a major part of the key is randomization, the random assignment to experimental and control groups. Then the manipulation coupled with this assignment becomes simply another variable that causes frustration, one which, because of its random character (subjects having been assigned randomly to categories differentially subjected to manipulation), can be assumed to be unrelated, except for chance, to alternative causes of prejudice besides frustration. The fact of control, manipulation of the subjects by the experimenter, accomplishes only one thing: It makes it fairly easy to locate or, rather, create a cause of frustration that is not related to other causes of prejudice.

It is also very important for the experimenter to be able to convince those who read his report that the manipulation could not have caused prejudice directly, thus competing with frustration as a possible cause of prejudice, but there is nothing built into the procedure of the experiment to guarantee that.

The experimenter makes use of this notion of random control, together with a bald assumption to the effect that the manipulation does not cause prejudice directly, in the following argument:

> If the manipulation, a cause of frustration, was unrelated to any unmeasured causes of prejudice and did not cause prejudice directly, it could be related to prejudice only by way of a causal link between frustration and prejudice. Therefore, if the experimental and control groups differed on prejudice or on change in prejudice, it must have been because of differences in frustration, or changes in frustration.

Suppose we designate level of frustration as X, level of prejudice as Y, and the presence or absence of experiences intended by the experimenter to be frustrating as Z. Alternatively, we could designate *change* in frustration as X, *change* in prejudice as Y, and *change* in the presence or absence of experiences intended to be frustrating as Z. In either case, if: (1) Z, a cause of X, does not cause Y except through X, and (2) Z is unrelated to any unmeasured causes of Y that do not operate solely through X, then any empirical association between Z and Y must be due to the effects of X on Y, since X is the only possible link between Z and Y (see Fig. 1.1). The argument would hold regardless of what other causes of prejudice there might be and regardless of what other causes of frustration there might be, including prejudice itself. *The two assumptions stated above, not the fact of manipulation per se, are the core of the experimental logic.*

We could, following out this argument a little further, assess the exact nature of the effect of frustration, X, on prejudice, Y, by computing the regression coefficient of Y on expected values of X given Z, the manipulation, using ordinary least squares. Let us see first exactly how this would be done and then look to the logic of its validity as a way to assess degree of causal effect.

First, we need the expected values of X, given Z. We regress X on Z by ordinary least squares and end up with the regression equation:

$$X = a + bZ$$

This is the first stage of two-stage least squares. For each case, we take this equation and the value of Z associated with the case and calculate the predicted (expected) value of X. Denoting the predicted value of X as $\hat{X}$, we then regress Y on $\hat{X}$ using ordinary least squares and end up with a regression equation:

$$Y = c + d\hat{X}$$

which is the second stage of two-stage least squares. The regression coefficient d represents the effect of X on Y, the increase in Y because of a unit increase in X.

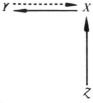

Figure 1.1. Causal relation of interest (⟶); possible causal relation not of interest (----→). Unmeasured variables omitted for simplicity.

Why would such a procedure give us the causal effect of X on Y? What is the sense in the procedure? The main problem in causal inference from the association of two variables is the possibility that at the same time the independent variable, X, is high, some unmeasured, possibly unthought of, cause of Y is also high, so that we mistakenly impute the effect of the unmeasured cause to X. Thus, if X is frustration, Y is prejudice, and an unmeasured cause of prejudice is the norms one has been taught with respect to intergroup relations, we would be in difficulty if it turned out that those who were very frustrated were also frequently people who had learned norms of intergroup relations in childhood that, quite aside from any connection with frustration, made prejudice a matter of course. Such norms might be part of a social structure that created severe frustration. People who were high on frustration might then be high on prejudice just because they had been taught to be prejudiced, not because they were frustrated. The solution, obviously, is to create analytically a situation where the value a person has on the independent variable, frustration, is unrelated to the values he may have on other, unmeasured causes of the dependent variable, such as norms. What we do in the laboratory is simply to determine each subject's value of Z by chance, in the randomization process, so that except for chance it will *not* be related to the offending unmeasured causes of Y. We also assume, without proof, that Z does not itself directly affect Y. We then use Z, the manipulation, to isolate a certain part of the variation in X, frustration, that we are sure is unrelated to unmeasured causes of Y, prejudice. We can do this by predicting X from Z and using the predicted values of X as variation in X not related to unmeasured causes of Y, as above. If Z is unrelated to unmeasured causes of Y, then the predicted values of X must be also, since the predicted values of X are an exact linear function of the values of Z.

In effect, we simply translate Z into X units. We have these experiences, failing an impossible test and missing a movie, that we think may cause prejudice, but only by way of causing frustration, which in turn causes prejudice. Our procedure is to express these experiences, to measure them if you will, in terms of units of frustration produced by them. To ascertain the effect of frustration, X, on prejudice, Y, we ask what effect an experience producing X units of frustration has on prejudice. In the laboratory, we might interpret this as meaning that we try to predict prejudice from that variation in frustration that *we* produced *in a random pattern* so as to be unrelated to other causes of prejudice, such as learned norms of intergroup relations. We exclude from consideration all other variation in frustration on the ground that it just might be related to some other causes of prejudice, such as learned norms of intergroup relations.

Note particularly that we do not have to assume that X, frustration, was not caused by Y. We use only variation in X that was ultimately caused by Z. The remaining variation in X, variation that we do not use, might have been caused by anything, including Y. Actually, the variation in X that we do use, that predicted by Z, may be partially caused by Y also. But the variation in Y that would have caused it would be variation in Y that had been caused in the first place by variation in X produced by Z. It would thus be variation ultimately caused by Z. It would not be variation in Y produced by the unmeasured causes of Y. The critical point is that the variation in X, on which we regress Y, not be confounded with variation in unmeasured causes of Y. The fact that it might have been produced in part by Y is not itself important. Y had to be caused by something, and if the variation we use in X is unrelated to other causes of Y, then our prediction of Y from that variation is representative of a causal relationship, the effect of X on Y. Note carefully that if X did not cause Y, we could not predict Y from variation in X *that was unrelated to unmeasured causes of Y.*[2] The regression coefficient of Y on such variation in X would equal zero.

Neither do we have to assume that the manipulation of Z, in our experiment the subjection to experience intended to be frustrating, completely determined the value of X in each and every subject. We simply estimate by regression what effect it did have and use the variation in X corresponding to that effect. We do not have to throw out cases that did not respond to Z exactly as we expected them to, as is sometimes done in experimental work. In fact, we would want to avoid throwing out cases as such a procedure would, as is well known, destroy the randomness of the allocation to experimental and control groups and might result in Z, which is, in effect, the distinction between the experimental group and the control group, being related to unmeasured causes of Y.

We do have to assume that Z is not caused by either X or Y. If we did not, we would necessarily violate the assumption already made that Z is unre-

---

[2] An alternative but related line of argument is to note that algebraically it can be shown that the slope of Y on $\hat{X}$ is the same as the slope of $\hat{Y}$ on $\hat{X}$, where both slopes are least-squares coefficients and $\hat{Y}$ is the expected value of Y given Z. Since $\hat{Y}$ is completely determined by $\hat{X}$, we make use of the fact that a relation without error may be estimated consistently, regardless of the presence or absence of feedback, by least squares, provided that there is not a singular matrix of regressors involved (Fisher, 1966: 87–88). The more technically inclined reader, incidentally, may enjoy applying this principle (of identification and consistent estimation by least squares of determinate relations where the regressors are not confounded) to nonstochastic versions of the models discussed in this chapter. He will find that a number of them actually depend on the presence of errors for identification. Practically, sociologists do no seem to be on the verge of trouble stemming from that fact except in a few areas such as status inconsistency or mobility research where definitional relationships are involved, since most sociological relations do involve error. Of course, it is also true that some models that are not identified when they have error are identified when they do not. Nonstochastic models are not discussed in this chapter because of the rarity of their occurrence in current sociological research. They can be dealt with, however, in terms of the framework discussed in this chapter.

lated to the unmeasured causes of Y. If Y caused Z, then the influence of the unmeasured causes of Y would be fed right into Z. If X caused Z and had been caused by Y or was related to unmeasured causes of Y, then the influence of the unmeasured causes of Y would again be fed right into Z. Thus, the assumption that Z is not caused by X or Y flows by necessity from the assumption that Z is not related to the unmeasured causes of Y.[3]

Let us look more closely at how we might go about making all these assumptions plausible in an experiment. The assumption that Z is unrelated to the unmeasured causes of Y is assured except for chance by randomizing values on Z. Frequently, that means nothing more than random allocation of subjects to experimental and control groups, as in our present, imaginary experiment. The other major assumption, that Z does not affect Y except through X, that is that the experiences do not cause prejudice except by producing frustration, is a completely unsupported assumption in the model as it stands, with one Z. It is one that the experimenter must assert as a given. Whether his colleagues believe him depends on the plausibility of a bald assertion, possibly supported in some way by previous research, which in turn was based on other, similar, bald assertions.

The assertion that Y is not directly caused by Z must stand unaided *unless* the researcher elects to use more than one Z (see Fig. 1.2) and make certain tests for the consistency of the several sets of resulting assumptions, one with another. We have, following Miller and Bugelski, said we would subject those of our subjects in the experimental group to the experience of failing an impossible test and missing bank night at the local movie. Unfor-

---

[3] We might point out that when significance is assessed with an F test in experimental design, the explained and unexplained variances are frequently derived from the regression of Y on Z, where Z is the distinction between the control group and the experimental group. A more powerful test, taking advantage of more variance in X, might be constructed, and usually is in econometrics, by computing the variance of the predicted values in Y where the prediction is from the observed values of X, using the regression coefficient obtained in two-stage least squares or a similar estimator. The variance of those predicted values is the variance in Y explained by X. The variance of the residuals from those predicted values is the variance in Y unexplained by X. These two variances are used in constructing an F test or t test (Christ, 1966: 503–520). It should be noted that should these variances be used to compute a measure of association, such a measure would be like a Beta weight rather than like a correlation coefficient, in that it could take values beyond the bounds of $+1$ and -1, since the unexplained variance, reflecting the effects of unmeasured causes of Y, is not assumed to be unrelated to X but only to the Z's. The measure would be the square root of the ratio of the explained variance to the total observed variance. The total observed variance is not equal to the simple sum of the explained and unexplained variances but rather to that sum plus twice the geometric mean of the variances times the correlation between them. The quantity is most easily obtained by simply computing the variance of Y. Note, also, that as long as *linear effects only* are estimated, the term *uncorrelated* would be sufficient in place of the term *unrelated* in the above discussion and throughout this chapter.

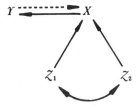

Figure 1.2. Curved arrow, possible correlation resulting from unspecified causal mechanisms.

tunately, if these two supposedly frustrating experiences always occur together, they are for all practical purposes a single experience. If the two experiences are introduced in such a manner as to be distinguishable, however, *some* subjects failing the impossible test not missing the movie and *some* subjects missing the movie not failing the test, then a partial test of the assumptions that the Z's did not affect Y directly and were unrelated to unmeasured causes of Y would be possible. The steps of the procedure can be stated:

1. Solve by ordinary least squares for the b in the equation:

$$Y = a + b\hat{X}$$

where $\hat{X} = c + dZ_1 + eZ_2$, coefficients estimated by least-squares regression of X on Z_1 and Z_2

2. Solve by ordinary least squares the equation:

$$(Y - bX) = f + gZ_1 + hZ_2$$

where g and h should be found to equal zero.

The logic is quite simply that if the Z's operate on Y only through X and are not related to unmeasured causes of Y, then if the effect of X is removed, all the variation explainable by the Z's should also have been removed (Christ, 1966: 531–542; Johnston, 1963: 263). *If* we had assumed that Z_1 was not directly a cause of Y and was unrelated to unmeasured causes of Y, we could have solved for b, the effect of X on Y, using only Z_1. Then, subtracting the effect of X from Y, any relation between Z_2 and the remaining variation in Y would be evidence that Z_2 either caused Y directly or was related to unmeasured causes of Y. If we had assumed that Z_2 was not directly a cause of y and was unrelated to unmeasured causes of Y, we could have solved alternatively for the effect of X on Y using only Z_2. Then, subtracting the effect of X from Y, any relation between Z_1 and the remaining variation in Y would be evidence that Z_1 either caused Y directly or was related to unmeasured causes of Y. In either case, the Z used to solve for the effect of X on Y would be unrelated to the remaining variation in Y (after the effect of X had been subtracted out) because the effect of X was solved for by regressing Y on an exact linear function of the Z, so that any separate effect of the Z, not through X, would not be distinguishable.

Using *both* Z's to get the effect of X on Y yields a kind of average of what would have been obtained using each separately. The procedure actually suggested is thus a way of symmetrically combining the tests that would follow from estimating the effect of X on Y using either Z and testing the assumptions about the other. The test is thus quite simply a test of the *consistency* of assuming that *both* Z's are not direct causes of Y and are unrelated to unmeasured causes of Y. It is quite possible to be consistent but wrong. Still, if the two Z's are not merely different measures of the same thing, the test strongly supports the assumptions about both Z's, even though not constituting proof. The more Z's used, obviously, the more compelling the support. In our experimental design with randomization, one assumption is, of course, satisfied except for chance by the process of randomization of the Z's. Thus, except for chance, failure of the design to pass this test would mean that the assumption that the Z's are not direct causes of Y is the one at fault.[4]

NONEXPERIMENTAL ANALYSIS

In nonexperimental research, we have exactly the same picture as in experimental research, except that the Z's are not conditions we have ourselves imposed in a random fashion, which makes the assumption that the Z's are unrelated to unmeasured causes of Y more of a substantive assumption and, except for the fact that the analysis may become more complicated, including more variables, in order to support that now more substantive assumption.

Lacking the device of randomization, what sort of picture of the world we are studying must we assume? The general model has been called "block recursive." The idea is of blocks, or categories, of variables where the blocks are numbered in such a way, and variables allocated to the blocks in such a way, that we can say that while variables in lower-numbered blocks may cause variables in higher-numbered blocks, variables in higher-numbered blocks are not causes of variables in lower-numbered blocks. Further, variables in lower-numbered blocks are not related to unmeasured causes of variables in higher-numbered blocks. Then we must be able to choose variables from lower-numbered blocks that are causes of some variables in

[4] Significance tests are also available for the test of the consistency of the assumptions about the Z's (Christ, 1966: 531–542).

higher-numbered blocks but not of other variables in those blocks, these chosen variables to act as the Z's did in our discussion in the preceding section. Nothing is said about the relationships among variables within the same block. Such variables may be reciprocally related or even spuriously related.

How realistic is such a conception of the world? How could we employ such a model of reality if we happen to believe that ultimately everything causes everything else to some degree? Consider a case where we have selected two variables out of an infinity of variables, these two being whether or not Mr. Jones insists on drinking milk and the success of the war effort of the nation wherein Mr. Jones resides. If the war effort is stepped up so as to be successful, Mr. Jones's supply of milk may be cut off and he may be compelled to stop drinking milk. On the other hand, if Mr. Jones and all other milk drinkers refuse to abide by the law and insist on getting their milk and drinking it, the war effort may fail. There is thus a reciprocal relationship between Mr. Jones's milk drinking and the war effort. But consider the effect of Mr. Jones's drinking milk independently of the effect of all other dissident citizens' drinking milk. Mr. Jones's drinking milk — by itself — has so little effect on the war effort as to be negligible. It takes the concerted action of thousands and thousands of milk drinkers to affect the war effort significantly enough to be measured. If Y refers to the war effort and X_1 refers to Mr. Jones's drinking milk, other X's referring to milk drinking by other persons, then Y affects X_1, and X_1 affects Y, but the effect of X_1 on Y is so small that it can be ignored, unless it is related to the other X's. In such a case Y could be taken for the purpose of a research project to be a cause of X_1 but uncaused by X_1.

Unless the world is a lot simpler than this example, which is simple enough, the idea that everything ultimately affects everything else should not prevent us from mapping the world into the block-recursive form for a particular research project. We should always be able to identify some variables that will serve as appropriate Z's with respect to the X's and Y's in which we are centrally interested.

A recently published empirical analysis using such a rationale is Scanzoni's study of aspiration and the need for achievement (1967). Aspiration is for us the Y, need for achievement the X, and childrearing practices known to produce need for achievement, the Z (see Fig. 1.3a). Each variable *could*

Figure 1.3a

Figure 1.3b

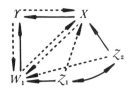

Figure 1.3c

have been defined as a change, alternatively, although at considerable inconvenience given the nature of the variables. Scanzoni assumes implicitly that the childrearing practices in question have no effect on aspirations except through need for achievement, and that they are unrelated to all unspecified causes of aspiration. His test of the effect of need for achievement on aspirations is simply to relate aspirations to the childrearing practices, need for achievement not being measured in the study, its relationship to childrearing practices being documented from the literature. Not having need for achievement as a measured variable meant that a regression coefficient showing the effect of need for achievement on aspiration could not be calculated. However, the existence or nonexistence of a relationship between childrearing practices and aspirations would reflect, respectively, the existence or nonexistence of an effect of need for achievement on aspiration. No assumption was needed regarding the effect of the aspiration on need for achievement.

Suppose that the X, need for achievement, had been measured, and that there had also arisen a question regarding the assumption that Z, childrearing practices, affected aspirations only through need for achievement. Or suppose that someone questioned the assumption that Z, childrearing practices, was not related to unmeasured causes of Y, aspirations. What would be the simplest way to handle the problem?

The first thing would probably be to introduce additional Z's into the model and to test the consistency of the assumptions about their relationships to Y and the unmeasured causes of Y. If this test showed the assumptions to be inconsistent, we would have to agree that the assumptions were wrong and alter the model.

One possibility would be to find a different Z, for which the necessary assumptions did in fact seem plausible. A perhaps more realistic strategy might be to try to figure out *how* the original Z affected Y aside from acting through X or *what* unmeasured causes of Y were related to Z. It is with the latter approaches that the model becomes a little more complicated. The additional links besides X connecting Z to Y must be included in the analysis, as must some *measure* of the to this point *un*measured causes of Y that are thought to be related to Z.

Let us first attend to the matter of Z affecting Y over and above its effect through X. Any causal relationship can be broken down into intervening links by more detailed specification of the causal mechanism. Thus, we should be able to describe the effect of Z on Y not through X by introducing W_1, a measure of a variable thought to constitute a link between Z and Y in addition to the link already constituted by X. Thus, we say that childrearing practices affect aspirations by way of need for achievement and also by way of W_1. W_1 might be belief in the moral necessity of high aspirations. If W_1 is not thought to be caused by either X or Y (see Fig. 1.3b) or to be in any other way related to unmeasured causes of Y, we can simply regress Y on the W_1

and the expected value of X, given Z and W_1. W_1 is thought of as being in the same block of the block recursive system as Z, and hence there is no need for any assumption regarding the nature of the causal connection between Z and W_1. W_1 can be treated as just another Z. Since W_1, like Z, is assumed to be uncaused by X or Y and unrelated to additional unmeasured causes of Y, we can use its observed value in the regression estimation procedure, rather than substituting an expected value as we did with X. Notice that W_1 is included among the givens for the expected values of X. This means that $\hat{X}$ includes variation coming from W_1, so that effects of W_1 passing through X instead of affecting Y directly will be controlled out of our estimate of the direct effect of W_1 on Y by the second stage of two-stage least squares.

In such a case, to test the consistency of our assumptions, given several Z's as causes of X but not Y and unrelated to unmeasured causes of Y, we would regress $(Y - bX)$ on W and the several Z's, where b is the effect of X on Y, and, as before, check to see that the coefficients of the Z's were equal to or close to zero. Thus, solving by least squares the equation

$$Y = a + b\hat{X} + cW_1$$

where $\hat{X} = d + eZ_1 + fZ_2 + gW_1$, coefficients estimated by least squares regression of X on Z_1 and Z_2, and W_1, and

$$(Y - bX) = h + iW_1 + jZ_1 + kZ_2$$

where j and k should equal zero.

Suppose that we cannot assume that W_1 is not caused by X or Y? If it is caused by Y, either directly or through X (see Fig. 1.3c), it will be related to all unmeasured causes of Y. We will then need to regress Y on the expected value of W_1 given our original Z, now called Z_1, and some other Z, say Z_2, and on the expected value of X, given Z_2 and our original Z, now called Z_1. Thus,

$$Y = a + b\hat{X} + c\hat{W}_1$$

where $\hat{X} = d + eZ_1 + fZ_2$ and $\hat{W}_1 = g + hZ_1 + iZ_2$

and where all coefficients are estimated by ordinary least squares.

What of the other problem, where Z is simply thought to be related to some unmeasured cause of Y? In effect, we have already solved that problem, because the case where Z causes Y through other channels than X is simply a routine example of that problem. We simply introduce the previously unmeasured variable, W_2, and treat it exactly as we did W_1, introducing its observed value if it is not caused by X or Y and is not related to unmeasured causes of Y, introducing an expected value if it is.

It will have been noticed that when we introduce expected values of W_1 or W_2, we introduce them given an additional Z. This is because if we introduced the expected values of X and W_1 given Z_1 in the same equation, they would be perfectly related to each other, both being exact linear functions of Z_1, which would prevent our being able to distinguish the effects of the two variables, X and W_1, unless we had an assumption on which we were willing to rely concerning the relative effects of the two variables on Y. In general, then, how many Z's do we have to round up to estimate a causal model? We need as many Z's assumed not to cause Y as we have independent variables thought likely to be caused by Y or likely to be related to unmeasured variables causing Y — that is, as many variables as we have included among the possible causes of Y that are classified as in the same block as Y in the block recursive system. In effect, for each variable that may be a cause of Y, for which we cannot assume independence of the unmeasured causes of Y, either because of common cause or because of reciprocal effects, we need a Z that is a cause of that variable but not directly a cause of Y.

Thus far, we have been concerned with the estimation of single equations — that is, ascertaining the effects of certain variables on one particular dependent variable, despite spuriousness or reciprocal causation. In practice, we would often be concerned with a whole system of equations representing the interdependence of an entire set of mutually dependent variables. The logic we have been discussing is suited to this kind of problem. It is referred to as a "limited-information" estimator or a single-equation estimator because it attacks such a system of equations, one equation at a time. The advantage is that errors in assumptions, sampling, or measurement have less comprehensive effects. Only errors affecting information actually required to estimate a particular equation affect the estimation of that equation. In full-information techniques, which estimate entire systems of equations in one operation, errors in any part of the system are more likely to ramify through the entire set of equations. It is a matter of choosing how many baskets to put one's eggs in. The advantage of the single basket, a full-information estimator, is that parts of the error terms can be eliminated for greater reliability and accuracy of results.

The strategy of applying the single-equation estimator we have been discussing to the problem of a set of simultaneous equations is no more complicated than the single-equation problems we have been discussing. One merely considers each equation in the set as if one really had no interest in the others except as a source of assumptions aiding in the solution of the equation at hand. Frequently, the same Z's can be used in estimating several equations, so that the number of such variables we have to dig up does not

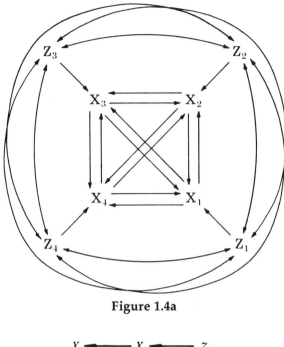

Figure 1.4a

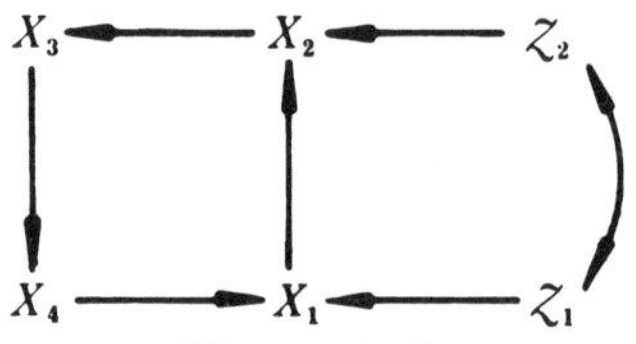

$X_3 \leftarrow X_2 \leftarrow Z_2$

$X_4 \rightarrow X_1 \leftarrow Z_1$

Figure 1.4b

necessarily increase drastically with the number of equations. If we had four
X's and each X caused every other X, we would require four Z's (see Fig.
1.4a). There are four equations involved. In the first equation, X_1 is dependent on Z_1, X_2, X_3, and X_4. It is regressed on the observed values of Z_1 and
the predicted values of X_2, X_3, and X_4 given Z_1, Z_2, Z_3, and Z_4. In the second
equation, X_2 is dependent on Z_2, X_1, X_3, and X_4. It is regressed on the
observed value of Z_2 and the predicted values of X_1, X_3, and X_4 given Z_1, Z_2,
Z_3, and Z_4. In the third equation, X_3 is dependent upon Z_3, X_1, X_2, and X_4. It
is regressed on the observed value of Z_3 and the predicted values of X_1, X_2,
and X_4 given Z_1, Z_2, Z_3, and Z_4. In the fourth and last equation, X_4 is
dependent on Z_4, X_1, X_2, and X_3. It is regressed on the observed value of Z_4
and the predicted values of X_1, X_2, and X_3 given Z_1, Z_2, Z_3, and Z_4.

If not every X causes every other X, even though there are still feedback
loops in the model the picture gets even simpler, as we do not need all four
Z's. Suppose X_1 causes X_2, which causes X_3, which causes X_4, which causes

X_1. Each X is caused directly by only one other X, though indirectly by all other X's. To estimate all four causal links in this circle of causation, we need a minimum of two Z's with certain specific relationships to the X's. Suppose Z_1 causes X_1 but no other X and is not related to unmeasured causes of any other X. Suppose Z_2 causes X_2 but no other X and is not related to unmeasured causes of any other X (see Fig. 1.4b). Then we can ascertain the effect of X_1 on X_2 by regressing X_2 on Z_2 and the expected values of X_1 given Z_1 and Z_2. We must include Z_2 because it is a cause of X_2 that may be related to Z_1. We can ascertain the effects of X_2 on X_3 by regressing X_3 on the expected values of X_2 given Z_2, or given Z_1 and Z_2, since Z_1 is related to X_3 only through X_2, by way of X_1. We can ascertain the effect of X_3 on X_4 by regressing X_4 on the expected values of X_3 given Z_2, since Z_2 is related to X_4 only through X_3 by way of X_2, or similarly on the expected values of X_3 given Z_1 and Z_2. Finally, we can ascertain the effect of X_4 on X_1 by regressing X_1 on Z_1 and the expected values of X_4 given Z_2 and Z_1. Introduction of additional Z's would allow us to test the consistency of all of the assumptions about the relationships of the Z's to the X's and to the unmeasured causes of the X's.

It should be noted that if one wanted to know the effect of Z_1 on X_2 and was unconcerned with the fact that X_1 was part of the mechanism by way of which Z_1 affected X_2, one could simply regress X_2 on Z_1 and Z_2. Since the Z's are assumed to be unrelated to unmeasured variables affecting the X's, such a procedure would not cause any difficulty. If we had wanted to speak, in an earlier section, of the effect of various experiences (Z) on prejudice (Y), not being concerned with whether the effect was by way of frustration, we could have simply regressed prejudice, Y, on experiences, Z. Such a development is called a "simple recursive" system, in contrast to the block-recursive system. No block, beyond the first, contains more than one measured variable. The difference in results is simply that intervening mechanisms are not specified.

INTERPRETATION WITH RESPECT TO TIME

It is frequently suggested that the measurement of all variables at the same point in time, and at only one point in time, gets the researchers into the awkward position of having to assume instantaneous causation and equilibrium in order to measure any causal effects at all. The problem stems from the attempt to predict a variable from a contemporaneous value of another variable and to interpret the result as a causal effect.

Consider the matter of equilibrium, where the effects of two variables on each other balance in such a way that the system is maintained without long-run change. Does measuring all variables at the same point in time compel us to make some sort of equilibrium assumption? Let us take the two variables X and Y and suppose that each causes the other. We will estimate the effect of X on Y by regressing Y on Z_2 and the expected value of X given

Figure 1.5

Z_1 and Z_2, and the effect of Y on X by regressing X on Z_1 and the expected value of Y given Z_2 and Z_1, where Z_1 does not cause Y directly and is not related to unmeasured causes of Y, and Z_2 does not cause X directly and is not related to unmeasured causes of X (see Fig. 1.5). Our estimate of the effect of X on Y is thus dependent on the observed association between Z_1 and X and between Z_1 and Y, controlling Z_2. These observed relationships place no logical constraint on the corresponding relationships between Z_2 and X and between Z_2 and Y, controlling Z_1, on the basis of which the effect of Y on X is estimated. There is thus no reason why this strategy should necessarily yield an estimate that describes a system as being in equilibrium, even if all variables are measured at the same point in time.

Measuring all the variables at one point in time does not constrain us to assume that all effects are instantaneous either, if we are willing to accept "arbitrarily close" approximations of effect over time. If we are assessing the effect of X on Y, assuming Z is a cause of X but not of Y and is unrelated to unmeasured causes of Y, then the only way Z could be related to Y would be for X at some point of time, not necessarily the present, to have caused Y (see Fig. 1.6). The b that we estimate by regressing Y on the expected value of X given Z in the present will approximate the b reflecting the effect of X on Y over time to the degree that the values of X in the present approximate the values of X at the point in the past when the relevant values of X occurred that affect Y in the present, or to the degree that changes in X have been nearly random with respect to Z. Bothersome changes in X are those brought

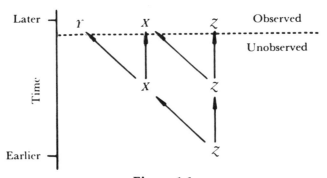

Figure 1.6

about by changes in Z or related variables and those brought about by feedbacks of X on itself, through Y or other variables. Both of these kinds of change in X are bothersome because they will be related to Z. All bothersome changes in X that an investigator considers likely should be thought through in the effort to anticipate their effect on the estimated b. If such changes in X are slight relative to the original variance of X, there is no great problem. If such changes are major, it is desirable not only to anticipate their effects on the estimated b but to compensate for them. If the changes in X come from Z, the b will be attenuated. If the changes are from a feedback loop that increases the variation of X, then the estimated b will again be attenuated, while if the variation in X has been decreased by a feedback loop, the estimated b will be too large. If a feedback has reflected X, then the sign of the estimated b will be reversed.

Frequently, but certainly not always, the researcher will have at least general knowledge of the existence of such processes to the extent that they have brought about major change. Fortunately, the changes referred to here as "bothersome" are likely to be minimal in many situations. Remember also that the presence or absence of an effect of X on Y, as opposed to its size and direction, is not in doubt. If Z is related to Y, so that any effect of any kind is estimated, X must have had some effect of some kind on Y. The problem is in pinning down the exact nature of that effect.

It should be remembered, of course, that any effects that are not in equilibrium necessarily mean that the effects are at least partly over time rather than instantaneous. If all effects were instantaneous, all changes would be over in an instant and the system would reach equilibrium or fluctuate with infinite speed for all of infinity. Practically, lack of equilibrium means over time change (i.e., delayed effect), and caution must be used, as suggested above, in interpreting such effects inferred from cross-sectional data without time lags.

These principles apply to both experimental and nonexperimental designs.

EXPLOITATION OF TIME IN THE USE OF CAUSAL VARIABLES FROM PRECEDING BLOCKS

It has been suggested, and seems valid at first glance, that a terribly simple approach would be the use of explicit time order in measurement, both in experimental and in nonexperimental designs. One would simply measure all variables at two points in time and regress each of the variables in turn, measured at the later time, on all the variables measured at the earlier time. The argument would be simply that the variable measured earlier could not have been caused by the value of the variables observed at a later time, since things do not cause other things that precede them. The earlier value could be thought of as being a preceding block in the block-re-

Figure 1.7

cursive system. Thus, we might measure X and Y at two points in time, denoting the measurement of X at the earlier time as X_1 and the measurement of X at the later time as X_2, and denoting the measurement of Y at the earlier time as Y_1 and the measurement of Y at the later time by Y_2. We simply regress the observed value of Y_2 on the observed value of X_1 and regress the observed value of X_2 on the observed value of Y_1 and conclude that we have neatly assessed the effect of X on Y and of Y on X (see Fig. 1.7).

Unfortunately, it is quite possible, however, for the regression of Y_2 on X_1 to reflect the effect of Y on X, rather than the effect of X on Y. The problem is serial correlation of Y with itself through time or serial correlation of unmeasured causes of Y with themselves over time. If Y at some prior time caused X_1 and also caused Y_2, it is obvious that the regression of Y_2 on X_1 would reflect the effect of Y on X (Y_1 on X_1 and Y_1 on Y_2) rather than the effect of X on Y (see Fig. 1.8). Similarly, if an unmeasured variable caused Y at an earlier time which in turn caused X_1, and if this same unmeasured variable caused itself at a later time and in turn caused Y_2, then, again, the regression of Y_2 on X_1 would reflect the effect of Y on X (see Fig. 1.9).

In the case of Y being serially correlated with itself, all we would have to do is control X_1 at the expense, however, of omitting from our estimate any immediate effect of X on Y, perhaps not usually such a serious loss but enough to reverse the direction of relationship in some cases where the effect of X on Y is immediate and temporary. What would be picked up would be the fading of the temporary effect, which would be interpreted as the effect itself. In the case of the serially correlated unmeasured causes of Y, the problem becomes more massive. Techniques for handling the problem, which we will not describe here, involve adding and subtracting exact mathematical equations from each other to generate new equations that contain the wanted regression parameters but not the unwanted serially correlated errors, these new equations being the ones finally solved by

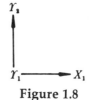

Figure 1.8

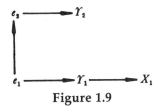

Figure 1.9

ordinary least squares (Christ, 1966: 481–494; Goldberger, 1964: 231–248; Johnston, 1963: 177–200; Malinvaud, 1966: 420–496). Such a solution requires that all variables be measured at four different points in time and that it be assumed that the same causal relationship obtains over the entire period of time involved. Use of time order and ordinary least squares is thus expensive in that it requires a great deal of data. It also is cumbersome in that the most practically workable of the techniques referred to may be sluggish, and in extreme cases totally ineffective, in dealing with the difficulty.

One last possibility that suggests itself must be disposed of. Suppose that we defined X_1, X_2, Y_1, and Y_2 as immediately above and, in order to assess the immediate or nearly immediate effects of X on Y and of Y on X, took the regression of Y_2 on Y_1 and the expected value of X_2 given X_1 and Y_1 and the regression of X_2 on X_1 and the expected value of Y_2 given Y_1 and X_1. Following the logic of the first two sections of this chapter, we would assume that X_1 caused X_2 but did not cause Y_2 except through X_2 and Y_1, and that Y_1 caused Y_2 but did not cause X_2 except through Y_2 and X_1 (see Fig. 1.10). Further, we would assume that X_1 was unrelated to all unmeasured causes of Y_2 and that Y_1 was unrelated to all unmeasured causes of X_2.

Obviously this solution, like the one above, is faulty on the count that serial correlation of unmeasured causes of X and Y will result in X_1 being related to unmeasured causes of Y_2 and Y_1 being related to unmeasured causes of X_2 as above. But this is a minor objection if we are willing to measure X and Y at four different points in time and assume that the relationship between X and Y and is the same over the entire period of time involved. At least, it is minor compared to a perhaps less obvious point. The assumption that X_1 causes X_2 and does not cause Y_2 except through X_2 and Y_1 is not consistent with the assumption that Y_1 causes Y_2 but does not cause X_2 except though Y_2 and X_1, unless it is also assumed that the effect of X on Y

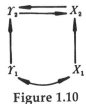

Figure 1.10

Figure 1.11a   Figure 1.11b

and of Y on X occurs only when the data are being gathered and not in between data gatherings. Suppose that it occurred at a time in between the two measurements we have been discussing and that we designate X at this point $X_{1\frac{1}{2}}$ and Y at the same time as $Y_{1\frac{1}{2}}$. Then X_1 causes $X_{1\frac{1}{2}}$, which causes $Y_{1\frac{1}{2}}$, which causes Y_2, which in other words means that X_1 causes Y_2 through other links than merely X_2 and Y_1. The same principle obtains for the effect of Y on X. Y_1 causes $Y_{1\frac{1}{2}}$, which causes $X_{1\frac{1}{2}}$, which causes X_2, which means that Y_1 causes X_2 by other links than merely Y_2 and X_1, contrary to our necessary assumption (see Fig. 1.11a and 1.11b).

It would, of course, be perfectly legitimate to regress Y_2 on the expected value of X_1 given Z, where, as usual, we assume Z to be a cause of X_1 but to be related to Y_2 only through X_1 and to be unrelated to unmeasured causes of Y_2, therefore, of course, not caused by Y_2 and not caused by X_1 (see Fig. 1.12). Such a procedure would give us the effect of X on Y over the specified time interval and would avoid the bias due to serial correlation. This is, in fact, probably the most workable solution and is merely the two-stage least-squares procedure we have been discussing all along, now with time intervals built into the data so that over time effects and disequilibrium analyses will be perfectly straightforward. This procedure is appropriate for estimating difference equations that may be transformed into differential equations — avoiding the usual difficulties with autocorrelated errors and similar problems encountered in solving for the coefficients of such equations. The procedure is not, however, an exploitation of time to provide a short cut and avoid assumptions. The existence of such a short cut seems doubtful at best.

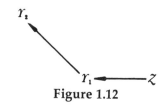

Figure 1.12

CONCLUSION

We began by pointing out that one would expect strong similarities between the mechanics of causal inference in experimental and nonexperimental settings. We found that such was, in fact, the case and that consistency tests of assumptions in experimental and nonexperimental research, together with ways of complicating nonexperimental designs to make the necessary assumptions tenable, make it not only theoretically possible but practically feasible to apply the same basic analysis to both kinds of research.

It may be added here that the approach described, two-stage least squares, is what is referred to in the statistical literature as a "consistent" estimator. That means that as the sample size is increased toward infinity, the estimates approach the population parameters. Two-stage least squares does have some sampling error problems on small samples, however.

When one more Z is used than is required for estimation, the results will be approximately unbiased (Christ, 1966: 470). The word *approximately* is necessary because of a technical problem in defining the expectation mathematically. On large sample analysis of the kind common in sociology, there should be no problem in any case. But with very small samples, such as 10 or 20 cases, one begins to worry a little about bias if one happens *not* to be using exactly one extra Z. The problem in that case becomes analogous to the bias of the common chi-square statistics on small samples, except that by using exactly one extra Z the problem can be bypassed.

It should also be pointed out that two-stage least-squares estimates have larger sampling variances than do ordinary least-squares estimates. This loss of efficiency, which is considerable on small samples, is the price paid for the gain of having a consistent estimate. On large samples, the price would seem to be a small one indeed.

While the capabilities of the approach described are very great, it must be stressed that it is not a means of getting something for nothing. It is a technique for putting existing theory into interaction with data in order to extend theory. In no case is it possible to determine causal relationships on the basis of data alone. However, the fact that the technique allows for consistency checks on assumptions does make trial and error on the basis of minimal theory a feasible procedure.

REFERENCES

Christ, Carl. *Econometric Models and Methods.* New York: John Wiley, 1966.

Fisher, Franklin M. *The Identification Problem in Econometrics.* New York: McGraw-Hill, 1966.

Goldberger, Arthur S. *Econometric Theory.* New York: John Wiley, 1964.

Johnston, J. *Econometric Methods.* New York: McGraw-Hill, 1963.

Malinvaud, E. *Statistical Methods of Econometrics.* Chicago: Rand McNally, 1966.

Miller, Neal E., and Bugelski, Richard. "Minor Studies of Aggression: II. The Influence of Frustrations Imposed by the In-Group on Attitudes Expressed Toward Out-Groups." *Journal of Psychology* 25 (1948): 437–442.

Scanzoni, John. "Socialization, Achievement, and Achievement Values." *American Sociological Review* 32 (1967): 449–456.

Wold, Herman O. A. "Forecasting by the Chain Principle." In *Econometric Model Building: Essays on the Causal Chain Approach,* edited by Herman O. A. Wold. Amsterdam: North Holland Publishing Co., 1964.

2

Causal Models Involving Unmeasured Variables in Stimulus–Response Situations*

H. M. Blalock, Jr.

We are rapidly accumulating an extensive literature dealing with causal approaches to the handling of measurement error, but most of this deals with situations where indicators are taken as effects rather than causes of the unmeasured variables. These models are especially appropriate whenever one is dealing with two or more postulated internal states of individuals (e.g., attitudes, values, or motives) that are being inferred on the basis of responses of one kind or another.

Chapter 1 by Miller points to another important kind of causal situation, though without dealing with the complications produced by imperfect measurement. Specifically, Miller has explicated the rationale for making causal inferences in experimental and nonexperimental situations in which the fundamental independent variable of interest (X) is manipulated by varying one or more of its causes (Z_i), under the assumption that these exogenous Z_i do not appear in the equation for the dependent variable Y. If the Z_i affect Y through any variables other than X, these latter variables must be explicitly introduced into the model. Miller shows that basically the same rationale applies to nonexperimental designs where it has not been possible to manipulate the Z_i independently of other sources of variation in X or Y.

* Chapter originally published in *Causal Models in the Social Sciences*, 1971.

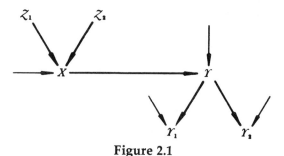

Figure 2.1

Miller also implies that X may sometimes be *measured* in terms of one or more of its causes Z_i. Thus, if one is attempting to manipulate frustration (X) in order to study aggression or prejudice (Y), one may not have obtained an independent measure of frustration, but he may merely assume that X varies with Z. For example, if the manipulation involves withholding food or sleep, the amount of frustration (or hunger or fatigue) may be taken as proportional to the duration of the period within which food or sleep has been withheld. Similarly, an investigator may attempt to induce frustration by insulting his subjects to varying degrees but without attempting to measure degree of frustration more directly. As Miller points out, it may be to one's advantage to have multiple manipulations in such instances so that there is some degree of insurance that the several Z_i are not all related to Y via unknown mechanisms in violation of the basic assumptions. If we take Y as indirectly measured by several indicators assumed to be effects of Y, we may diagram this very simple model as in Fig. 2.1.

The purpose of this chapter is to explore the implications of models of this type by developing elaborations of various kinds.[1] These elaborations will involve the addition of effect measures of X and possible disturbances between measures taken to be causes and effects of X and the dependent variable Y. For simplicity, however, we shall always assume that Y is measured by two effect indicators subject only to random errors.

This particular kind of model arises very frequently in political science, psychology, and sociology. The stimulus – response (S – R) tradition in psychology has sometimes, though not always, involved a rather extreme form of operationalism in which the causal connections involving the unmeasured intervening variables have been conceived in terms of an impenetrable "black box." Stimuli have been conceived as having more or less direct effects on responses, or at least researchers have proceeded as though this were the case. But a similar tradition also prevails within political science

---

[1] Land has independently reached essentially the same conclusions as those to be elaborated in the present chapter. Land's models involve the single unmeasured variable X, measured by both causes and effects (see K. Land, 1970).

and sociology, though it might not have been recognized as such. Many so-called "background" variables such as race, sex, occupation of father, religion, community, region, and even "age" are basically crude indicators of stimuli that are thought to influence behavior. But the intervening psychological mechanisms may not be spelled out, particularly in empirical research. Usually, one tries out various combinations of background factors to see which predict most satisfactorily to behavior or attitudes, with no serious effort being made to spell out the causal mechanisms involved. It is hoped that the orientation made possible by the explicit introduction of unmeasured variables into a causal model will help to overcome some of the shortcomings produced by this type of rather atheoretical research.

MODEL I. ALL INDICATORS OF X ARE CAUSES OF X

Let us begin very simply with Model IA of Fig. 2.2, which is basically the same as the model of Fig. 2.1 except that the notation has been made to coincide with that of Costner's (1969) Fig. 4, which is reproduced (without the primes) as Model IB of our Fig. 2.2. We have relabeled the causes of X as X_1 and X_2 in order to emphasize that these causes of X are being used as

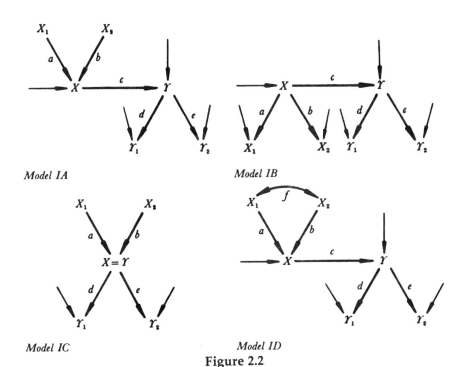

Model IA

Model IB

Model IC

Model ID

Figure 2.2

measures of X. In Models IA and IB of Fig. 2.2, we are assuming that other sources that produce variation in X, Y, and the two measures Y_1 and Y_2 have aggregate effects that are approximately random. This is implied by the side arrows that have not been connected with the other variables in the system. In Model IA, the absence of an arrow linking the two causes of X implies that $r_{X_1X_2} = 0$, except for sampling error. The path coefficients, here all total correlations, have been labeled a, b, c, d, and e (following Costner) in both diagrams.

The equations linking the measured correlations to the unknown path coefficients are as follows:

Model IA	Model IB (Costner's model)
(1) $r_{X_1X_2} = 0$	(1) $r_{X_1X_2} = ab$
(2) $r_{Y_1Y_2} = de$	(2) $r_{Y_1Y_2} = de$
(3) $r_{X_1Y_1} = acd$	(3) $r_{X_1Y_1} = acd$
(4) $r_{X_1Y_2} = ace$	(4) $r_{X_1Y_2} = ace$
(5) $r_{X_2Y_1} = bcd$	(5) $r_{X_2Y_1} = bcd$
(6) $r_{X_2Y_2} = bce$	(6) $r_{X_2Y_2} = bce$

We see that Eqs. (2)–(5) are identical for both models, and that they differ only with respect to the first equation. Recall that Costner's first consistency criterion involves the implied relationship

$$r_{X_1Y_1}r_{X_2Y_2} = r_{X_1Y_2}r_{X_2Y_1} = abc^2de$$

which is obtained by using only Eqs. (3)–(6). We immediately see that this test criterion is satisfied by Model IA as well as Model IB, and we have one more example of a model that implies the same empirical prediction as IB.

It turns out, however, that we cannot estimate the path coefficient c connecting X to Y in Model IA. In Costner's Model IB, it will be recalled, one may estimate c^2 as follows:[2]

$$c^2 = \frac{r_{X_1Y_1}r_{X_2Y_2}}{r_{X_1X_2}r_{Y_1Y_2}} = \frac{(acd)(bce)}{(ab)(de)}$$

[2] We also could have used the numerator $r_{X_1Y_2}r_{X_2Y_1}$, which, if the first Costner consistency criterion has been satisfied, will be approximately equal to $r_{X_1Y_1}r_{X_2Y_2}$. Common sense would suggest using some kind of average of the two expressions. Robert Hauser and Arthur S. Goldberger (1971) indicate that it is optimal to use a weighted average involving the standard errors of the coefficients, but for exploratory research a simple arithmetic mean should suffice.

Notice that this procedure involves dividing by $r_{X_1X_2}$, which is taken to be zero in Model IA. The basic problem is that there is no way to isolate c in any of the Eqs. (3)–(6), and in Model IA we cannot obtain a separate expression for the product ab, as is possible in Model IB. Looking at the matter another way, in Model IA we really only have five equations and five unknowns, since the first equation is completely trivial (though of course not automatically satisfied by the data). But among these five equations is one redundant equation, which may be used as a test criterion but which means that the five equations are not completely independent. Therefore, we shall not be in a position to solve for all of the unknowns, and in particular we cannot solve for c.

Another way of seeing this is to note that if X and Y were identical, so that $c = 1$, we would have Model IC of Fig. 2.2, which implies a set of predictions that do not involve c but that could not be distinguished empirically from those of Model IA.[3] In fact, we could have replaced Model IA by any number of alternative models involving a series of unmeasured variables interrelating X and Y, and none of these models could have been distinguished empirically from Model IA. We have here another example of the identification problem, one stemming from the existence of unmeasured variables in a recursive system.

Of course, the simple Model IA could be distinguished empirically from IB by the absence of a correlation between the two causal variables X_1 and X_2. In nonexperimental situations, we generally expect such stimulus variables to be intercorrelated as in Model ID of Fig. 2.2. For example, if X_1 were race and if X_2 were occupation of father, with X being the conceptual variable "exposure to educational discrimination," we would anticipate a correlation between the two indicators of X, as represented by the curved arrow in Model ID. The equations for Model ID are somewhat more complex and are as follows:

(1) $r_{X_1X_2} = f$

(2) $r_{Y_1Y_2} = de$

(3) $r_{X_1Y_1} = cd(a + bf)$

(4) $r_{X_1Y_2} = ce(a + bf)$

(5) $r_{X_2Y_1} = cd(b + af)$

(6) $r_{X_2Y_2} = ce(b + af)$

Again, the first Costner consistency criterion is satisfied since

$$r_{X_1Y_1}r_{X_2Y_2} = r_{X_1Y_2}r_{X_2Y_1} = c^2de(a + bf)(b + af)$$

The coefficient f is given directly by the correlation between X_1 and X_2, and

---

[3] These predictions are as follows: $r_{X_1X_2} = 0$; $r_{Y_1Y_2} = de$; $r_{X_1Y_1} = ad$; $r_{X_1Y_2} = ae$; $r_{X_2Y_1} = bd$; and $r_{X_2Y_2} = be$.

we may solve for d and e by obtaining the ratio d/e by dividing Eq. (3) by Eq. (4) or by dividing Eq. (5) by Eq. (6). Multiplying either of these ratios (which should be identical except for sampling error) by de we can obtain an expression for d^2. A similar expression for e^2 can likewise be obtained. But we shall not be able to use the remaining equations to disentangle c from a and b. If we were to use the estimate appropriate for Costner's Model IB, we would obtain the result

$$\frac{r_{X_1Y_1}r_{X_2Y_2}}{r_{X_1X_2}r_{Y_1Y_2}} = \frac{c^2de(a + bf)(b + af)}{def} = c^2\frac{(a + bf)(b + af)}{f}$$

which is certainly not equal to c^2. Furthermore, Models IB and ID could not be distinguished on purely empirical grounds unless the temporal sequences linking X to X_1 and X_2 could be used to reject one or the other model. The implication is that if one cannot decide whether the indicators are causes or effects of X, he should not attempt to estimate the path coefficient c linking X or Y.

MODEL II. A SINGLE CAUSE AND SINGLE EFFECT INDICATOR OF X

Having failed to estimate the effects of X on Y when both measures of X are taken as causes, let us next examine a very simple model involving a single cause of X and a single effect that are not linked by any path other than through X. This model, Model IIA, is represented in Fig. 2.3. It can readily be seen that the equations for Model IIA are identical with those for Costner's Model IB. Therefore, we may utilize the same test for compatibility of the data with the model, and we may also legitimately estimate c^2 using the equation

$$\frac{r_{X_1Y_1}r_{X_2Y_2}}{r_{X_1X_2}r_{Y_1Y_2}} = \frac{(acd)(bce)}{(ab)(de)} = c^2$$

Thus, if we are able to locate a single indicator of X that is assumed to be an effect of X, we may utilize this second indicator in conjunction with the indicator causing X to estimate all of the coefficients in this very simple model.[4]

---

[4] The method of instrumental variables may also be used in this particular model, though it is somewhat more sensitive to specification error than is ordinary least squares in instances where there may be an additional path from X_1 to Y (see Blalock, Wells, and Carter, 1970).

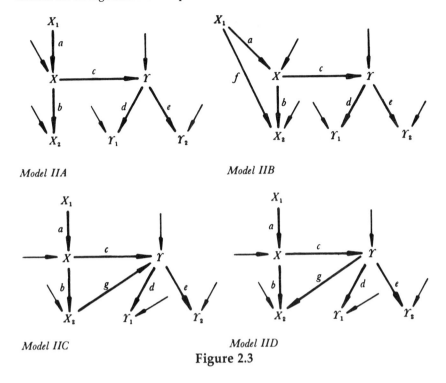

Model IIA

Model IIB

Model IIC

Model IID

Figure 2.3

Let us next see what complications are introduced if we allow for two kinds of disturbances involving X_2, namely (1) the possibility that X_1 affects X_2 by some additional path f not involving X and (2) the possibility that X_2 is linked to Y by a path other than that through X. The first of these possibilities is represented as Model IIB and the second as Models IIC and IID. In the case of Model IIB, where there is an additional path f from X_1 to X_2, we have the following six equations involving six unknowns:

(1) $r_{X_1X_2} = ab + f$ (4) $r_{X_1Y_2} = ace$
(2) $r_{Y_1Y_2} = de$ (5) $r_{X_2Y_1} = cd(b + af)$
(3) $r_{X_1Y_1} = acd$ (6) $r_{X_2Y_2} = ce(b + af)$

Once again it turns out that Costner's first consistency criterion is satisfied since

$$r_{X_1Y_1}r_{X_2Y_2} = r_{X_1Y_2}r_{X_2Y_1} = ac^2de(b + af)$$

but for familiar reasons we cannot disentangle c from a, b, and f. If we were to try to estimate c^2 utilizing the same function of the correlations appropriate for Models IB and IIA, we would obtain the result

$$\frac{r_{X_1Y_1}r_{X_2Y_2}}{r_{X_1X_2}r_{Y_1Y_2}} = \frac{ac^2de(b+af)}{(ab+f)(de)} = c^2\frac{ab+a^2f}{ab+f}$$

which would approximate c^2 if f were very small or if a^2 were almost unity, but which would otherwise not be an appropriate estimate.

In the cases of Models IIC and IID involving direct causal linkages g between the effect indicator X_2 and the dependent variable Y, we reach the same conclusions. The equations for these two models are as follows:

Model IIC	Model IID
(1) $r_{X_1X_2} = ab$	(1) $r_{X_1X_2} = a(b + cg)$
(2) $r_{Y_1Y_2} = de$	(2) $r_{Y_1Y_2} = de$
(3) $r_{X_1Y_1} = ad(c + bg)$	(3) $r_{X_1Y_1} = acd$
(4) $r_{X_1Y_2} = ae(c + bg)$	(4) $r_{X_1Y_2} = ace$
(5) $r_{X_2Y_1} = d(bc + g)$	(5) $r_{X_2Y_1} = d(bc + g)$
(6) $r_{X_2Y_2} = e(bc + g)$	(6) $r_{X_2Y_2} = e(bc + g)$

These equations satisfy Costner's first criterion, but we cannot obtain a separate estimate of c^2. The same result holds for models involving more complex relationships between X_2 and Y. We conclude that the device of utilizing a single cause of X and a single effect indicator works only in the very simple case of Model IIA. If we were to *assume* the correctness of this model when, in fact, one of the alternatives IIB, IIC, or IID were actually more appropriate, we would obtain a biased estimate of c^2 calculated on the basis of the ratio

$$r_{X_1Y_1}r_{X_2Y_2}/r_{X_1X_2}r_{Y_1Y_2}$$

These results are comparable to those obtained by Costner for nonrandom errors in instances where there are only two indicators of each variable, and the obvious suggestion is to introduce additional indicators. Let us, therefore, turn to a comparison of the relative merits of using one effect and two causal indicators of X versus using one causal and two effect indicators.

MODEL III. TWO CAUSE, ONE EFFECT INDICATORS OF X

In Model IIB, we considered the case where there is one cause and one effect indicator connected by an additional path f. Let us modify this model

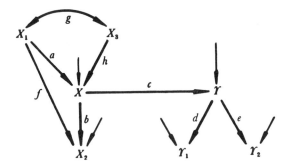

Model III

Figure 2.4

by adding another cause indicator X_3 that is permitted to be correlated with X_1 as in Model III in Fig. 2.4. The equations for this model are as follows:

(1) $r_{X_1X_2} = f + b(a + gh)$

(2) $r_{X_1X_3} = g$

(3) $r_{X_2X_3} = bh + g(ab + f)$

(4) $r_{Y_1Y_2} = de$

(5) $r_{X_1Y_1} = cd(a + gh)$

(6) $r_{X_1Y_2} = ce(a + gh)$

(7) $r_{X_2Y_1} = cd[b + f(a + gh)]$

(8) $r_{X_2Y_2} = ce[b + f(a + gh)]$

(9) $r_{X_3Y_1} = cd(h + ag)$

(10) $r_{X_3Y_2} = ce(h + ag)$

We encounter exactly the same difficulty; although the test criterion is satisfied we cannot estimate c^2. Suppose we now set $g = 0$, meaning that we have been able to find a second cause of X (namely, X_3) that is completely unrelated to X_2 except through X. It might now be expected that we could solve for c^2, just as we did in the case of Model IIA where there was no link between the indicators of X except through X itself. But even where $g = 0$ and where we ignore the indicator X_1, we discover that we cannot estimate c^2 utilizing the simple Costner estimate since

$$\frac{r_{X_2Y_1}r_{X_3Y_2}}{r_{X_2X_3}r_{Y_1Y_2}} = \frac{cd(b + af)ceh}{(bh)(de)} = c^2[1 + af/b]$$

Of course if $f = 0$, in addition, then we have the very simple model for which there is no link between X_2 and either cause of X (except through X) and estimation of c^2 becomes possible. In fact, if $f = 0$ with $g \neq 0$, we can also estimate c^2 as would be expected.

The important point is that if the effect indicator X_2 is linked with *any* causal indicator of X by any path other than through X, we are in difficulty.

This is an extremely significant problem if we keep in mind that, in any particular application, a causal variable such as X_1 may be unknown to the investigator. The implication is that with a single effect indicator we cannot rely on multiple indicators that are causes of X unless we make the extreme assumption that the effect indicator is unrelated to all such variables except through X.

MODEL IV. TWO EFFECTS, ONE CAUSE INDICATOR OF X

Having found difficulties with each of the preceding models, let us turn to the situation where we have more than one effect indicator. As we would certainly anticipate by now, the situation will prove hopeless if all such effect indicators are linked in unknown ways either to the causal indicator(s) of X or to Y or its indicators. Our basic hope in using multiple effect indicators is that there may be one or more such indicators that are *not* so linked to the other variables in the system. But if this were in fact the case, how would we tell which effect indicators have the desirable properties and which do not? If we use multiple effect indicators, and if all but one or two give almost identical results, then *perhaps* we can muster some faith that, having removed the indicators that yield different results, the remaining indicators have the desired properties. This is essentially the strategy followed in the application of Costner's procedure by McPherson, Welch, and Clark (Chapter 11, this volume).

If we let X_3 be a second effect indicator of X, it can be shown that if X_3 is linked to X_1 via an additional path, it will once more be impossible to isolate c^2 from the remaining unknown coefficients. Let us therefore confine our attention to Model IVA in Fig. 2.5, where the causal indicator X_1 is linked to X_2 via the path f but is not linked to X_3 except through X. The equations for this model are as follows:

(1) $r_{X_1X_2} = ab + f$	(6) $r_{X_1Y_2} = ace$
(2) $r_{X_1X_3} = ag$	(7) $r_{X_2Y_1} = cd(b + af)$
(3) $r_{X_2X_3} = g(b + af)$	(8) $r_{X_2Y_2} = ce(b + af)$
(4) $r_{Y_1Y_2} = de$	(9) $r_{X_3Y_1} = cdg$
(5) $r_{X_1Y_1} = acd$	(10) $r_{X_3Y_2} = ceg$

In applying Costner's first criterion, we can of course utilize all three pairings of the X_i, namely (X_1, X_2), (X_1, X_3), and (X_2, X_3). It can immediately be seen that this consistency criterion should be satisfied, except for sampling errors, in all three pairings. However, if we then estimate c^2 using the

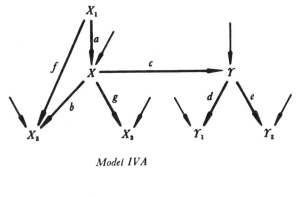

Model IVA

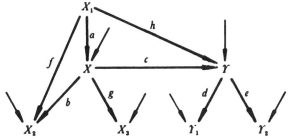

Model IVB

Figure 2.5

three pairings, as we might do if we made the erroneous assumption that $f = 0$, we would obtain the following results:

$$\frac{r_{X_1Y_1}r_{X_2Y_2}}{r_{X_1X_2}r_{Y_1Y_2}} = \frac{(acd)(ce)(b+af)}{(ab+f)(de)} = c^2 \frac{ab+a^2f}{ab+f}$$

$$\frac{r_{X_1Y_1}r_{X_3Y_2}}{r_{X_1X_3}r_{Y_1Y_2}} = \frac{(acd)(ceg)}{(ag)(de)} = c^2$$

$$\frac{r_{X_2Y_1}r_{X_3Y_2}}{r_{X_2X_3}r_{Y_1Y_2}} = \frac{cd(b+af)(ceg)}{g(b+af)(de)} = c^2$$

We see that two of the three possible pairings give the correct estimate, whereas the pairing involving (X_1, X_2) does not (as we previously saw in the case of Model IIB). If we were willing to assume that only one of the effect indicators is linked with X_1, then we could infer which of the two has the nonzero link by looking for the estimate that differs from the remaining two.

Of course the more indicators that appear in the role of effect indicators, the more faith we would have in this procedure. It should be emphasized, however, that it will *always* be necessary to make a number of *a priori* simplifying assumptions that are inherently untestable. The more indicators we have in relation to the number of unmeasured variables, the more tests of compatibility between the model and the data we can make.

Finally, we must return to a point made by Miller that it will be advisable to utilize multiple causal indicators, as well as multiple effect indicators, to guard against alternatives involving linkages of one or more of these variables with Y. In Model IVB, we have complicated Model IVA by adding a path h from X_1 to Y, and it can easily be shown that this again makes it impossible to isolate the path c. In this particular model, the compound path $(c + ah)$ will replace c, but since the existence of h may be unknown, it will be difficult to discover the bias without additional causal indicators. We see that multiple causal indicators help guard against alternatives involving causal connections between stimuli and responses, other than through X, whereas multiple effect indicators guard against very different kinds of nonrandom errors. Obviously, the investigator should be aware of both possibilities and design his research and measurement procedures with each in mind.

CONCLUDING REMARKS

In introducing unmeasured intervening variables into a stimulus–response setup, one is attempting to avoid the extreme operational orientation that, in many practical instances, has characterized much empirical research in sociology and other social sciences. This makes it possible to work explicitly with constructs and measurement errors in causal models in order to guide one's research. Ideally, one should formulate a series of reasonably plausible alternative models that allow for the possibility of nonrandom measurement errors. The causal connections between unmeasured variables and their indicators should also be made explicit so that implications for tests and estimating procedures can be noted. This should then tell the investigator what pieces of data he will need to collect, given the models under consideration. For example, it might suggest that one should obtain at least two effect measures of X along with any indicators taken as causes of X.

But we obviously pay a price for the introduction of such unmeasured variables. In effect, we introduce additional unknowns into the system and are likely to encounter identification problems as a result. Discussions of the identification problem in the econometrics literature have centered around the k-equation system, where we have seen that there must be at least $k - 1$ restrictions on the parameters for any equation that is to be identified. Such discussions usually presume that all variables have been perfectly measured, however. The kinds of identification problems presently under consideration are basically similar to those encountered in factor analysis, where the underlying factors are taken as unknowns. Nevertheless, we can profit from the discussions of identification in the econometrics literature, where one essential strategy is that of introducing exogenous variables into the causal system.

If one thinks in terms of models of the type discussed by Costner, where all indicators are effect variables, then additional causal indicators such as X_1 may be considered as exogenous variables that are presumed to affect X but not Y. Similarly, one might attempt to locate causal indicators of Y that are assumed unrelated to X or any of its indicators. In models involving additional unmeasured variables, a similar strategy of locating both causal indicators and effect indicators would also apply. In general, the more complex and numerous the linkages among the unmeasured variables, the simpler the required assumptions about the indicators and the more numerous these indicators must be in order to avoid identification problems.

It would be helpful to develop necessary and sufficient conditions for the general model involving unmeasured as well as measured variables, but in the absence of such general criteria, one can readily investigate the properties of specific models that seem most appropriate in a given context. Obviously, it would also be useful to attempt to catalog the various kinds of causal models that are most likely to be utilized in different substantive areas, so that investigators can be alerted to a wide range of possible complications and ways of coping with each. It is undoubtedly unwise to expect too much of this kind of model-building enterprise, which can only sensitize one to his untested assumptions rather than doing away with them completely. But this approach does have the very great advantage of bringing these assumptions into the open, where they can be studied and modified if necessary.

REFERENCES

Blalock, H. M., Wells, Caryll S., and Carter, Lewis F. "Statistical Estimation in the Presence of Random Measurement Error." In *Sociological Methodology 1970*, edited by Edgar F. Borgatta and George Bohrnstedt. San Francisco: Jossey-Bass, 1970.

Costner, Herbert, L., "Theory, Deduction and Rules of Correspondence." *American Journal of Sociology* 75 (1969): 245–263.

Hauser, Robert M., and Goldberger, Arthur S. "The Treatment of Unobservable Variables in Path Analysis." In *Sociological Methodology 1971*, edited by Herbert L. Costner. San Francisco: Jossey-Bass, 1971.

Land, Kenneth. "On the Estimation of Path Coefficients for Unmeasured Variables from Correlations among Observed Variables." *Social Forces* 48 (1970):506–511.

3

Utilizing Causal Models to Discover Flaws in Experiments*

Herbert L. Costner

Changes in the language of experimental design appear in response to new conceptions of what constitutes a plausible rival hypothesis (Campbell, 1969). While a concern for the "demand characteristics" of experiments (Orne, 1962), for "experimenter bias" (Rosenthal, 1966), and for "evaluation apprehension" effects (Rosenberg, 1969) does not reflect new logical discoveries, it does give rise to new substantive conceptions of how variables are interrelated and hence new conceptions of plausible rivals to the theoretical hypothesis under examination in a given experiment. If a rival hypothesis is to provide a plausible alternative interpretation for experimental results, it must identify a variable (a) that has effects on the dependent variable or its measurement and (b) that is correlated with (e.g., is affected by) the experimental manipulations without being affected by the independent variable of the underlying theory being tested. In this chapter, we consider such rival hypotheses abstractly by representing the basic features of an experiment and of potential rival hypotheses in the form of a causal model.

* Reprinted by permission of the author and publisher from *Sociometry* 34:398–410. Copyright 1971, the American Sociological Association. This chapter is also a revised version of a paper presented at the meetings of the American Sociological Association, 1970, in Washington, D.C.

In a simple experiment, one variable is manipulated and the degree to which variation in another variable covaries with these manipulations is observed. If our interest lies simply in the effects of the specific manipulations employed, we may be minimally concerned with the causal path by which such effects occur, but this is not the usual purpose of an experiment. Experiments are typically designed, not to document the effects of specific manipulations, but to serve as a test of a more abstract causal theory. The appropriate causal model, then, is not the simple proposition that the manipulation has an effect on the dependent variable; the appropriate causal model entails a minimum of four variables, as shown in Figure 3.1.

In Figure 3.1, X' is the variable actually manipulated by the investigator. For example, he may vary the instructions and "rationale" given to subjects in accord with some prearranged plan. This manipulation, in the total context of the experimental setting, is presumed to produce variations in an unmeasured theoretical variable, X (e.g., to induce varying degrees of cognitive dissonance). The theory proposes that the unmeasured variable, X, has an effect on another unmeasured variable, Y. For example, the theory may propose that variation in cognitive dissonance has an effect on attitudes toward the experimental task. The unmeasured variable, Y, in turn, is presumed to have an effect on an indicator or reflector, Y', that serves as a measure of Y. The reflector in this instance might be a set of questions about the experimental task, for example. What the investigator observes is the covariation (or lack of it) between X' and Y' (i.e., between his manipulations and his measures). What he infers, if the covariation is as anticipated, is an effect of X on Y (i.e., an effect of cognitive dissonance on attitude). To phrase all conclusions simply in terms of the specific variables manipulated and measured instead of in terms of abstract theoretical dimensions would make it difficult if not impossible to arrive at any coherent general principles.

It is evident that an experiment may fail to generate the anticipated outcome in the data even though the theory is correct. This may occur because of an "operational flaw" (i.e., X' may not actually produce variation

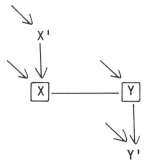

Figure 3.1

in X and variation in Y may not be reflected in Y'). But can the anticipated covariation emerge in the data even though the theory is wrong? It may, and this may be true even though "extraneous" variables have been controlled or randomized in the manner advised in treatises on experimental design. Simply put, the producer of the independent variable (X') may have an effect on the reflector of the dependent variable (Y') for reasons that have nothing to do with the theory that the experiment was designed to test (i.e., that X has an effect on Y). The remainder of this chapter is devoted to considering one technique that may be utilized to determine whether such has, in fact, occurred. In this discussion, we have occasion to utilize causal models and path coefficients. Although these techniques have been utilized by sociologists primarily in nonexperimental studies, this discussion points to the potential utility of the same set of principles in experimental studies.

Originally developed by Sewall Wright for working with problems in genetics (Wright, 1921, 1934), path analysis consists in making assumptions about causal structure explicit and, on the basis of those assumptions, estimating the effect of one variable on another by appropriate regression procedures. Although the term *path analysis* is not generally used in economics, essentially the same analytic procedures were independently developed in econometrics more than four decades ago, and it is in econometrics that these procedures, known as the method of "structural equation models," have been most extensively developed and most widely utilized (Christ, 1966; Goldberger, 1964). Drawing especially on the tradition in econometrics, Blalock is primarily responsible for the introduction of this style of reasoning into sociology (Blalock, 1960, 1961, 1962, 1969b). More recently, the term *path analysis* has been introduced into sociology primarily through the work of Duncan (1966) and into psychology by the work of Werts and Linn (1970). A number of recent discussions have examined the basic reasoning of path analysis and emphasized its basic assumptions (Duncan, 1969; Heise, 1969; Land, 1969). Procedures for estimating path coefficients in simple systems in which all variables are measured variables are presented and illustrated in Nygreen (1971).

The applications and discussions of "path analysis," "structural equation models," or "causal models" in sociology have, until recently, concentrated very heavily on the estimation of effects for systems in which all variables are measured variables. Unmeasured variables in path models have now been given considerable attention (Blalock, 1963, 1968, 1969a; Costner, 1969; Hauser and Goldberger, 1971; Heise, 1970; Jöreskog, 1969, 1970; Land, 1970; Wiley and Wiley, 1970). The inclusion of unmeasured variables in path models may render a model "underidentified" (i.e., insufficient information to estimate the parameters). Estimation then requires that more information be added, either in the form of additional measured variables suitably situated in the causal structure or in the form of *a priori* assumptions about the magnitude of selected parameters. In Fig. 3.1, for example, since X

and Y are unmeasured variables, there is only one observed correlation (between X' and Y'), and that is insufficient to estimate the three path coefficients of the model. If one assumes that the standardized path coefficient from X' to X is 1.0 (i.e., that all variation in the unmeasured variable X is accounted for by the manipulation of X') and that the standardized path coefficient from Y to Y' is also 1.0 (i.e., that Y' is an error-free measure of Y), the model would then be identified (i.e., one observed correlation and one path coefficient to be estimated). If one hesitates to make such *a priori* assumptions about parameters (as one certainly would in most social psychological experiments), an alternative way to achieve identification would be to add other measured variables so situated in the causal structure that they make estimation possible. The advantage of doing so derives not simply from the quantitatively precise estimates of effect that are thereby made possible but from the fact that the model may then become "overidentified" (i.e., more information than is minimally required to estimate the parameters). This, in turn, makes problematic the "goodness of fit" between the model, with the parameters estimated, and the observed correlations. A poor "fit" indicates that the model represents an inaccurate or incomplete specification of the causal relations actually obtaining among the several variables. Among the set of possible reasons for incomplete specification of the model for an experiment is the omission of effects of the experimental manipulation that are not channeled through the theoretical independent variable (e.g., the effects of "demand characteristics," "experimenter bias"). Hence, a good fit will indicate that such unanticipated effects are not evident in the data, whereas a fit that is poor in specific ways will suggest that such unanticipated effects are present.

Two papers have also examined path models in ways that pertain specifically to experiments. Miller (1971) has explored the potential advantage of including multiple experimental manipulations of a single independent variable in the design of an experiment but does not address directly the problem of measurement error (i.e., there are no unmeasured variables in his models). Utilizing a two-stage least-squares estimating procedure, Miller shows that such a multiple manipulation design allows one to discern effects of the experimental manipulation that are not channeled through the theoretical independent variable if such "unwanted" effects are present. Blalock (1971), expanding on an earlier discussion by Land (1970), has explored a number of different models in which the unmeasured independent variable of interest is either manipulated or "measured" by variations in its causes, with or without additional measures based on variations in its effects. The principal focus of Blalock's discussion is on the identification problems encountered in such models. The conclusions clearly lead to a consideration of the kind of models that are examined below.

Before proceeding to consider a workable model for discerning the unanticipated effects of experimental manipulations, if they are present, it will be useful to examine in greater detail how the effects of "demand characteristics," "experimenter bias," or "evaluation apprehension" can be represented in a path model. The models of Fig. 3.2 represent causal connections between the producer (X') of the independent variable and the reflector (Y') of the dependent variable even though the theory is false (i.e., even though there is no effect of the theoretical independent variable, X, on the theoretical dependent variable, Y).

In Fig. 3.2A, the producer, X', has an effect (through V) on the dependent variable, Y, variation in which is reflected in the reflector, Y'; hence, X' has an effect on Y', and the covariation anticipated by the theory would be observed even though the theory (X → Y) is wrong. In Fig. 3.2B, X' also has an (indirect) effect on Y' even though it has no effect on the dependent variable, Y. Note that in either case, interpretation of the experimental results as support for the underlying theory that X has an effect on Y would be incorrect. The effect of the manipulation is real, so this is not a problem of mistaking spurious effects for real effects. Furthermore, we do not have an "operational flaw" in the commonly understood meaning of that term (i.e., X' really does create variation in X, and Y' really does reflect variation in Y. In either of the circumstances represented in Fig. 3.2 we might have occasion to refer to an effect due to the "demand characteristics" of the experiment rather than an effect due to the validity of the underlying theory. The concept of *demand characteristics* suggests that, in creating variations in the independent variable of theoretical interest, the investigator inadvertently creates variation in social expectations that are perceived by the subjects who respond accordingly. The experimental variation has thus created the anticipated effect in the dependent variable reflector, not because of the validity of the theory that the experiment was designed to test, but because of other processes that have inadvertently been set in motion by the experimental variation.

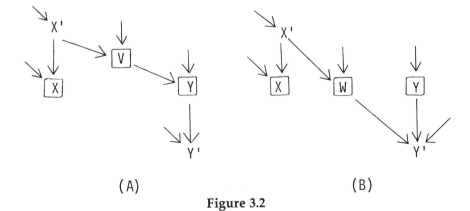

(A)   (B)

Figure 3.2

But if such "demand characteristics" could arise in any experiment involving human subjects, what is an experimenter's defense? How can he assure his potential critics (and himself) that his "supportive" data do indeed support the abstract theory under test rather than being a result of "demand characteristics" that he has inadvertently created? What evidence can he present to suggest that the causal model of Fig. 3.1 is more tenable than either of the alternative causal models of Fig. 3.2? In the usual experiment, with no reflectors of the independent variable (only a producer) and only one reflector of the dependent variable, the decision between these alternatives is largely a matter of intuition and faith. Intuition and faith may not always mislead us, but with additional reflectors for each of the variables there is no need to rely solely on faith and on one's intuitive grasp of the experimental situation.

Consider the model of Fig. 3.3, in which multiple reflectors have been provided for both the independent and the dependent variables. Procedurally, this means that the experimenter not only manipulates conditions that are presumed to produce variations in the theoretical independent variable, X, but that he also measures the variations thus produced in at least two different ways. Furthermore, he also measures variation in the dependent variable, Y, in at least two different ways also. It is then possible, utilizing the estimation procedures described in Jöreskog (1969, 1970), to estimate each of the path coefficients in the model and to utilize those estimates to check the "goodness of fit" between the model thus estimated and the observed correlations. If the fit is satisfactory, the experimenter would be reassured that the effects of the experimental manipulations were all channeled through the unmeasured independent variable (i.e., no effects of "demand characteristics," "experimenter bias") because the model "fits" the data and includes no such "unwanted" effects. If the fit were not satisfactory, however, the interpretation of the poor overall fit for the model would be uncertain since flaws in the specification of the model other than

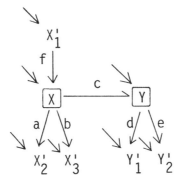

Figure 3.3

the "unwanted" (and unanticipated) effects of the experimental manipulation might be responsible for the poor fit. Hence, if the overall fit is poor, it will be useful to check the fit of the model in three stages. First, consider the "submodel" within Fig. 3.3 that omits the experimental manipulation and its path. Again, the techniques described by Jöreskog (1969, 1970) may be utilized to estimate the coefficients a, b, c, d, and e in Fig. 3.3 (i.e., the paths that do not entail the experimental manipulation). If the fit for this "submodel" is poor, suggesting the existence of "differential bias" among the reflectors of X and Y (Costner, 1969), certain alternative models, some indicating "unwanted" effects of the experimental manipulation, are suggested (discussed below). If the fit at this stage is satisfactory, however, one may proceed to a second stage of the goodness-of-fit check.

The second stage focuses on still another "submodel" of Fig. 3.3, that consisting of the experimental manipulation and the reflectors of the unmeasured independent variable (i.e., paths a, b, and f). The question to be answered at this stage is not simply whether the experimental manipulation is creating variation in the unmeasured independent variable (i.e., does $f = 0$) but whether all of the covariation between the experimental manipulation and the reflectors of the unmeasured independent variable is channeled through that unmeasured independent variable. A careful experimenter may seek assurance that the coefficient f is non-zero by conducting a pretest. The relevant pretest for this purpose would evidently entail a determination of the correlation between the experimental manipulation on the one hand and reflectors of the *independent* variable on the other (i.e., of $r_{X_1'X_2'}$ and $r_{X_1'X_3'}$ in Fig. 3.3). If such pretest correlations turn out to be zero, the experimenter is properly doubtful of the efficacy of his experimental manipulations in producing the intended variation in X. But even if such pretest correlations are non-zero, this does not imply that all of the effects of the experimental manipulation on the reflectors of the independent variable have been channeled through the unmeasured independent variable, and if they are not, the fit for the model of Fig. 3.3 will be poor. In practice, furthermore, a pretest sometimes means something quite different; frequently, it means a preliminary check on the correlation between the experimental manipulations and some reflector of the *dependent* variable (i.e., $r_{X_1'Y_1'}$ or $r_{X_1'Y_2'}$ in Fig. 3.3). Such a preliminary running of the experiment, even if encouraging, does not, of course, have any bearing in the point at issue in this second stage of the goodness-of-fit check, nor, for that matter, any bearing on the more general issue of "unwanted" effects of the experimental manipulations.

An estimate of the path coefficient f may be obtained by utilizing the estimates of coefficients a and b (from the first stage above) and certain correlations that can be computed directly from the data. The model of Fig. 3.3 implies:

$$r_{X_1'X_2'} = af \tag{3.1}$$

$$r_{X_1'X_3'} = bf \tag{3.2}$$

Having estimates for a and b, we may obtain two estimates for f as follows:

$$f = \frac{r_{X_1'X_2'}}{a} \tag{3.3}$$

$$f = \frac{r_{X_1'X_3'}}{b} \tag{3.4}$$

Should these two estimates of f turn out to be inconsistent (i.e., to differ from each other beyond tolerable limits), we would conclude that there is some causal connection between the experimental manipulation, X_1', and at least one of the reflectors, X_2' or X_3', other than that provided by the unmeasured independent variable, X. Such inconsistent estimates should lead to the consideration of alternative models incorporating such additional connections (not discussed in this chapter). Consistent estimates of f, on the other hand, allow one to proceed to the third stage of the goodness-of-fit check for the model of Fig. 3.3.

The third stage bears directly on the question of "unwanted" effects of the experimental manipulation on the dependent variable. For the model represented in Fig. 3.3, the correlations between the experimental manipulation, X_1', and each indicator of the dependent variable, Y_1' and Y_2', may be expressed as the product of the path coefficients connecting the correlated variable. Thus, for Fig. 3.3:

$$r_{X_1'Y_1'} = fcd \tag{3.5}$$

$$r_{X_1'Y_2'} = fce \tag{3.6}$$

But if the experimental manipulation has effects on the indicators of the dependent variable that are not channeled through the unmeasured independent variable (such as those represented in Fig. 3.2), Eqs. (3.5) and (3.6) cannot be expected to hold. If the overall fit for the model of Fig. 3.3 is poor and the fit is satisfactory in the two preceding stages, we should then expect Eqs. (3.5) and (3.6) to fail to hold.

What models stand as alternatives to the model of Fig. 3.3 and what kind of evidence might be utilized to discredit or support them? It would be exceedingly tedious to represent all possible alternatives. We restrict atten-

tion here to alternatives that entail an effect of the experimental manipulation on the reflectors of the unmeasured dependent variable that is not
channeled through the unmeasured independent variable (i.e., alternative
models that include the effects of "demand characteristics," "experimenter
bias"). With this restriction, the models of Fig. 3.4 are the relevant alternatives to the model of Fig. 3.3.

Evidently, the models in Fig. 3.4 do not represent the experimenter's
assumptions in originally designing the experiment; those assumptions are
represented in Fig. 3.3. But if the model of Fig. 3.3 turns out to be untenable,
then the experimenter may seek some understanding of what is responsible
for his experimental results by attempting to ascertain which of the several

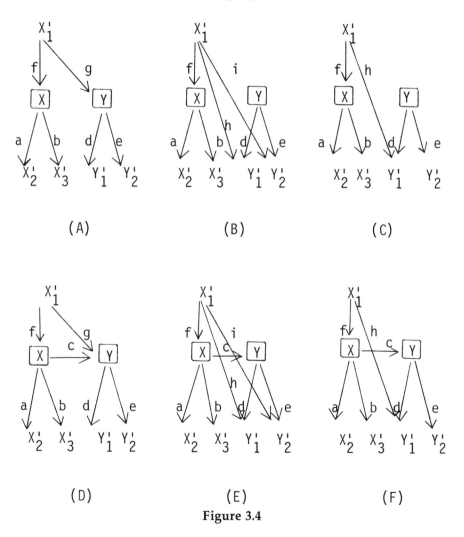

Figure 3.4

possible alternatives represented in Fig. 3.4 fits his data best. An understanding of what has gone on in the experiment requires that one give a
substantive meaning to the models abstractly represented in Fig. 3.4. By
themselves, such abstract models yield no substantive understanding of
how the "unwanted" effects of the experimental manipulation work but
provide instead simply a representation of the paths through which they
work.

In Figs. 3.4A and D, the only connections between the reflectors of X, on
the one hand, and the reflectors of Y, on the other, stem from the correlation
(partially "spurious" in Fig. 3.4D and completely "spurious" in A) between
the corresponding unmeasured variables. The implication is that a satisfactory fit should be obtained in the first stage of the three-stage goodness-of-
fit check outlined above (i.e., there is no "differential bias" entailed in the
reflectors of X and Y). For analogous reasons, the second stage should
likewise yield a satisfactory fit. But a lack of fit should appear in the third
stage (i.e., Eqs. [3.5] and [3.6] should fail to hold). This pattern of results thus
suggests that Fig. 3.4A or D probably represents the appropriate alternative
model, and a new set of estimates for the path coefficients of Fig. 3.4D, using
the procedures described by Jöreskog (1969), may be computed. The results
will indicate which of these two alternatives is more appropriate (i.e., is the
coefficient c zero or non-zero) and may further be used to check for the
goodness of fit of this alternative model. The models of Figs. 3.4A and D
suggest that the "unwanted" effects of the experimental manipulation appear as effects on the unmeasured dependent variable itself and not simply
as measurement errors in the reflectors of it; a substantive interpretation of
such a model may therefore yield new theoretical insights into the determinants of the unmeasured dependent variable.

The remaining models in Fig. 3.4 (i.e., B, C, E, and F) may yield a different
pattern of results in the three-stage goodness-of-fit check outlined above
and furthermore, when substantively interpreted, may yield insights into
the problems of measuring Y rather than into the determinants of Y. In each
of these models, the experimental manipulation creates a connection between the reflectors of X and Y in addition to whatever connection may exist
between these two unmeasured variables themselves. Given three reflectors for both X and Y (instead of the two shown in the figures), an unsatisfactory fit would be expected at the first stage of the goodness-of-fit check
because of the "differential bias" thus created (see Costner, 1969); with only
two reflectors for each of the unmeasured variables, however, these models
should yield a satisfactory fit at the first stage but an unsatisfactory fit at the
third stage in the goodness-of-fit check. Even with three reflectors for each
unmeasured variable, the failure to achieve a satisfactory fit at this first
stage, however, may arise from circumstances quite different from those
represented in these models, and it is therefore appropriate to make estimates and check the goodness of fit before proceeding to interpret them. A

new set of estimates for the model of Fig. 3.4E will suffice since it includes all paths included in the other three models. If the fit is satisfactory, the magnitudes of selected coefficients (e.g., is c zero or non-zero, is i zero or non-zero) will indicate which of the four models is tenable.

As is evident in the models represented in Figs. 3.4D, E, and F, the theory underlying the original design of the experiment (i.e., that X has an effect on Y) may be supported by the data even though "demand characteristics," "experimenter bias," etc., have intruded to partially distort the experimental results. Evidently, then, the mere existence of such "unwanted" effects of the experimental manipulation need not completely invalidate an experiment. Hence, the representation of an experiment in the form of a path model and the quantitative estimation of the several paths may allow one to emerge with sound and theoretically relevant conclusions despite very real threats to internal validity.

In summary, the procedures sketched here allow a test of the tenability of a set of assumptions about the causal structure by which experimental manipulations have observed effects and thereby may be used to render experimental studies more clearly relevant to the theories they are designed to test. If the usual assumptions about the causal structure underlying experimental results are found to be untenable, the tenability of alternatives may also be checked, and the results may yield new substantive insights as well as data supporting or failing to support the theory underlying the original design of the experiment.

REFERENCES

Blalock, Hubert M., Jr. "Correlation Analysis and Causal Inferences." *American Anthropologist* 62 (1960):624–631.

Blalock, Hubert M., Jr. *Causal Inferences in Nonexperimental Research*. Chapel Hill: University of North Carolina Press, 1961.

Blalock, Hubert M., Jr. "Four-Variable Causal Models and Partial Correlations." *American Journal of Sociology* 68 (1962):182–194.

Blalock, Hubert M., Jr. "Making Causal Inferences for Unmeasured Variables from Correlations among Indicators." *American Journal of Sociology* 69 (1963):53–62.

Blalock, Hubert M., Jr. "The Measurement Problem: A Gap between the Language of Theory and Research." In *Methodology in Social Research*, edited by Hubert M. Blalock, Jr. and Ann B. Blalock. New York: McGraw-Hill, 1968.

Blalock, Hubert M., Jr. "Multiple Indicators and the Causal Approach to Measurement Error." *American Journal of Sociology* 75 (1969):264–272. (a)

Blalock, Hubert M., Jr. *Theory Construction: From Verbal to Mathematical Formulations*. New York: Prentice-Hall, 1969. (b)

Blalock, Hubert M., Jr. "Causal Models Involving Unmeasured Variables in Stimulus–Response Situations." In *Causal Models in the Social Sciences*, edited by Hubert M. Blalock, Jr. Chicago: Aldine Atherton, 1971, and this volume.

Campbell, Donald T. "Prospective: Artifact and Control." In *Artifact in Behav-*

ioral Research, edited by Robert Rosenthal and R. L. Rosnow. New York: Academic Press, 1969.

Christ, Carl. *Econometric Models and Methods.* New York: John Wiley & Sons, 1966.

Costner, Herbert L. "Theory, Deduction and Rules of Correspondence." *American Journal of Sociology* 75 (1969):245–263.

Duncan, Otis Dudley. "Path Analysis: Sociological Examples." *American Journal of Sociology* 72 (1966):1–16.

Duncan, Otis Dudley. "Contingencies in Constructing Causal Models." In *Sociological Methodology 1969,* edited by Edgar F. Borgatta. San Francisco: Jossey-Bass, 1969.

Goldberger, Arthur S. *Econometric Theory.* New York: John Wiley & Sons, 1964.

Hauser, Robert M., and Goldberger, Arthur S. "The Treatment of Unobservable Variables in Path Analysis." In *Sociological Methodology 1971,* edited by Herbert L. Costner. San Francisco: Jossey-Bass, 1971.

Heise, David R. "Problems in Path Analysis and Causal Inference." In *Sociological Methodology 1969,* edited by Edgar F. Borgatta. San Francisco: Jossey-Bass, 1969.

Heise, David R. "Separating Reliability and Stability in Test–Retest Correlation." *American Sociological Review* 34 (1970):93–101 and this volume.

Jöreskog, K. G. "A General Approach to Confirmatory Maximum Likelihood Factor Analysis." *Psychometrika* 34 (1969):183–202.

Jöreskog, K. G. "A General Method for Analysis of Covariance Structures." *Biometrika* 57 (1970):239–251.

Land, Kenneth C. "Principles of Path Analysis." In *Sociological Methodology 1969,* edited by Edgar F. Borgatta. San Francisco: Jossey-Bass, 1969.

Land, Kenneth C. "On the Estimation of Path Coefficients for Unmeasured Variables from Correlations among Observed Variables." *Social Forces* 48 (1970):506–511.

Miller, Alden D. "Logic of Causal Analysis: From Experimental to Nonexperimental Designs." In *Causal Models in the Social Sciences,* edited by Hubert M. Blalock, Jr. Chicago: Aldine Atherton, 1971, and this volume.

Nygreen, G. T. "Interactive Path Analysis." *American Sociologist* 6 (1971):37–43.

Orne, M. T. "On the Social Psychological Experiment: With Particular Reference to Demand Characteristics and Their Implications." *American Psychologist* 17 (1962):776–783.

Rosenberg, Milton J. "The Conditions and Consequences of Evaluation Apprehension." In *Artifact in Behavioral Research,* edited by Robert Rosenthal and R. L. Rosnow. New York: Academic Press, 1969.

Rosenthal, Robert. *Experimenter Effects in Behavioral Research.* New York: Appleton-Century-Crofts, 1966.

Werts, C. E., and Linn, R. L. "Path Analysis: Psychological Examples." *Psychological Bulletin* 74 (1970):193–212.

Wiley, David E., and Wiley, James A. "The Estimation of Measurement Error in Panel Data." *American Sociological Review* 35 (1970):112–117 and this volume.

Wright, Sewall. "Correlation and Causation." *Journal of Agricultural Research* 20 (1921):557–585.

Wright, Sewall. "The Method of Path Coefficients." *Annals of Mathematical Statistics* 5 (1934):161–215.

4

Causal Models, Unobserved Variables, and Experimental Data*

Duane F. Alwin

Richard C. Tessler

INTRODUCTION

For more than a decade, there has been much attention devoted to causal analysis in the social sciences (e.g., Blalock, 1964, 1971b). Most of this attention has focused on the analysis of *nonexperimental* data in which the causal relationships are assumed to be recursive. One problem sometimes encountered in the causal analysis of nonexperimental data is that relationships between the variables of interest may be causally reciprocal, and in some substantive domains reciprocal causation is regarded as common-place. Support can often be advanced for hypotheses that X causes Y *and* that Y causes X. For example, social psychologists often maintain that atti-

*Reprinted by permission of the authors and publisher from the *American Journal of Sociology* 80: 58–86. Copyright 1974, the University of Chicago Press. Portions of this chapter were written while the authors were postdoctoral fellows at the University of Wisconsin. Support was provided by Professors David Mechanic, William H. Sewell, and Robert M. Hauser from National Institute of Mental Health grant MH-07413, National Institutes of Health grant M-6275, and American College Testing Program research funds. Research reported here was supported by the NIMH grant. Computing facilities were provided by the Madison Academic Computing Center.

tudes are both causes and consequences of overt behavior. Where reciprocal causation characterizes a substantive problem, the analyst is often advised to separate the variables temporally (Blalock, 1964), leave the causal connections unspecified (Sewell, Haller, and Ohlendorf, 1970; Sewell, Haller, and Portes, 1969) or allow for simultaneous causation between the variables involved (see Duncan, Haller, and Portes, 1968; Kohn and Schooler, 1973). A limitation of the latter approach is that simultaneous reciprocal causal parameters are often underidentified. The obvious problem with leaving causal connections unspecified is that it yields virtually no information regarding causation, except when both reciprocal effects are zero.

A second problem encountered in the causal analysis of nonexperimental data is that observed effects may be spurious. The possibility exists that neither X causes Y nor Y causes X, but rather that the association observed between them results from the operation of some third variable that affects both X and Y. Insofar as measures of such antecedent variables are available, the analyst can examine the issue of spuriousness. However, the number of possible prior variables may be large, and therefore some might be left unmeasured. Thus, the possibility of spuriousness cannot always be ruled out in the analysis of nonexperimental data.

This chapter is concerned with possible applications of causal modeling techniques in the analysis of *experimental* data. One of the virtues of experimental data for causal analysis is that the two problems noted above are minimized if not entirely eliminated (Aronson and Carlsmith, 1968; Wiggins, 1968). In experimental data, the temporal ordering of independent and dependent variables is unequivocal. Since the independent variable, X, is ordinarily induced temporally prior to the measurement of the dependent variable, Y, the possibility of reciprocal causation can be ruled out, and the causal directionality of an association between X and Y can usually be interpreted unambiguously.

Experimental analysis can also be seen as a potential solution to the problem of underidentification due to presumed simultaneity. If X and Y are believed to have reciprocal effects in a nonexperimental design, and the coefficients expressing these effects are not identified, it is, in principle, possible to design an experiment in which first X, and then Y, is the experimental variable, with the other being the outcome. In many cases, this may not be practical, but when it is, it may offer a solution to the problem of underidentification due to simultaneity.

Experimental analysis can also circumvent the problem of spuriousness. By random assignment of subjects to treatment groups (levels of X), it becomes highly unlikely that some third variable will be correlated with X. Hence, if a relationship is observed between X and Y, the analyst can confidently offer a causal interpretation of the result.[1] For these reasons,

---

[1] Of course any observed relationship between X_m and Y_1 may admit of alternative interpretations, for example, demand characteristics (Orne, 1962), experimenter

Kish (1959) has described the experiment as the scientific method par excellence, when it is feasible.

While we endorse a view that underscores the special virtues of experimental data for causal analysis, we do not want our presentation to be construed as downplaying the importance of techniques of causal analysis for nonexperimental data. Despite the methodological problems sometimes encountered in the causal analysis of nonexperimental data, such analyses have had clear and significant payoffs. Our contention is simply that the application of techniques of causal modeling ought not be limited to nonexperimental data, and that their use in the analysis of experimental data may yield estimates of causal parameters that are superior to estimates based upon conventional methods.

One of the early concerns of causal analysts working with nonexperimental data was with the treatment of unobserved or unobservable variables in structural equation models representing causal systems (Blalock, 1963; Land, 1970). A major use of unobserved variables in sociology has been to represent various types of error in the measurement of variables (Althauser and Heberlein, 1970; Alwin, 1973a, 1973b; Blalock, 1969, 1970; Costner, 1969; Hauser and Goldberger, 1971; Heise, 1969). A second major use, noted by Land (1970) and discussed by Hauser and Goldberger (1971), is the case where one or more unmeasured variables intervene between sets of measured variables. This chapter extends the treatment of unobserved variables in path analysis to the analysis of experimental data. Previous attention to this problem by Costner (1971) and Blalock (1971a) provides both a background to the problem and a stimulus for applying some specific estimation procedures in the analysis of experimental data. Our discussion of the problem, however, places an emphasis on a somewhat different set of issues; and, unlike earlier investigators, we estimate a model with data from a recent experiment (Tessler, 1973).

THE PARAMETERS OF SIMPLE EXPERIMENTS

Blalock (1971a) and Costner (1971) have emphasized the importance of viewing experiments in terms of unobserved causal processes. Experiments are usually designed to estimate general causal relationships and consequently should accomplish more than simply measuring the effects of a manipulation per se on measurements of the dependent variable. In social psychological experiments, the experimenter typically wishes to create differences among subjects exposed to different experimental conditions in some psychological state (e.g., affect, goals, intentions). This is usually

---

bias (Rosenthal, 1966), other types of reactivity (Campbell and Stanley, 1963), or confounding variables (Aronson and Carlsmith, 1968). Such alternative interpretations, however, do not dispute the fact that a relationship between X_m and Y_1 has been observed.

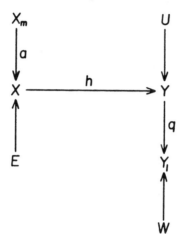

Figure 4.1. Underidentified model of a simple experiment.

achieved by manipulating the instructions or other stimulus material that subjects encounter upon entering the formal experimental situation.

Blalock (1971a) and Costner (1971) have suggested that this aspect of an experiment — the induction of an experimental treatment — be expressed in terms of two separate variables, one representing the manipulation and one representing the unobserved psychological state. We will refer to the first variable as a *manipulated independent variable* and the second as an *unobserved independent variable*. The effect of the manipulated independent variable on the unobserved independent variable reflects the extent to which the experimental treatment has been successfully induced. This parameter is denoted by a in Fig. 4.1, linking X_m (the manipulated independent variable) and X (the unobserved independent variable) causally. The experimenter ordinarily desires this parameter to approach unity.[2] (Note that the disturbances in Fig. 4.1 and in all subsequent models are uncorrelated with all other variables in the model, including other disturbances. All models are stated for the population.)

The theory underlying an experiment ordinarily involves some predicted relationship between an unobserved independent variable and an attitudinal or behavioral outcome. We refer to such an outcome as an *unobserved dependent variable* and represent it by Y in Fig. 4.1. The effect of the unobserved independent variable on the unobserved dependent variable is de-

---

[2] Blalock (1971a: 336) discusses the possibility of multiple manipulated variables for each unobserved independent variable. Since we think this situation is rather rare in behavioral experiments, we will include only one manipulated independent variable for each unobserved independent variable in all models discussed in this chapter.

noted by h in Fig. 4.1. This parameter is of primary interest to the experimenter, since its magnitude will lead him to accept or reject his theoretical hypothesis.

Since the effect of X on Y cannot be assessed in any direct sense, an indicator of Y is needed in order to assess the effect indirectly. We refer to this indicator of Y as an *observed dependent variable* and represent it by Y_1 in Fig. 4.1. The measurement adequacy of this indicator of Y is represented by the symbol q in Fig. 4.1. We can think of this parameter in terms of conventional definitions of reliability and validity.[3]

In summary, a minimum of four variables is required to explicitly represent the appropriate causal model for simple experiments: a manipulated independent variable, an unobserved independent variable, an unobserved dependent variable, and an observed dependent variable. This requirement is usually ignored in the analysis of experimental data. Ordinarily, the experimenter uses some measure of the relationship between X_m and Y_1 as an estimate of h.[4] It should be clear, however, that more is involved in this relationship than the causal parameter h, since

$$r_{X_m Y_1} = ahq$$

Therefore, any attempt to equate

$$r_{X_m Y_1}$$

(or some analogous measure of association) with the parameter h amounts to the assumption that $a = q = 1.0$. In other words, it would be necessary to assume that the unobserved independent variable (X) is isomorphic with the manipulated independent variable (X_m) and that the unobserved dependent variable (Y) is perfectly measured. Unless one is dealing with a highly unusual experimental situation, these parameters will doubtless not equal unity.

---

[3] Here we view variation in Y_1 as due to two orthogonal components—a true or reliable component, Y, and a random error component, E. Given this definition, it follows that q^2 is an estimate of the reliability of Y_1 (see Lord and Novick, 1968). If we assume that Y_1 measures Y and no other reliable sources of variation, then q can be thought of as a validity coefficient.

[4] This statement may be somewhat misleading. In fact, one rarely sees experimental analyses in which the magnitudes of relationships are estimated. The most frequent statistical analysis presented in experimental journals is the F-test for the overall difference of means. However, it is not uncommon for analysts to interpret the magnitude of the F-ratio as a measure of association or as an estimate of the magnitude of the effects.

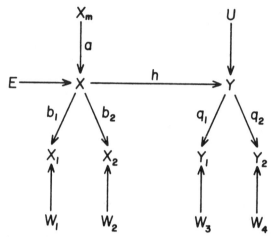

Figure 4.2. Overidentified model of a simple experiment.

The causal model for the simple experiment diagrammed in Fig. 4.1 is underidentified, that is, there are three unknown parameters in one observed correlation. In order to allow the parameters to be estimated, it is sufficient to include at least one measurable indicator of the unobserved independent variable and multiple indicators (at least two) of the unobserved dependent variable (Blalock, 1971a; Costner, 1971). These additional variables are included in the model depicted in Fig. 4.2. This model is overidentified and is estimable using confirmatory factor analysis (Jöreskog, 1969, 1970; Jöreskog, Gruvaeus, and van Thillo, 1970). Before estimating a model of this type for a more complex experiment, we will pursue some general aspects of experimental analysis in greater detail. First, we will consider the problem of evaluating experimental manipulations and suggest some methods for assessing their effectiveness. Second, we will consider the question of how to evaluate the adequacy of measures of the dependent variable(s). Third, we will review Costner's discussion of the problem of detecting "flaws" in the analysis of experimental data and present some observations of our own. Finally, we will pursue the estimation of an entire model of the type portrayed in Fig. 4.2 with data from a recent social psychological experiment.

EVALUATING EXPERIMENTAL MANIPULATIONS

The use of measures of X (see Fig. 4.2) as *manipulation checks* in experiments and experimental pretests is commonplace. Indeed, the typical approach to estimating the parameter *a* involves gathering data at some point after the manipulation in the form of questions pertaining to the subjects' perceptions of the manipulated independent variable. The subjects' responses to these questions are presumed to be caused in part by the underlying psychological state that the experimenter has attempted to induce. The model in Fig. 4.2 depicts the manipulation checks as X_1 and X_2 and denotes the effects of the underlying state on the manipulation checks as b_1 and b_2. The parameters represent information on the reliability and validity of the manipulation checks as measures of X.[5]

The experimenter typically estimates the relationship between X_m and X_1 and/or X_2 in order to get some idea of the event to which he has effectively manipulated X. In other words, he often thinks of the relationship here as an estimate of a.[6] It is clear, however, that

$$r_{X_m X_1} = ab_1$$

and

$$r_{X_m X_2} = ab_2$$

The correlations involved depend not only on the parameter a but also on the parameters representing the validity of the manipulation checks, b_1 and b_2.

If the experimenter is pretesting his manipulations and wishes to carry out some assessment of the effectiveness of his manipulations, it is possible to estimate this aspect of the general model in advance of the actual experiment with pretest data. (We assume that the entire experiment is not carried out in the pretest.) The structural equations for this part of the model, represented in Fig. 4.3a, are as follows:

$$X = a\,X_m + \sqrt{1 - a^2}E$$

$$X_1 = b_1\,X + \sqrt{1 - b_1^2}W_1$$

$$X_2 = b_2\,X + \sqrt{1 - b_2^2}W_2$$

The terms E, W_1, and W_2 represent random disturbances and as such are uncorrelated with the prior variables in the equations and with each other. It is now possible to write the correlations among the observed variables as

---

[5] See footnote 3.

[6] Again, the usual practice is to evaluate the overall difference in means by an F-test rather than to estimate the magnitude of the relationship involved. However, since the magnitude of the F-ratio is often interpreted as an indication of the size of the relationship, our point is probably valid.

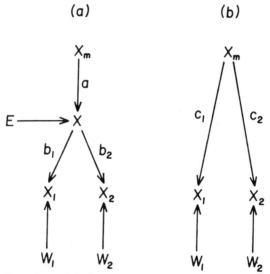

Figure 4.3. Causal models for evaluating experimental manipulations.

$$r_{X_1X_2} = b_1b_2$$

$$r_{X_1X_m} = ab_1$$

$$r_{X_2X_m} = ab_2$$

The parameters of the model in Fig. 4.3a are just-identified, so it is possible to solve uniquely for the unknown parameters in straightforward algebraic fashion as

$$a = \sqrt{r_{X_1X_m}r_{X_2X_m}/r_{X_1X_2}}$$

$$b_1 = \sqrt{r_{X_1X_m}r_{X_1X_2}/r_{X_2X_m}}$$

$$b_2 = \sqrt{r_{X_2X_m}r_{X_1X_2}/r_{X_1X_m}}$$

This simple model is equivalent to a one-factor model for the correlations among three variables (see Duncan, 1972; Hauser; 1969; Land, 1970). It can be made overidentified by adding more manipulation checks. It should be obvious that a model with only one manipulation check is underidentified.

It is possible that the model in Fig. 4.2 is misspecified in important ways. Specifically, the experimenter may be concerned with such things as "demand characteristics" (Orne, 1962) and "experimenter effects" (Rosenthal,

1966) which could invalidate his inferences. In Fig. 4.2, any effect of X_m that operates directly on the manipulation checks, X_1 and X_2 rather than through the unobserved independent variable X, can be considered an experimental artifact or "flaw" (Costner, 1971) of the form described by the above terms.[7]

The effects discussed in the preceding paragraph are not included in Fig. 4.2, and we should note that their inclusion there would render the model underidentified. Blalock (1971a: 340–341) and Costner (1971: 404–405) discuss this problem in some detail. One possible approach is to phrase the issue in terms of a model that does not include an unobserved independent variable and compare the estimates of this model with those provided for Fig. 4.3a. In such a model, the effects of the manipulated independent variable on the manipulation checks would all be direct, not mediated by an unobserved variable. The diagram in Fig. 4.3b represents such a model, where c denotes the demand or experimenter effects (hereafter referred to simply as demand effects).

The model in Fig. 4.3b implies that the partial correlation $r_{12 \cdot m}$ should be zero in the population; that is, $r_{12} = r_{m1}r_{m2}$. Since this equality is not implied by the model in Fig. 4.3a — that is, $r_{12} \neq r_{m1}r_{m2}$ — we have a way of choosing between a model that contains nothing but demand effects and one that allows for the transmission of the effects of X_m through an unobserved variable. Superficially, then, we can compare the relative fit of the two models using sample data. Unfortunately, the comparison is not always definitive, since as the parameter a approaches unity (a desirable circumstance), the two models will be indistinguishable empirically. Moreover, if we reject the model in Fig. 4.3b, we have in no sense confirmed the model in Fig. 4.3a, since there are other reasons why the partial correlation in question might be non-zero. For example, there could be some effect of X_1 on X_2 or vice versa. There could be some unknown, uncontrolled factor causing both X_1 and X_2. However, as we pointed out earlier, if the subjects have been randomly assigned to treatments, this interpretation can ordinarily be ruled out. Finally, it is possible that some combination of the models in Fig. 4.3a and b might be the most appropriate for the data in a given situation. This possibility is illustrated in Fig. 4.4. Indeed, the models in Fig. 4.3a and b are special cases of the model in Fig. 4.4, where certain parameters are equal to zero. Here, the manipulated independent variable affects the manipulation checks both directly and indirectly via the unobserved independent variable. Unfortunately, this model does not lend itself to a tractable solution. Any model of this type that includes three unknown parameters in all

---

[7] The terms *demand characteristics* and *experimenter effects* are ordinarily used in connection with artifactual effects of the independent variable on measures of the dependent variable rather than on its effects on such things as manipulation checks. However, the terminology appears general enough to permit the inclusion of the type of effects being considered here.

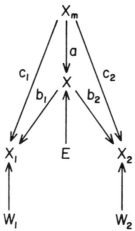

Figure 4.4. Causal model for evaluating experimental manipulations.

of the correlations between the manipulated independent variable and each manipulation check and two unknown parameters in each of the correlations among the manipulation checks is grossly underidentified. It is feasible, however, to construct a model in which we can estimate some (but not all) demand effects. The model in Fig. 4.5 represents this alternative. This model includes three measures of X and allows us to estimate one demand effect c. The correlations among the observed variables are as follows:

$$r_{X_m X_1} = ab_1$$

$$r_{X_m X_2} = ab_2$$

$$r_{X_m X_3} = ab_3 + c$$

$$r_{X_1 X_2} = b_1 b_2$$

$$r_{X_1 X_3} = b_1(b_3 + ac)$$

$$r_{X_2 X_3} = b_2(b_3 + ac)$$

All of the parameters of the model in Fig. 4.5 are identifiable, and some are overidentified. It is possible to estimate the parameters a, b_1, and b_2 as above (using r_{m1}, r_{m2}, and r_{12}). Then, by writing $c = r_{m3} - ab_3$ and substituting this term into the equations for r_{13} and r_{23}, we can obtain two estimates for b_3; that is, there is an overidentifying restriction.

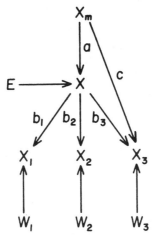

Figure 4.5. Causal model for evaluating experimental manipulations.

$$b_1/b_2 = r_{X_1X_3}/r_{X_2X_3}$$

Finally, returning to the equation for r_{m3}, we have two estimates for c. Efficient estimates for all these parameters should be possible. Note also that besides the model discussed here, two other such models are possible: one allowing for a demand effect on X_1 and one allowing for a demand effect on X_2.

As one adds measures of X, that is, manipulation checks, the ability to estimate the c's is increased. With four such manipulation checks, two c's can be estimated, while with five, three c's can be estimated. While it is clearly possible to estimate such models, it is unclear whether the associated gains in terms of identification outweigh the practical costs of obtaining multiple measures. Moreover, it is uncertain whether such demand effects would operate on some measures of X and not on others. As noted earlier, the problem does not lend itself to satisfactory solution, since any general model that includes both direct and indirect effects for all manipulation checks is underidentified. Perhaps the only tangible indication of the presence of demand effects, aside from the fit of the extreme case in Fig. 4.3b (which does not always work), is when one is unable to fit the desired model in Fig. 4.3a.

EVALUATING THE ADEQUACY OF MEASURES OF THE DEPENDENT VARIABLE

The model proposed for the purposes of identifying the key parameters of the simple experiment was presented in Fig. 4.2. This model includes at least one measurable indicator of X, namely, X_1, and at least two such measures if this part of the model is studied separately as in the preceding section. Moreover, the model in Fig. 4.2 includes multiple measures (at least two) of Y, specifically Y_1 and Y_2. It is important to evaluate the measures of Y as well, and this is the subject of this section.

Any attempt to evaluate the adequacy of measures of Y (either during pretesting or upon completion of the experiment) will be concerned with the extent to which the several measures covary. More specifically, the concern is with the extent to which a single factor can account for their intercorrelations. (Obviously, if the model involves more than a single dependent variable, then an m-factor solution would be of interest.) In order to identify such a single-factor model for the measures of Y, it is necessary to incorporate at least three such measures to estimate the parameters of this part of the model. This model is presented in Fig. 4.6. The estimates of q_1, q_2, and q_3 are formally equivalent to those presented for a, b_1, and b_2 in the model in Fig. 4.2. These estimates are as follows:

$$q_1 = \sqrt{r_{Y_1Y_2}r_{Y_1Y_3}/r_{Y_2Y_3}}$$

$$q_2 = \sqrt{r_{Y_1Y_2}r_{Y_2Y_3}/r_{Y_1Y_3}}$$

$$q_3 = \sqrt{r_{Y_1Y_3}r_{Y_2Y_3}/r_{Y_1Y_2}}$$

As additional measures of Y are included, the parameters become overidentified, and efficient estimates for the q's can be obtained by Jöreskog's confirmatory factor analysis procedure (Jöreskog et al., 1970). It is possible to examine the statistical fit of the single-factor model in terms of its ability to reproduce the correlations among the Y_j. The logic of statistical hypothesis testing in factor analysis is described by Maxwell (1959) and Lawley and Maxwell (1971). The general strategy involves testing the hypothesis that m

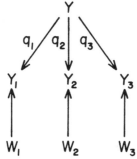

Figure 4.6. Causal model for evaluating dependent–variable measures.

factors adequately reproduce the correlation matrix (see Lawley and Maxwell, 1971: 37).

The difference between the present strategy and those usually taken to examine the adequacy of the Y_j's as measures of some single underlying factor is that the present approach explicitly sets forth a model for their intercorrelation and proposes a test of that model. If a single factor fits the correlations among the Y_j items, one can have some confidence that they all measure the same thing. If this model does not fit the data, a number of alternative strategies are possible. The most fruitful of these is probably an exploratory unrestricted factor analysis of the items.[8] This will indicate the clusters of linear dependence in them. Then it will be possible to decide, according to some *a priori* scheme, which cluster(s) of items measures the concept(s) involved as a dependent variable(s).

EVALUATING RIVAL HYPOTHESES

An important contribution Costner's (1971) paper makes is the suggestion that one can examine the presence of "demand characteristics" and/or "experimenter" effects within the framework of the causal modeling approach. Costner's strategy is first to estimate the causal model of interest, for example, the model in Fig. 4.2, and if the fit to the data is poor, to consider several other models.

One possible reason for the lack of fit that Costner discusses is the presence of the type of demand effects discussed at length under Evaluating Experimental Manipulations above. While such effects can often be detected and, one hopes, eliminated in the analysis of pretest data, they may not be entirely absent in the actual experiment. It is important, therefore, to entertain such effects in the alternative specification of the model. The ways in which such effects can be included are discussed above.

A second possible reason for the lack of fit that Costner discusses is the presence of direct effects of the manipulated independent variable on the unobserved or observed dependent variables. This type of effect has conventionally been referred to as "experimenter" and/or "demand characteristics" effects. Following our above usage, we will simply refer to this category as demand effects.

Costner suggests that we consider six models that incorporate some form of this second kind of demand effect. Figure 4.7 presents a general model under which all of Costner's models can be subsumed. We have used Costner's effect notation but our own variable notation (see Fig. 4.2).

[8] If only three measures of Y are included in a pretest, only a single-factor model will fit the correlations, if any. Except for the Heywood case (see Harman, 1967: 117–118), a single-factor model will always fit the correlations among three variables. It may be desirable, therefore, to include at least four variables as measures of Y.

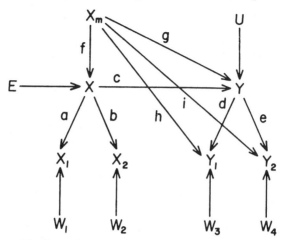

Figure 4.7. Causal model for evaluating rival hypotheses.

Costner presents two general classes of models — one in which the parameter g is zero, but h and i are potentially nonzero; and one in which the parameters h and i are zero, but g is potentially non-zero. In other words, the demand effect can operate in one of two ways, either directly on the observed dependent variables or indirectly via the unobserved dependent variable.

Table 4.1 presents the correlations among the observed variables in terms of the unknown parameters for each of Costner's six models and for the models in Figs. 4.2 and 4.7. We have labeled the models 2, A, B, C, D, E, F, and 7 to be consistent with both Costner's symbols and our own. Table 4.1 indicates that in model 2, $g = h = i = 0$; in model A, $c = h = i = 0$; in model B, $c = g = 0$; in model C, $c = g = i = 0$; in model D, $h = i = 0$; in model E, $g = 0$; and in model F, $g = i = 0$. Moreover, it can be deduced from Table 4.1 that models 2 and A are special cases of model D, and that models B, C, and F are special cases of model E. So there are two subtypes of the model in Fig. 4.7 that Costner treats in his consideration of rival hypotheses. Model D involves the general case in which X_m affects Y but not Y_1 and Y_2 directly, and model E involves the general case in which X_m affects Y_1 and Y_2 directly but not Y.

If the model in Fig. 4.2 does not provide a reasonable fit to the data, then it is possible to estimate versions of Costner's models D and E using the Jöreskog approach. Since Costner's other models are special cases of these models, these estimates should indicate which model, if any, will provide the best fit.[9] Jöreskog (1970) and Lawley and Maxwell (1971) discuss a

[9] In some cases, models D and E may be indistinguishable. For instance, when the parameters h and i in model E are proportional to the parameters d and e, such that the ratio of estimates for h and i approximates (within sampling error) the ratio of estimates for d and e, we essentially have the case of model D for Eqs. (5)–(10) of Table 4.1.

Table 4.1. Correlations among observed variables in the simple experiment expressed in terms of the unknown parameters for eight alternative causal models[a]

Correlation	Model							
	2	A	B	C	D	E	F	7
(1) $r_{X_m X_1}$	af	af	af	af	af	af	af	af
(2) $r_{X_m X_2}$	bf	bf	bf	bf	bf	bf	bf	bf
(3) $r_{X_1 X_2}$	ab	ab	ab	ab	ab	ab	ab	ab
(4) $r_{Y_1 Y_2}$	de	de	$de + hi$	de	de	$d(e + icf)$ $de + h(i + ecf)$	$de + hecf$	$d[e + i(g + cf)]$ $de + h[i + e(g + cf)]$
(5) $r_{X_m Y_1}$	fcd	gd	h	h	$d(g + fc)$	$h + fcd$	$h + fcd$	$h + d(g + cf)$
(6) $r_{X_1 Y_1}$	acd	$afgd$	afh	afh	$d(c + fg)a$	$a(fh + cd)$	$a(fh + cd)$	$da(gf + c) + hfa$
(7) $r_{X_2 Y_1}$	bcd	$bfgd$	bfh	bfh	$d(c + fg)b$	$b(fh + cd)$	$b(fh + cd)$	$db(gf + c) + hfb$
(8) $r_{X_m Y_2}$	fce	ge	i	0	$e(g + fc)$	$i + fce$	fce	$i + e(g + cf)$
(9) $r_{X_1 Y_2}$	ace	$afge$	afi	0	$e(c + fg)a$	$a(fi + ce)$	ace	$ea(gf + c) + ifa$
(10) $r_{X_2 Y_2}$	bce	$bfge$	bfi	0	$e(c + fg)b$	$b(fi + ce)$	bce	$eb(gf + c) + ifb$

[a] See Figure 4.7 for variable and effect notation.

69

goodness-of-fit test for the adequacy of the obtained estimates in reproducing the observed correlation matrix. This test, which depends on maximum-likelihood estimates, is distributed as χ^2 for large samples, assuming multivariate normality. This test can be used for comparisons of relative fit to the data (see Burt, 1973).

AN EMPIRICAL ILLUSTRATION: CLIENTS' REACTIONS TO INITIAL INTERVIEWS

This section provides an illustration of the estimation of the parameters of a complex causal model for data from a recent experiment (Tessler, 1973). An experimental investigation of the determinants of clients' reactions to initial interviews was structured around a simulation of a first meeting between a counselor and a client. The experiment extended earlier research on clients' reactions (Kounin, Polansky, Biddle, Coburn, and Fenn, 1956; Polansky and Kounin, 1956) by examining determinants of relationship-centered and problem-centered satisfaction.[10] Three independent variables were manipulated. They were (1) experience: the length of time the counselor is reputed to have acted in his professional capacity; (2) value similarity: the degree to which the client perceives herself as similar to the counselor in values and life-style preferences; and (3) formality: the extent to which the counselor exercises the maximum level of social distance permitted by norms governing a counseling relationship.

Ninety-six female subjects were randomly assigned to two levels of experience, two levels of value similarity, and two levels of formality so that 12 subjects were exposed to each of eight experimental conditions. All subjects were exposed to the same male counselor. Experience (E_m) and value similarity (S_m) were manipulated in advance of the interview through variations in the information communicated to subjects about the counselor. In the *low-experience* condition, subjects were informed that the counselor had virtually no experience in counseling or in any related field, and that this was to be his first encounter with a client. In the *high-experience* condition, by contrast, subjects were told that they would be meeting with a "full-fledged" counselor who had 6 years of experience in clinical settings.

Subjects in the *low-value-similarity* condition were given information designed to lead them to believe that the counselor's philosophy of life deviated sharply from their own, while those in the *high-value-similarity* condition were provided information that suggested greater commonality. Manipulation checks for the experience and value-similarity manipulations ($E_1 - E_3$ and $S_1 - S_3$) were obtained immediately prior to the interview. These

---

[10] The theoretical rationale for the present experiment is presented in Tessler (1973) and will not be pursued here.

manipulation checks were composed of items designed to assess whether the manipulations had been accurately perceived and whether they had been credible.

Formality (F_m) was manipulated through variations in the amount of social distance exercised by the counselor during the interview. In the *informal* condition, the counselor wore sport clothes, used first names exclusively, and reclined in a lounge chair next to the subject. In the *formal* condition, by contrast, the counselor wore a suit, used surnames exclusively, and sat in a straight-back chair behind a large desk. Following the interview, a reaction form was administered to subjects that included manipulation checks for formality ($F_1 - F_3$) and indicators of the dependent variables, relationship-centered and problem-centered satisfaction ($R_1 - R_4$ and $P_1 - P_4$). Relationship-centered satisfaction was measured by items designed to assess subjects' perceptions of the counselor's personalism, warmth, friendliness, and concern. Problem-centered satisfaction was measured by items that dealt with subjects' perceptions of the counselor's thoroughness, skillfulness, impressiveness, and success in helping clarify the problem.[11] The zero-order correlations among the variables representing the manipulated independent variables, the manipulation checks, and the observed dependent variables are presented in Table 4.2.

The causal model postulated for the relationships among the variables noted above is presented in Fig. 4.8. The model includes three unobserved independent variables, experience (E), value similarity (S), and formality (F), each of which depends upon its corresponding experimental manipulation and each of which causes a set of manipulation checks. The model also includes two unobserved dependent variables, relationship-centered satisfaction (R) and problem-centered satisfaction (P). The two unobserved dependent variables depend upon the three antecedent unobserved variables, and in addition each causes a set of observed dependent variables.

The following factor model is consistent with the model described in Fig. 4.8:

$$Z = BF + UW$$

where Z is a $p \times n$ matrix of standardized observed scores (p = the number of variables, n = the number of observations), B is a $p \times m$ factor pattern matrix (m = the number of latent factors), F is an $m \times n$ matrix of hypothetical factor scores, U is a $p \times p$ diagonal matrix of residual variances, and W is a $p \times n$ matrix of hypothetical residual scores. In such a model, we do not deal with F and W directly, but we do estimate the matrices B and $E(FF')$

---

[11] The actual indicators used may be found in Tessler (1973).

Table 4.2. Correlation matrix for observed variables in clients' reactions experiment[a]

Variable[b]	S_m	S_1	S_2	S_3	E_m	E_1	E_2	E_3	F_m	F_1	F_2	F_3	R_1	R_2	R_3	R_4	P_1	P_2	P_3	P_4
(1) S_m	1																			
(2) S_1	98	1																		
(3) S_2	87	88	1																	
(4) S_3	71	73	79	1																
(5) E_m	00	04	09	09	1															
(6) E_1	01	05	10	09	99	1														
(7) E_2	07	09	11	13	73	74	1													
(8) E_3	01	00	10	15	52	51	51	1												
(9) F_m	00	01	00	06	00	-01	-05	-21	1											
(10) F_1	-03	-02	-04	04	01	00	-04	-23	98	1										
(11) F_2	00	01	00	06	00	-01	-05	-20	99	98	1									
(12) F_3	-08	-05	-12	01	-08	-09	-12	-27	84	82	84	1								
(13) R_1	15	13	21	20	09	08	08	27	-35	-39	-35	-50	1							
(14) R_2	11	13	12	26	-02	-03	04	26	-25	-30	-25	-22	56	1						
(15) R_3	15	14	15	21	00	00	02	28	-22	-30	-22	-23	56	70	1					
(16) R_4	07	07	08	15	07	06	16	15	07	01	07	02	45	60	54	1				
(17) P_1	13	14	13	16	16	17	27	25	-06	-07	-06	-01	15	25	16	24	1			
(18) P_2	08	08	10	07	13	15	17	22	-08	-08	-08	-07	28	23	13	16	46	1		
(19) P_3	07	08	17	22	21	20	20	19	15	14	15	05	23	29	33	30	31	29	1	
(20) P_4	04	07	07	22	57	58	47	26	00	03	00	-03	05	20	05	19	41	28	35	1

[a] Decimals have been omitted from the matrix.
[b] See text for variable abbreviations.

72

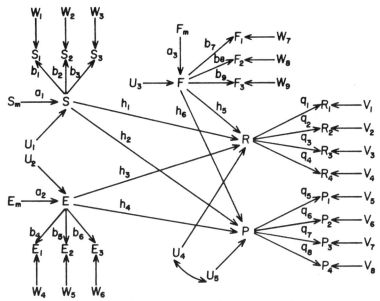

Figure 4.8. Causal model for clients' reactions to initial-interviews experiment.

from sample data. The matrix U does not represent independent information — it is determined given B.[12]

Consistent with the model depicted in Fig. 4.8, the model makes the usual assumptions in factor analysis that $E(FW') = E(WF') = 0$, and that $E(WW') = I_p$. In other words, the common factors are uncorrelated with the residual factors, and the residual factors are mutually uncorrelated. In addition to these assumptions, certain restrictions are placed on the B matrix and the variance–covariance matrix for the factors, $E(FF')$, in the form of zero constraints on some of the parameters of the model. (See matrices B and $E[FF']$ below.) The factor analytic procedures used to estimate the model in Fig. 4.8 allow the estimation of the model under these constraints (see Jöreskog et al., 1970).[13] Least-squares estimates were obtained for the parameters.[14]

---

[12] The reader should not confuse the notation for the matrix of factor scores with the notation used to denote the variable formality.

[13] Note that since we have specified $r_{ES} = r_{FS} = r_{EF} = 0$, the h's in the model represented in Fig. 4.8 are simply equal to the true correlations among E, S, and F, on the one hand, and R and P, on the other.

[14] The least-squares solution obtained from the Jöreskog et al. (1970) program minimizes the trace of the matrix $(R - R^*)^2$, where R is the observed correlation matrix and R^* is the reproduced correlation matrix. The reason the least-squares solution is used here rather than a maximum-likelihood solution is that the original correlation matrix (Table 4.2) is not positive–definite, and it is necessary to invert this matrix in obtaining maximum-likelihood estimates.

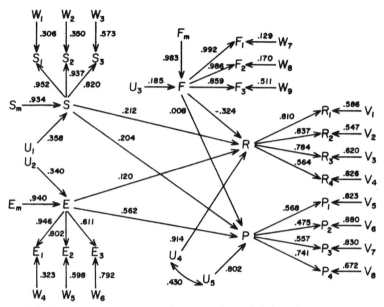

Figure 4.9. Parameter estimates for causal model for clients' reactions to initial-interviews experiment.

The causal diagram in Fig. 4.9 presents the estimates of the parameters of the model. Note that we have represented the residuals on R and P as correlated, obviating the specification of a causal linkage between them. There are three general aspects of the parameter estimates in Fig. 4.9 that deserve attention: the effects of the manipulations on the unobserved independent variables; the reliability/validity of the manipulation checks and the observed dependent variables; and the estimates of the parameters of the causal theory underlying the experiment.

According to the estimates for a_1, a_2, and a_3, the manipulations of the independent variables appear to be quite effective. These results essentially indicate that, on the average, the subjects in each experimental condition perceived the characteristics of the condition in a manner consistent with the intentions of the experimenter. Because of the high magnitude of these estimated effects, this part of the model cannot easily be distinguished from one that excludes the unobserved variables in favor of simple direct effects of the manipulations on the manipulation checks (see Fig. 43).[15]

---

[15] Although the correlation among the manipulations and their corresponding manipulation checks are well reproduced by the model, some attempt was made to estimate several models including "demand effects" discussed in an earlier section. Our conclusion from this analysis was that it is unnecessary to include such effects in the present data. Still, since the estimates of the effects of the manipulations on the unobserved independent variables are quite high, it is impossible to distinguish the model proposed in Fig. 4.8 from one which allows for direct effects only.

The second feature of the estimated model in Fig. 4.9 that deserves comment has to do with the reliability/validity of the manipulation checks and the dependent-variable measures. With one exception, the estimated coefficients for the parameters $b_1 - b_9$ are all greater than .8, indicating a reasonable amount of consistency in the responses to the items involved. The estimates of the parameters $q_1 - q_s$ range from .48 to .84, which indicates reliability estimates in the range of .23 - .70. These are generally lower than those reported for the manipulation checks.[16]

The third important feature of the estimates in Fig. 4.9 is the estimates of the parameters of the causal theory. The model originally specified in Fig. 4.8 allows for non-zero effects of all three independent variables on the two dependent variables. From the estimates presented in Fig. 4.9, it appears that the major determinant of problem-centered satisfaction is the experience of the counselor, $\hat{h}_4 = .562$, while the similarity of the counselor has only a moderate effect, $\hat{h}_2 = .204$, and the formality of the counseling situation has a near-zero effect, $\hat{h}_6 = .008$. In contrast, the major determinant of relationship-centered satisfaction appears to be the formality of the interview situation, $\hat{h}_5 = -.324$, while the similarity and experience of the counselor have only moderate or small effects, $\hat{h}_1 = .212$ and $\hat{h}_3 = .120$. These findings suggest that there are two distinct kinds of client-centered satisfaction in initial interviews and that they depend upon different features of the interview situation. Assuming such findings were to hold up in repeated studies, they would be considered important for professional counselors, particularly those charged with the responsibility of training clinical personnel.

It is important to note that the coefficients for the parameters of the theory, $h_1 - h_6$, are estimates of "true" parameters in the sense that they are specified in the model to be free of random measurement error. As such, they are logically similar, but not equivalent, to coefficients corrected for attenuation, in the conventional meaning of the phrase.[17] The analysis of experimental data, by whatever method, should take into account the unreliability of the dependent-variable measures, particularly when measures of association are used. Otherwise, serious bias is likely to result. The present

---

[16] It should be emphasized that the interpretation of these coefficients in terms of the reliability and validity of the observed variables depends upon the assumption that the only systematic or nonrandom determinant of the observed variable is the underlying dimension of interest, and that all other determinants of the observed variable are random with respect to this underlying dimension. It follows from this that any variable that systematically influences an observed variable must exert its influence through the unobserved variable.

[17] An approach that is sometimes used in situations where estimates of the true parameters are desired is the correction of all bivariate correlations for attenuation using conventional correction formulae. Then estimates of the true parameters are calculated from these corrected correlation coefficients. While this approach is similar in purpose to the one advocated here, the two are not equivalent.

approach explicitly includes the issue of measurement reliability in the theoretical model and therein attempts to avoid such bias. Indeed, the present approach not only estimates the true parameters but also provides estimates of the reliabilities involved.

The adequacy of the model depicted in Fig. 4.8 can be evaluated in terms of the ability of the parameter estimates presented in Fig. 4.9 to reproduce the correlations among the observed variables (Table 4.2). This criterion was alluded to earlier when we discussed evaluating the measures of the dependent variable in the pretest. Table 4.3 presents the correlations among the variables that are generated by the least-squares estimates of the parameters presented in Fig. 4.9, and Table 4.4 presents the observed correlation matrix minus the reproduced correlation matrix. While some of the correlations appear not to be well reproduced, the overall fit of the model appears to be reasonably good.

As noted earlier, Jöreskog (1970) and Lawley and Maxwell (1971) present a goodness-of-fit test for the adequacy of the estimates in reproducing the observed correlation matrix. The test, however, depends on the availability of maximum-likelihood estimates, and we have only been able to obtain least-squares estimates in the present analysis. While we encourage the cautious use of such goodness-of-fit tests where efficient estimates are obtained, we are in no position to justify their use in the present case, so we have not made use of the test to examine fit.

Although we have judged the overall fit of the model to be reasonably good, there are some parts of the observed correlation matrix that are poorly reproduced. In particular, the correlations of E_3 with several variables (mainly F's and R's), and the correlations of R_4 with several variables (mainly F's) are not well reproduced. In essence, the common variation that E_3 and R_4 share with other variables in the system is not entirely accounted for by the model as specified. One possible approach to improving the fit of the model is to include some additional factors in the model. This can be done implicitly by allowing for correlated error among the variables whose correlations are not well reproduced. This yields little information, however, regarding the actual processes that produce the relationships. A second approach to improving the fit of the model is to include some additional effects of the type discussed in the section devoted to evaluating rival hypotheses. In the present case, there may be room for the specification of some demand effects of the manipulated independent variables on some of the dependent-variable measures, for example, F_m on R_4 and P_3. However, this type of specification is unlikely to improve the fit relative to the relationships in question. Finally, a third approach to improving the fit of the model is to exclude the variables that are creating the problems (E_3 and R_4), reestimating the model in their absence. The results of this approach in the present case (not presented here) indicate a general improvement in the fit of the model. Such an approach may not, however, offer a general solution

Table 4.3. Reproduced correlation matrix for observed variables in clients' reactions experiment[a]

									Variable[b]											
Variable[b]	S_m	S_1	S_2	S_3	E_m	E_1	E_2	E_3	F_m	F_1	F_2	F_3	R_1	R_2	R_3	R_4	P_1	P_2	P_3	P_4
(1) S_m	1																			
(2) S_1	89	1																		
(3) S_2	88	89	1																	
(4) S_3	77	78	77	1																
(5) E_m	00	00	00	00	1															
(6) E_1	00	00	00	00	89	1														
(7) E_2	00	00	00	00	75	76	1													
(8) E_3	00	00	00	00	57	58	49	1												
(9) F_m	00	00	00	00	00	00	00	00	1											
(10) F_1	00	00	00	00	00	00	00	00	98	1										
(11) F_2	00	00	00	00	00	00	00	00	97	98	1									
(12) F_3	00	00	00	00	00	00	00	00	84	85	85	1								
(13) R_1	16	16	16	14	09	09	08	06	−26	−26	−26	−22	1							
(14) R_2	17	17	17	15	09	10	08	06	−26	−27	−27	−23	68	1						
(15) R_3	16	16	16	14	09	09	08	06	−25	−25	−25	−22	64	66	1					
(16) R_4	11	11	11	10	06	06	05	04	−18	−18	−18	−16	46	47	44	1				
(17) P_1	11	11	11	10	30	30	26	20	00	00	00	00	19	20	19	14	1			
(18) P_2	09	09	09	08	25	25	21	16	00	00	00	00	16	17	16	11	27	1		
(19) P_3	11	11	11	09	29	30	25	19	00	00	00	00	19	20	18	13	32	26	1	
(20) P_4	14	14	14	12	39	39	33	25	01	01	01	01	25	26	25	18	42	35	41	1

[a] Decimals have been omitted from the matrix.
[b] See text for variable abbreviations.

Table 4.4. Residual correlation matrix for observed variables in clients' reactions experiment[a]

Variable[b]	S_m	S_1	S_2	S_3	E_m	E_1	E_2	E_3	F_m	F_1	F_2	F_3	R_1	R_2	R_3	R_4	P_1	P_2	P_3	P_4
(1) S_m	0																			
(2) S_1	09	0																		
(3) S_2	−01	−01	0																	
(4) S_3	−06	−05	02	0																
(5) E_m	00	04	09	09	0															
(6) E_1	01	05	10	09	11	0														
(7) E_2	07	09	11	13	−02	−02	0													
(8) E_3	01	00	10	15	−06	−06	02	0												
(9) F_m	00	01	00	06	01	−01	−05	−21	0											
(10) F_1	−03	−02	−04	04	01	00	−04	−23	04	0										
(11) F_2	00	01	00	06	00	−01	−05	−21	03	00	0									
(12) F_3	−08	−05	−12	01	−08	−09	−12	−27	00	−03	−01	0								
(13) R_1	−01	−03	05	06	−01	−01	00	21	−10	−13	−10	−27	0							
(14) R_2	−06	−04	−05	12	−11	−12	−04	20	02	−03	02	01	−12	0						
(15) R_3	−01	−02	00	08	−09	−09	−06	23	03	−05	02	−02	−07	04	0					
(16) R_4	−05	−04	−03	05	00	00	10	10	24	19	25	17	00	12	10	0				
(17) P_1	02	03	02	06	−14	−13	02	05	−07	−07	−07	−01	−04	05	−03	10	0			
(18) P_2	−01	−02	01	−01	−12	−10	−04	06	−09	−09	−09	−08	11	06	−03	05	19	0		
(19) P_3	−04	−02	07	13	−09	−09	−05	00	14	14	14	05	04	10	14	17	−01	02	0	
(20) P_4	−10	−08	−07	09	18	19	14	01	−01	03	−01	−03	−21	−06	−20	02	−01	−07	−06	0

[a] Decimals have been omitted from the matrix.
[b] See text for variable abbreviations.

to the problem, since it depends on having more than two measures of each underlying construct.

SUMMARY AND DISCUSSION

This chapter began by commenting on the appropriateness of techniques of causal modeling for the analysis of experimental data. Experimental data are especially amenable to causal analysis because of the unambiguity of the temporal ordering of independent and dependent variables, and because observed relations between variables are unlikely to be spurious. While techniques of causal modeling have been employed in the analysis of non-experimental data, they have been largely ignored by social scientists who deal with experimental data. Therefore, the major purposes of this chapter have been to discuss ways in which causal models may be fruitfully used in the analysis of experimental data and to illustrate their uses.

Building on the work of Costner (1971) and Blalock (1971a), we have introduced a working terminology for the description of simple experiments. Central to our exposition is the inclusion of unobserved variables in the representation of social–psychological experiments. In this way, we encourage the treatment of theoretical constructs apart from their empirical referents and deemphasize the exclusive attention to the effects of manipulated independent variables on observed dependent variables.

In addition to the treatment of the social experiment in terms of a causal process involving unobservables, we have focused on two key experimental issues in greater detail: the evaluation of both experimental manipulations and the adequacy of indicators of the dependent variable. One aim of these discussions is to sensitize the experimenter to the possibility of pretesting manipulations and dependent-variable measures prior to the actual experiment. We have attempted here to provide some workable procedures for evaluating these aspects of the experiment. Also, we have reviewed Costner's (1971) suggestions regarding the examination of rival hypotheses in simple experiments.

In order to illustrate the utility of the estimation procedures involved in confirmatory factor analysis for experimental data, we have presented an estimated model for data from a recent experiment. Data on clients' reactions to initial interviews are used to illustrate the approach. A causal model that includes both observed and unobserved variables is set forth to represent the causal process underlying the experiment. The model is estimated, and the results are taken to be theoretically interpretable, thereby suggesting the feasibility of the general approach.

The analysis of experimental data in this manner constitutes a significant departure from conventional methods (see Kirk, 1968, for a definitive exposition of conventional statistical procedures). One advantage of this approach is that the reliability of measurement is explicitly taken into account in the analysis. This permits estimates of "true" parameters to be obtained. A second advantage of the causal modeling approach is that it yields information about the magnitudes of effects, making it possible to assess the relative importance of the independent variables. A third advantage is that, in assessing the effects of the independent variables, the degree to which the manipulations have "taken" is explicitly taken into account. Thus, if a manipulation is only weakly induced, this is reflected in the results. Finally, a fourth advantage of this approach is that it provides a framework for examining alternative interpretations of observed differences. These causal modeling techniques permit the analyst to assess empirically the plausibility of rival interpretations such as demand characteristics and experimenter bias.

There are, of course, a number of assumptions inherent in the approach taken here to the analysis of experimental data. Two major assumptions are the linearity and additivity of effects. Also, the example provided involves only orthogonal relationships among independent variables (a balanced design). This approach, however, is not limited to situations in which independent variables are orthogonal and additive in their effects, but linearity must be assumed. We should caution the reader not to consider the approach set forth here as a panacea for all problems inherent in experimental analysis. Indeed, it can be argued that in some situations conventional procedures may be preferable. We feel, however, that greater attention should be given to this approach, both as a viable alternative to conventional experimental methods and as a set of tools that can be used to supplement conventional methods in the constructive analysis of experimental data.

ACKNOWLEDGMENTS

We wish to acknowledge William M. Mason, Robert M. Hauser, Gerald Marwell, and the participants in the summer 1973 Seminar of the Methodology Training Program at the University of Wisconsin for helpful criticisms on an earlier version of the chapter.

REFERENCES

Althauser, Robert P., and Heberlein, Thomas A. "A Causal Assessment of Validity and the Multitrait–Multimethod Matrix." In *Sociological Methodology 1970*, edited by E. F. Borgatta and G. W. Bohrnstedt. San Francisco: Jossey-Bass, 1970.

Alwin, Duane F. "Approaches to the Interpretation of Relationships in the Multitrait–Multimethod Matrix." In *Sociological Methodology 1973*, edited by H. L. Costner. San Francisco: Jossey-Bass, 1973.

Alwin, Duane F. "Making Inferences from Attitude-Behavior Correlations." *Sociometry* 36 (1973): 253–278.

Aronson, Elliot, and Carlsmith, J. M. "Experimentation in Social Psychology." In

The Handbook of Social Psychology, edited by G. Lindzey and E. Aronson. Vol. 2. Reading, Mass.: Addison-Wesley, 1968.

Blalock, Hubert M., Jr. "Making Causal Inferences for Unmeasured Variables from Correlations among Indicators." *American Journal of Sociology* 69 (1963): 53–62.

Blalock, Hubert M. *Causal Inferences in Nonexperimental Research.* Chapel Hill: University of North Carolina Press, 1964.

Blalock, Hubert M. "Multiple Indicators and the Causal Approach to Measurement Error." *American Journal of Sociology* 75 (1969): 264–272.

Blalock, Hubert M. "Estimating Measurement Error Using Multiple Indicators and Several Points in Time." *American Sociological Review* 35 (1970): 101–111, and this volume.

Blalock, Hubert M. "Causal Models Involving Unmeasured Variables in Stimulus–Response Situations." In *Causal Models in the Social Sciences,* edited by Hubert M. Blalock, Jr. Chicago: Aldine-Atherton, 1971a, and this volume.

Blalock, Hubert M. *Causal Models in the Social Sciences.* Chicago: Aldine-Atherton, 1971b.

Burt, Ronald S. "Confirmatory Factor-analytic Structures and the Theory Construction Process." *Sociological Methods and Research* 2 (1973): 131–190.

Campbell, Donald T., and Stanley, Julien, "Experimental Designs and Quasi-Experimental Designs for Research on Teaching, In *Handbook of Research on Teaching,* edited by N. L. Gage. Chicago: Rand McNally, 1963.

Costner, Herbert L. "Theory, Deduction, and Rules of Correspondence." *American Journal of Sociology* 75 (1969): 245–263.

Costner, Herbert L. "Utilizing Causal Models to Discover Flaws in Experiments." *Sociometry* 34 (1971): 398–410, and this volume.

Duncan, Otis D. "Unmeasured Variables in Linear Models for Panel Analysis." In *Sociological Methodology 1972,* edited by H. L. Costner. San Francisco: Jossey-Bass, 1972.

Duncan, Otis D., Haller, Archibald O., and Portes, Alejandro. "Peer Influences on Aspirations: A Reinterpretation." *American Journal of Sociology* 74 (1965) 119–137.

Harman, Harry. *Modern Factor Analysis.* Chicago: University of Chicago Press, 1967.

Hauser, Robert M. "On 'Social Participation and Social Status.' " *American Sociological Review* 34 (1969): 549–553.

Hauser, Robert M., and Goldberger, Arthur S. "The Treatment of Unobservable Variables in Path Analysis." In *Sociological Methodology 1971,* edited by H. L. Costner. San Francisco: Jossey-Bass, 1971.

Heise, David R. "Separating Reliability and Stability in Test–Retest Correlation." *American Sociological Review* 34 (1969): 93–101, and this volume.

Jöreskog, Karl G. "A General Approach to Confirmatory Maximum Likelihood Factor Analysis." *Psychometrika* 34 (1969): 183–202.

Jöreskog, Karl G. "A General Method for Analysis of Covariance Structures." *Biometrika* 57 (1970): 239–251.

Jöreskog, Karl G., Gruvaeus, G. T., and van Thillo, M. *ACOVS: A General Computer Program for Analysis of Covariance Structures.* Research Bulletin 70–15. Princeton, N.J.: Educational Testing Service, 1970.

Kirk, Roger E. *Experimental Design Procedures for the Behavioral Sciences.* Belmont, Calif.: Brooks/Cole, 1968.

Kish, Leslie, "Some Statistical Problems in Research Design." *American Sociological Review* 24 (1959): 328–338.

Kohn, Melvin L., and Schooler, Carmi. "Experience and Psychological Functioning: An Assessment of Reciprocal Effects." *American Sociological Review* 38 (1973): 97–118.

Kounin, J., Polansky, N., Biddle, B., Coburn, H., and Fenn, A. "Experimental Studies of Clients' Reactions to Initial Interviews." *Human Relations* 9 (1956): 256–292.

Land, Kenneth C. "On the Estimation of Path Coefficients for Unmeasured Variables from Correlations among Observed Variables." *Social Forces* 48 (1970): 506–611.

Lawley, D. N., and Maxwell, A. E. *Factor Analysis as a Statistical Method.* London: Butterworth. New York: American Elsevier, 1971.

Lord, Frederick M., and Novick, Melvin R. *Statistical Theories of Mental Test Scores.* Reading, Mass.: Addison-Wesley, 1968.

Maxwell, A. E. "Statistical Methods in Factor Analysis." *Psychological Bulletin* 56 (1959): 228–235.

Orne, M. T. "On the Social Psychology of the Psychological Experiment: With Particular Reference to Demand Characteristics and Their Implications." *American Psychologist* 17 (1962): 776–783.

Polansky, Norman, and Kounin, Jacob. "Clients' Reactions to Initial Interviews: A Field Study." *Human Relations* 9 (1956): 237–264.

Rosenthal, Robert. *Experimenter Effects in Behavioral Research.* New York: Appleton-Century-Crofts, 1966.

Sewell, William H., Haller, Archibald O., and Ohlendorf, George W. "The Educational and Early Occupational Status Attainment Process: Replication and Revision." *American Sociological Review* 35 (1970): 1014–1027.

Sewell, William H., Haller, Archibald O., and Portes, Alejandro. "The Educational and Early Occupational Attainment Process." *American Sociological Review* 34 (1969): 82–92.

Tessler, Richard C. "Clients' Reactions to Initial Interviews: Determinants of Relationship-centered and Problem-centered Satisfaction." Manuscript, University of Massachusetts, 1973.

Wiggins, James A. "Hypothesis Validity and Experimental Laboratory Methods." In *Methodology in Social Research,* edited by H. M. Blalock and A. B. Blalock. New York: McGraw-Hill, 1968.

ADDENDUM: THE ANALYSIS OF EXPERIMENTAL DATA USING STRUCTURAL EQUATION MODELS[1]

Causal modeling and the application of structural equation techniques have enjoyed considerable popularity among social and behavioral scientists who analyze nonexperimental data from either cross-sectional or longitudinal designs. This has, however, not been true of those using experimental and quasi-experimental designs (psychologists and psychological social psychologists, primarily), despite some potential advantages for doing so. The classical experimental design with randomization resolves certain issues of model specification by procedurally fixing the expected correlation of the disturbance with both measured and unmeasured deter-

---

[1] Prepared by Duane F. Alwin, The University of Michigan.

minants of the dependent variable to zero. Thus, experimentalists are not attracted to structural equation methods in the way nonexperimentalists are because there are few gains to be had in model specification. In addition, the conventional view is that experimental techniques readily lend themselves to analysis by standard statistical techniques, specifically the "analysis of variance" and the "analysis of covariance."

Despite these factors affecting the role of structural equation innovations in the analysis of experimental data, several writers have recently argued that conventional techniques for the analysis of covariance structures (e.g., analysis of variance and covariance) become problematic in the social–psychological experiment, where sources of measurement error and the potential response biases involved in the induction of experimental states (or levels) call into question the assumptions of the conventional models (Alwin and Tessler, 1974; Bagozzi, 1977, 1980; Blalock, 1971; Costner, 1971; Jöreskog and Sörbom, 1982; Sörbom, 1974, 1978).

Measurement error is known to affect the power of statistical analyses of the effects of experimental manipulations using analysis of variance techniques (Cleary; Linn, and Walster, 1970 and the references contained therein), and there is ample evidence for random errors of measurement in many of the types of variables used in social-psychological experiments. However, it is rare to find a paper published in an experimental journal in social psychology that concerns itself with the reliability of measurement where experimental data are involved. It is also rare to find very much concern with the measurement of unobserved variables presumed to be induced by experimental manipulations, but which are in fact not assessed even through indirect measurement, in the social-psychological experiment. Bronfenbrenner's (1979: 28 – 36) discussion of this issue in the context of experimental research in human development demonstrates an uncommon sensitivity to this problem.

The 1974 paper, "Causal Models, Unobserved Variables, and Experimental Data," by Tessler and Alwin represents an attempt (1) to apply the logic of causal modeling to the analysis of the dynamics of the social–psychological experiment, and (2) to illustrate how the parameters of a causal model for experimentally derived data could be estimated using Jöreskog's methods of covariance structure analysis (Jöreskog, 1970). Our efforts in these areas were preceded by the work of Costner (1971) and Blalock (1971), and building upon this work is Bagozzi's (1977, 1980) more recent research in the area of experimental marketing (see also Jöreskog and Sörbom, 1982).

The emphasis in all of this work is on the need to obtain measures of experimentally induced variables, referred to as "manipulation checks," in order to assess the extent to which the manipulations were effective, plus the need to take random measurement error into account in measures of dependent variables (as well as in the measures of the manipulated or induced variables). The general strategy in the analysis of this type of model is to incorporate experimental manipulations as "0-1" exogenous variables that determine (with some error) the unobserved latent variables representing the "induced" psychological experimental state. The effectiveness of the experimental inducement can be assessed if measures of the induced variable (manipulation checks) are included. This involves the straightforward application of confirmatory factor analysis to the measurement models involved.

A second aspect of this general approach is the specification of the dependent-variable measures as imperfect reflections of an unobserved latent variable. Again, these patterns of relationships can be modeled using conventional confirmatory factor analysis techniques. Then, the "effect parameters" of the model are examined as the associations among the exogenous latent variable(s) and the latent variable(s) underlying the measured dependent variables. Thus, in the analysis of Tessler's experimental data on clients' reactions to initial interviews, we specified the model simply as a confirmatory factor analysis problem.

The analysis of this type of experimental data relies entirely on the covariance structure of the variables (the second moments of the joint distribution) and does not directly take the observed first moments, the observed means, into account. Thus, the model has no way of specifying the actual mean levels of the latent dependent variables. Also, this type of model does not permit the investigation of nonadditive effects where more than one experimental factor is manipulated. In other words, while these models may allow one to strengthen the level of confidence in the resulting inferences from the data, they do have some limitations. There are other limitations as well, and the problematic nature of these assumptions requires the exploration of alternative methods of analyzing experimental data in some cases.

The work of Sörbom (1974, 1978, 1982) has been particularly useful in the development of models that permit the examination of factor means within the context of the above models by incorporating the observed means into the analysis. And it is possible, using state-of-the-art techniques, to estimate such models using LISREL (see Jöreskog and Sörbom, 1978, 1981). In the remainder of this addendum, I summarize the general parameters of a model that incorporates the means of the observed variables and briefly discuss the kinds of analytic models that can benefit from the application of these techniques. The following discussion draws heavily on the treatment of these models by Jöreskog and Sörbom.

STRUCTURED MEANS IN LISREL

I take this opportunity to review the application of LISREL to the use of structured means because it demonstrates the applicability of the general model not only to the analysis of experimental data but to the analysis of multiple-group data generally, including quasi-experimental and non-experimental data. This model allows the incorporation of categoric variables into the LISREL framework in a somewhat different manner from that described above. In this discussion, we adopt the use of Jöreskog and Sörbom's notation in order to facilitate the translation of the models such as these into the LISREL framework.

The model presented involves the general case that represents alternatives to both the analysis of variance and the analysis of covariance (Sörbom, 1974, 1978, 1982). The former represents a special case of the latter, wherein there are preexisting differences among the groups involved, and these differences are assessed by measured variables.

For this model, we adopt the following symbolic notation:

y $= a\ (p \times 1)$ vector of measured dependent variables
x $= a\ (q \times 1)$ vector of measured independent variables
η $= a\ (m \times 1)$ vector of latent dependent variables
ξ $= a\ (n \times 1)$ vector of latent independent variables
ϵ $= a\ (p \times 1)$ vector of random disturbances on the measured dependent variables
δ $= a\ (q \times 1)$ vector of random disturbances on the measured independent variables
v_y $= a\ (p \times 1)$ vector of location parameters (or intercepts) for the measured dependent variables
v_x $= a\ (q \times 1)$ vector of location parameters (or intercepts) for the measured independent variables
ζ $= a\ (m \times 1)$ vector of disturbances in the regression of η on variables in η and ξ
α $= a\ (m \times 1)$ vector of intercepts in the regression of η on variables in η and ξ
κ $= a\ (n \times 1)$ vector of means of the latent independent variables
Λ_y $= a\ (p \times m)$ matrix of regression parameters linking the measured and latent dependent variables
Λ_x $= a\ (q \times n)$ matrix of regression parameters linking the measured and latent independent variables
β $= a\ (m \times m)$ matrix of regression parameters linking variables in η
Γ $= a\ (m \times n)$ matrix of regression parameters linking variables in η with those in ξ

In order to develop this model in the environment of LISREL, the x and y vectors of the LISREL model are combined into a single $[(p + q) \times 1]$ vector, z, and the measurement model for this vector can be written as:

$$z = \begin{bmatrix} y \\ x \end{bmatrix} = \begin{bmatrix} \Lambda_y & 0 & v_y \\ 0 & \Lambda_x & v_x \end{bmatrix} \begin{bmatrix} \eta \\ \xi \\ 1 \end{bmatrix} + \begin{bmatrix} \epsilon \\ \delta \end{bmatrix}$$

This means that we can write x and y as follows:

$$y = \Lambda_y \, \eta + v_y + \epsilon$$

$$x = \Lambda_x \, \xi + v_x + \delta$$

The structural equation representation for the latent variables of the LISREL model may be written as follows:

$$
\begin{bmatrix} \eta \\ \xi \\ 1 \end{bmatrix} = \begin{bmatrix} \beta & \Gamma & 0 \\ 0' & 0 & 0 \\ 0' & 0' & 0 \end{bmatrix} \cdot \begin{bmatrix} \eta \\ \xi \\ 1 \end{bmatrix} + \begin{bmatrix} \alpha \\ \kappa \\ 1 \end{bmatrix} + \begin{bmatrix} \zeta \\ \xi - \kappa \\ 0 \end{bmatrix}
$$

Thus, we can write equations for η and ξ as follows:

$$\eta = \beta \, \eta + \Gamma \, \xi + \alpha + \zeta$$

$$\xi = \kappa + \xi - \kappa$$

Note, this model assumes that (a) both the x and y variables are included in the endogenous-side of LISREL; (b) both the η and ξ vectors are treated as latent endogenous variables in LISREL; and (c) there is a single fixed exogenous variable equal to 1. This fixed exogenous variable is also included as the last endogenous latent variable. Thus, the vector $[\eta \; \xi \; 1]'$ is of order $[1 \times (m + n + 1)]$ (See Jöreskog and Sörbom, 1978:B5–B10, 1981:V.15–V.18). Notice also that this model incorporates the intercepts for the endogenous-variable equations.

The case that concerns us here is one in which the above model can be written for *multiple groups*—in the case of the two-group experimental design, a model for the experimental group and one for the control group. Thus, we might rewrite the model for η in the above equation as pertaining to the gth group, as follows:

$$\eta^g = \beta^g \eta^g + \Gamma^g \xi^g + \alpha^g + \zeta^g$$

Here we assume an equivalence of the Λ_x, Λ_y, v_x, and v_y matrices across groups in order to impose a set of constraints sufficient to identify the model (see Jöreskog and Sörbom, 1981:V18–V30; Sörbom, 1982). Then, by fixing the α values for one group to zero, the α values for the remaining group(s) are interpretable as *differences* among groups in intercepts in the latent-dependent-variable equations. The logic of examining these equations closely parallels the logic involved in evaluating differences of intercepts and slopes in regression models (e.g., see Pedhazur, 1982).

In order to estimate the parameters of this type of model, it becomes necessary to analyze a "moments matrix" in LISREL rather than the more conventional "covariance matrix." The moments matrix for some general population of interest may be defined as:

$$\Omega = \begin{bmatrix} (\Sigma + \mu\mu') & \mu \\ \mu' & 1 \end{bmatrix}$$

where Σ is the population covariance matrix (in this case of order $[(p + q) \times 1]$) and μ is a vector of population means for these variables. For instructions on how to read such a matrix into the LISREL program, see Jöreskog and Sörbom (1978:B9–B10).

SUMMARY

In this addendum, I have summarized major recent developments in the application of structural equation models to experimental data. One of the major areas of concern in this literature has been with the social-psychological experiment in which errors occur not only in the indicators of the dependent variables but in the inducement of experimental levels. The approach that has been taken to these models has relied on conventional covariance structure analysis techniques (LISREL) without incorporating information on the observed means. Here, I have briefly reviewed Sörbom's (1974, 1978, 1982; see also Jöreskog and Sörbom, 1978, 1981) approach to the analysis of experimental data which incorporates means and intercepts into the analysis. In this model, the equations for the latent variables have both slopes and intercepts, and within a multiple-groups framework this model has a number of potential advantages for the analysis of experimental effects.

REFERENCES

Alwin, D. F., and Tessler, R. C. "Causal Models, Unobserved Variables, and Experimental Data." *American Journal of Sociology* 80(1974):58–86.

Bagozzi, R. P. "Structural Equation Models in Experimental Research." *Journal of Marketing Research* 14(1977):209–226.

Bagozzi, R. P. *Causal Models in Marketing.* New York: John Wiley and Sons, 1980.

Blalock, H. M., Jr. "Causal Models Involving Unmeasured Variables in Stimulus–Response Situations." In *Causal Models in the Social Sciences*, edited by H. M. Blalock, Jr. Chicago: Aldine-Atherton, 1971, and this volume.

Bronfenbrenner, U. *The Ecology of Human Development.* Cambridge, Mass.: Harvard University Press, 1979.

Cleary, T. A., Linn, R. L., and Walster, G. W. "Effect of Reliability and Validity on Power of Statistical Tests. "In *Sociological Methodology 1970*, edited by E. F. Borgatta and G. W. Bohrnstedt. San Francisco: Jossey-Bass, 1970.

Costner, H. L. "Utilizing Causal Models to Discover Flaws in Experiments." *Sociometry* 34(1971):398–410, and this volume.

Jöreskog, K. G. "A General Method for Analysis of Covariance Structures." *Biometrika* 57(1970): 239–251.

Jöreskog, K. G., and Sörbom, D. *LISREL—Analysis of Linear Structural Relationships by the Method of Maximum Likelihood*. User's Guide, Version IV. Chicago: National Educational Resources, 1978.

Jöreskog, K. G., and Sörbom, D. *LISREL—Analysis of Linear Structural Relationships by the Method of Maximum Likelihood*. User's Guide, Version V. Chicago: National Educational Resources, 1981.

Jöreskog, K. G., and Sörbom, D. "Recent Developments in Structural Equation Modeling." *Journal of Marketing Research* 19(1982):404–416.

Pedhazur, E. J. *Multiple Regression in Behavioral Research*. New York: Holt, Rinehart and Winston, 1982.

Sörbom, D. "A General Method for Studying Differences in Factor Means and Factor Structures between Groups." *British Journal of Mathematical and Statistical Psychology* 27(1979):229–239.

Sörbom, D. "An Alternative to the Methodology for Analysis of Covariance." *Psychometrika* 43(1978):381–396.

Sörbom, D. "Structural Equation Models with Structured Means." In *Systems under Indirect Observation—Causality, Structure, Prediction*, edited by K. G. Jöreskog and H. Wold. Amsterdam: North-Holland, 1982.

5

Inadvertent Manipulations of Dependent Variables in Research Designs

H. M. Blalock, Jr.

In the idealized experimental design, one manipulates a set of independent variables and then looks for changes in one or more dependent variables. As Miller (Chapter 1, this volume) has noted, randomization then may make it possible to assume that other possible causes of the dependent variable are nearly independent of these manipulations. The admittedly less satisfactory substitute for randomization that must be employed in nonexperimental situations is that of identifying the principal alternative causes that may be confounded with the independent variables under consideration, measuring them nearly perfectly, and then making paper-and-pencil adjustments in the form of statistical controls based on a causal model of the social processes presumed to be at work.

There are many situations, however, in which one may introduce controls in an improper fashion, either because the underlying causal structure has not been correctly modeled or because it is sufficiently complex that it is far from obvious how to proceed. Indeed, there appear to be a number of very practical and seemingly sensible rules of thumb that, if uncritically applied, can lead to inadvertent manipulations that increase variances and covariances of dependent variables in such a way as to lead to serious misinterpretations of one's results. In the present chapter, I confine my attention to some *design* features that produce such inadvertent manipulations, though the problem is by no means confined to questions of proper design.

Before turning to these problems of design, let us examine certain implications of a simple recursive system that are patently obvious once one has explicitly formulated the model. Consider, for example, the four-variable model in which the variables have been labeled such that X_1 is the causally most prior variable and X_4 the ultimate dependent variable. In the linear equation system, represented in conventional ordinary least-squares (OLS) notation but with all intercepts assumed to be zero, we would have the OLS estimating equations:

$$X_1 = e_1$$

$$X_2 = b_{21}X_1 + e_2$$

$$X_3 = b_{31 \cdot 2}X_1 + b_{32 \cdot 1}X_2 + e_3$$

$$X_4 = b_{41 \cdot 23}X_1 + b_{42 \cdot 13}X_2 + b_{43 \cdot 12}X_3 + e_4$$

where the dot notation indicates explicitly which variables are and are not to be controlled.

The causal interpretations given to such recursive systems by Wold and Juréen (1953), Simon (1954), and Blalock (1964) involve the assumption that a manipulation of a particular X_i cannot affect any X_j with a lower-numbered subscript. Thus, someone who gains control over X_4 cannot

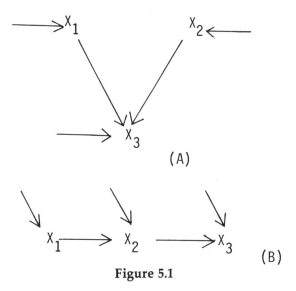

Figure 5.1

thereby modify X_1, X_2, or X_3. Someone who controls X_3 cannot affect X_1 or X_2 (by this means), though X_4 can indeed be modified. Nor would it ever occur to anyone, with such a model explicitly laid out, to control for a dependent variable such as X_4 when interrelating X_1, X_2, and X_3. If one believes that grandmothers have influenced mothers' later behaviors, with these mothers in turn influencing their own daughters, one does not control for the daughters' behaviors in studying the relationships between their grandmothers and mothers. Nor, indeed, would one want to select one's sample by using information about the daughters if one were primarily interested in the grandmother–mother relationship.

One can see the absurdity of introducing controls for such dependent variables by examining the two extremely simple models given in Fig. 5.1. In Model A, we have the situation in which X_1 and X_2 are completely unrelated causally, though both independently affect X_3. Although r_{12} would be zero in this instance (apart from sampling errors), the value of $r_{12 \cdot 3}$ would be given by

$$r_{12 \cdot 3} = \frac{r_{12} - r_{13}r_{23}}{\sqrt{1 - r_{13}^2}\,\sqrt{1 - r_{23}^2}} = -\frac{r_{13}r_{23}}{\sqrt{1 - r_{13}^2}\,\sqrt{1 - r_{23}^2}} \neq 0$$

which would be negative if X_1 and X_2 affect X_3 in the same direction but positive if they have opposite effects on X_3. If one were to introduce a statistical control for X_3, the relationship between X_1 and X_2 would be disturbed, contrary to the rationale for recursive modeling. We simply have no business manipulating a variable that is causally dependent on the two variables whose relationship we are trying to study.

Similarly, in Fig. 5.1B, if we are examining the link between the two "end" variables X_1 and X_3, it makes sense to control for X_2 to see if the relationship disappears, as predicted by the model. If we were to study the linkage between X_2 and X_3 and control for X_1, this would be foolish in that it would reduce the variance in X_2 relative to that in the other causes of X_3, and therefore the correlation between X_2 and X_3 would be reduced. The expected value of the slope b_{32} would be unaffected, however. The crucial point to note is that if we were looking at the linkage between X_1 and X_2, it would make *no* sense to control for X_3 and, in fact, such a control would modify not only the correlation r_{12} but also the slope b_{21} (Blalock, 1964).

What if one does not "control" for these dependent variables but, instead, merely manipulates them somehow in one's design? For instance, suppose that one finds it necessary to use a sampling frame involving the daughters (here representing X_3) in order to study the relationships between their mothers and grandmothers. Or suppose one selects the employees of a particular factory in order to study the relationships among occupational prestige, job performance, income, and perhaps a set of morale or alienation variables. If one constructs a causal model involving certain prior "background" variables such as the workers' educations, religious preferences, or parental educations and occupations, what exactly is going on, if we assume that such background factors might have affected the workers' selection into the sample? Or suppose one is dealing with data based on a cluster sample involving blocks within a city or location within a geographically dispersed rural area. Is it reasonable to assume that actors' locations in space are not dependent on at least some of the variables to be included in one's recursive model?

Let us begin with the very simple situation in which only the *variance* of a dependent variable, say X_3, is manipulated in one's sample design. In such situations, common sense would suggest (misleadingly) that relationships with prior variables such as X_1 and X_2 will not be disturbed. For instance, it used to be common in social psychological research to oversample extreme cases on a dependent variable such as antiminority prejudice. Having done so, one could then undertake an intensive study of the persons at either extreme of the prejudice continuum in order to locate independent variables that differentiated among these extreme groupings. It was apparently not recognized that an oversampling of such extremes tends to *confound* the effects of included independent variables with those of neglected variables, with the result that the effects of the former are overestimated.

Consider the simple case where there are only two causes of X_3, say prejudice. One of these is X_1 which is explicitly measured by the investigator. Suppose, for example, that X_1 represents level of authoritarianism, a variable whose impact was investigated in hundreds of empirical studies in the 1940s and 1950s. But suppose X_2 also positively affects X_3, with X_1 and X_2 being virtually uncorrelated in the population. Perhaps X_2 represents degee of prior exposure to the minority in competitive contact situations. Now suppose we oversample persons at both ends of the prejudice continuum, assuming only these two causes of prejudice. Those who are high on prejudice will tend to be high on *both* X_1 and X_2, and those who score low on prejudice will tend to be low on both of these independent variables. Thus, an oversampling of extremes on the dependent variable will also produce an oversampling of individuals who are *simultaneously* low or high on X_1 and X_2.

If both of these independent variables have been measured, then unless their sample correlation approaches unity, it will still be possible to disentangle their effects provided that measurement is nearly perfect and the sample size is large. It will obviously be impossible to anticipate and measure *all* of the important causes of prejudice X_3, however, and indeed our usual experience is that even where a considerable number of independent variables have been brought into the picture, the proportion of unexplained variance (with random samples) remains substantial. Thus, there will nearly always be important variables in the role of X_2 that have had to be omitted from consideration. We see that an overselection of extreme cases on the dependent variable will tend to confound their effects with whatever independent variables have been singled out for investigation. Furthermore, the confounding will be such that the investigator's independent variable will be made to look good, almost no matter what it is!

If one designs a study by sampling individuals who have been self-selected on some basis (e.g., students at a particular university or workers in a given factory), it will be much less clear what has actually taken place. One possibility is that the entire population will be relatively homogeneous, say with respect to level of education or occupational status. In order to achieve greater heterogeneity in one's sample, the temptation then may be to oversample extremes, (e.g., those who occupy managerial/professional positions and those who perform very unskilled duties). If one then also collects and analyzes data pertaining both to past experiences (e.g., parental education, prior socialization, or entry-level characteristics) and to variables that are assumed to depend on occupation (e.g., alienation scores or future plans), the picture is likely to become extremely confusing. In effect, one will have manipulated variances and perhaps covariances involving some of the intermediate variables, such as X_2 or X_3 in our four-variable system.

The more general point is that a reasonably complete recursive system will contain a number of variables, most of which will be taken as dependent in one of the equations in the system. Manipulations of variances in those few variables that are strictly independent or exogenous will be legitimate in the sense that expected values of unstandardized regression coefficients will not be affected. This fact may be used to improve design features (e.g., making sure that X_1 has a substantial variance relative to unknown causes of X_2). But if one's design in any way manipulates variances in one of the subsequent variables in the system, one must be far more cautious, especially when estimating any of the coefficients interrelating the prior variables in the causal sequence.

Unfortunately, design considerations must inevitably involve tradeoffs relating to costs and convenience. Thus, multistage survey designs practically always involve cluster samples that take, as given, the spatial locations of the individuals or families that become the ultimate units of analysis. Yet, these same surveys utilize information about past characteristics that *might* have influenced these very same locations in space. Similarly, a low-budget study of workers or hospital patients will almost necessarily be confined to at most two or three organizations, as will an inexpensive study of high school students. We must remember, however, that considerations of research expediency, although important for obvious reasons, cannot legitimately be used to justify a set of *theoretical* assumptions unless, by coincidence, the expediency has no impact on the adequacy of one's assumptions. Sweeping assumptions under the rug does not make their implications disappear.

So as to make some of these general observations somewhat less abstract we shall next turn to two very different kinds of specific design situations that will be examined in some detail. In the next section, the focus is on matching designs in which there is selection on a combination of dependent and independent variables. The following section then deals with the confounding likely to occur whenever one uses aggregated data based on geographic proximity.

SOME COMPLICATIONS IN MATCHING DESIGNS[1]

In *ex post facto* designs, one often obtains control and experimental groups, or other comparison groups, by essentially matching individuals with respect to combinations of scores on several independent or dependent variables. Suppose, for example, that one is studying some relatively rare phenomenon such as mental disorders, suicides, or other forms of deviant behavior. Random sampling might not produce enough such deviant cases, whereas it is often true that public records or institutional files can be utilized to obtain an adequate number of cases for statistical analysis. A control group can then be selected from the larger population by individual matching, frequency–distribution matching, or some other device. In effect, the particular independent variables used in the matching process are made unrelated to the dependent variable in one's sample. One then may compare the deviant and control samples with respect to *other* variables, noting whether or not the differences are significantly different from zero or attempting to assess which of these other independent variables have the greatest explanatory power.

In these examples, one is in effect obtaining disproportionate stratified samples by stratifying by a *combination* of variables (e.g., education *and* occupation). Sampling specialists are careful to emphasize that disproportionate stratified samples require the use of weighting procedures whenever one wishes to obtain unbiased estimates of population parameters. (Kish, 1965.) If the ideal sampling practice has been followed, the proper substratum weights will be known and can be used in the subsequent analysis. However, in the case of the kinds of "quasi-experiments" illustrated above, certain practical considerations often interfere. One may not be able to locate delinquents except for those who have officially appeared in police courts. Even if the deviant population is clearly defined, an investigator may not have bothered to ascertain the weights that should be applied to the control group. Someone wishing to make a secondary analysis may not have been given these weights or (more likely) may fail to use them.

The basic difficulty in the nonexperimental type of matching is that one

[1] This section is excerpted from Blalock (1967) with the permission of the publisher. Copyright 1967, the American Sociological Association.

may inadvertently disturb the relationships among independent variables, many of which will not be measured. Consider once more the very simple causal model of Fig. 5.1A in which X_3 is dependent on X_1 and X_2, which are completely unrelated (causally and empirically). Suppose one were to select a sample so as to "force" X_1 to be unrelated to X_3 in the sample. What will happen to the sample measures of association involving the *other* independent variable X_2?

For a concrete illustration, suppose that X_1 is a measure of socioeconomic status and that X_2 represents some socialization variable associated with familial control over a deviant's behavior. Suppose, also, that this form of deviance is more prevalent in the lower classes. Then in selecting equal or proportional numbers of each subtype for X_1 and X_3, one will be oversampling middle-class deviants and lower-class nondeviants. But who are the higher-status deviants likely to be? Those experiencing minimal familial control. Similarly, the lower-class nondeviants are more likely to come from families with strong controls. Hence, family control (X_2) and status (X_1) will be negatively related in the *sample*, though we are assuming they are unrelated in the population. This will also affect the association between family control (X_2) and deviance (X_3) in the sample, so that unless one is extremely careful, one is likely to make faulty inferences concerning this relationship. Obviously, there will be a number of additional determinants of deviance (X_3), and these will be variously related to X_1. Depending on the signs and magnitudes of these relationships with X_1, their relationships with X_3 will be affected in different ways.

If one wishes to study the relative magnitudes of the distortions introduced in such matching designs, it is ordinarily not possible to make use of real data for which the population parameters are unknown. Artificially constructed or computer-generated data are ideal for this purpose, since repeated samples can be taken and sampling errors estimated by "Monte Carlo" techniques.

In the case of very simple models, expected values of estimates can be computed mathematically and then compared with results obtained from artificially constructed data. I have explored only the simplest of cases involving three variables, each of which was dichotomized at the median.[2]

---

[2] A procedure for obtaining expected values can be outlined as follows: Set up three 2 × 2 tables, one for each pair of variables. For example, in the case of X_1 and X_2, we would have:

		X_1	
	W	$.5 - W$	$.5$
X_2			
	$.5 - W$	W	$.5$
	$.5$	$.5$	1.0

(continued)

"Population" data were constructed using specific parameter values. Samples of size 200 each were then drawn in such a way as to make X_1 and X_3 unrelated in each sample design by selecting 50 cases in each cell of the fourfold table. Table 5.1 contains the expected values for the relationships between the remaining independent variable X_2 and both X_1 and X_3. Empirical figures are also provided (in parentheses) for those combinations for which samples were actually drawn. Given the relatively small size of the samples, the closeness of fit seems reasonably good.

All of the figures in Table 5.1 are derived from models in which the two independent variables X_1 and X_2 are uncorrelated in the hypothetical "pop-

---

This gives a difference of proportions d_{21} (or d_{12}) = $4W - 1$. (In the special case where $d_{12} = 0$, $W = .25$.) Similarly,

$$d_{31} = 4Y - 1 \text{ and } d_{32} = 4Z - 1$$

where Y and Z replace W in the corresponding cells of the remaining tables for total associations. Turning to the joint effects, consider a table of "high" X_1's in which X_2 and X_3 are related:

High X_1
X_2

	X	$Y - X$	Y
X_3	$W - X$	$.5 + X - W - Y$	$.5 - Y$
	W	$.5 - W$	$.5$

For the "low" X_1 category, a similar table could be constructed, with the upper left-hand cell being $Z - X$. If we now impose the condition that there be no interaction, then

$$X = .5(W + Y + Z - .5)$$

Using these relationships, we now imagine drawing samples so that there will be equal numbers in all of the cells for the table relating X_1 and X_3. It is then easy to show that for random selection within each of the subcells, the expected value of d_{32} will be $(X - 2WY)/Y(1 - 2Y)$. The *random* sample formula for a partial slope $b_{32 \cdot 1}$, when applied to differences of proportions as a special case, gives

$$b_{32 \cdot 1} = (X - 2WY)/W(1 - 2W)$$

Thus, the two quantities will not generally be equal. In the special case where $W = .25$, equality requires that $Y = .25$, that is X_1 must be unrelated to X_3.

Table 5.1. Distortions produced by matching "control" and "experimental" groups by X_1, where independent variables X_1 and X_2 are uncorrelated[a]

Population correlation between variables X_1 and X_3	Relationships (d_{32}) between X_2 and X_3 after matching		
	True value	True value	True value
	$d_{32} = .6$	$d_{32} = .4$	$d_{32} = .2$
.6	.94	.62 (.63, .66)	.31 (.33, .34)
.4	.71 (.70, .68)	.48	.24
.2	.62 (.63, .66)	.42	.21
Population correlation between variables X_1 and X_3	Relations (d_{21}) between X_1 and X_2 after matching (true value, $d_{21} = 0$)		
	$d_{32} = .6$	$d_{32} = .4$	$d_{32} = .2$
.6	$-.56$	$-.38$ ($-.37, -.34$)	$-.19$ ($-.15, -.10$)
.4	$-.29$ ($-.30, -.32$)	$-.19$	$-.10$
.2	$-.12$ ($-.05, -.12$)	$-.08$	$-.04$

[a] Figures in parentheses represent actual sample values obtained with samples of size 200, with 50 cases in each subcell of the fourfold table relating X_1 and X_3. Remaining figures are mathematically computed expected values.

ulation." The measure used is a simple difference of proportions, which represents a direct analogue to a slope in a regression equation. Notice that the difference of proportions d_{32} (analogous to b_{32}) is always *larger* than the true population value, with this differential increasing with the size of the population correlation between X_1 and X_3. In other words, if through matching we force a dependent variable to be unrelated to an independent variable with which it is highly correlated in the population, this will substantially increase correlations with *other* independent variables originally uncorrelated with this particular independent variable. Intuitively, in making X_1 and X_3 unrelated in one's sample, one is taking out some of the variation in X_3 due to this source, variation that would be considered "unexplained" by X_2.

This is consistent with what one would expect if one had drawn a random sample and had used partial correlations, comparing the numerical values of r_{23} and $r_{23 \cdot 1}$. Given the model of Fig. 5.1A, for which r_{12} should be approximately zero, an examination of the formula for $r_{23 \cdot 1}$ will show that the expected value of the absolute value of $r_{23 \cdot 1}$ should be greater than that of r_{23} (except when $r_{13} = 0$), since with $r_{12} = 0$ we have

$$r_{23 \cdot 1} = \frac{r_{23} - r_{12} r_{13}}{\sqrt{1 - r_{12}^2} \sqrt{1 - r_{13}^2}} = \frac{r_{23} - 0}{1 \sqrt{1 - r_{13}^2}} = \frac{r_{23}}{\sqrt{1 - r_{13}^2}}$$

But the expected value of the slope $b_{32 \cdot 1}$ should be the same as that for b_{32}, as can again be seen by setting $r_{12} = 0$. Thus,

$$b_{32 \cdot 1} = \frac{b_{32} - b_{31} b_{12}}{1 - b_{12} b_{21}} = \frac{b_{32} - 0}{1 - 0} = b_{32}$$

These results can be interpreted to mean that in controlling for a cause of X_3 that is unrelated to X_2, we improve our accuracy of prediction, but there is no bias introduced in estimating the slope. The fact that the results given in Table 5.1 indicate that the expected values of d_{32}, with X_1 and X_3 made unrelated, are greater than the (zero-order) population value is a reflection that in 2×2 tables the behavior of a difference of proportions is generally more similar to that of correlation coefficients than to that of slopes (Blalock, 1964, Chap. 4).

This illustrates the major point that matching procedures do not necessarily lead one to erroneous conclusions, provided that one pays attention to what is happening. But unlike the case where the investigator has available the correlations between X_1 and X_2, and between X_1 and X_3, this information is likely to be missing, or ignored, in the case of the matching design.

Notice in Table 5.1 that the predicted and actual associations between the two independent variables X_1 and X_2 become negative in the samples obtained in the matching design. In general, the stronger the association between the matching variable X_1 and the dependent variable X_3 in the population, the more pronounced this negative relationship. Likewise, the stronger the original association between X_2 and X_3, the larger the negative association between X_1 and X_2 in the sample. These results have the simple intuitive explanation suggested above in the case of deviance. If we force X_1 and X_3 to be unrelated, then we in effect manipulate X_3 in some systematic way so as to counteract the effects of X_1. The values of X_1 and X_3 can be made independent, for example, by counteracting high values of X_1 with low values of X_2, assuming all relationships to be positive. This will produce a negative relationship between X_1 and X_2 in the sample.

X_1 AND X_2 CORRELATED IN THE POPULATION

If one could be assured that the population relationship between X_1 and X_2 is always zero, then the problem would be straightforward, at least in the sense that the association between X_2 and X_3 would always be overestimated. But unfortunately this will generally not be the case. Assuming that both independent variables are positively linked with X_3, then sample relationships between X_2 and X_3 will be increased whenever X_1 and X_2 are negatively associated in the population. But they will be *decreased* if X_1 and X_2 are positively correlated in the population.

Table 5.2. Distortions in d_{32} produced by different population relationships between independent variables X_1 and X_2, with true values of d_{31} and d_{32} equal to .40 and with X_1 and X_3 made uncorrelated in the sample

	True relationship (d_{21}) between X_1 and X_2							True value of d_{32}
	.60	.40	.20	0	−.20	−.40	−.60	
Expected sample relationships (d_{32}) between X_2 and X_3	.19	.29	.38	.48	.57	.67	.76	.40

Some specific examples are given in Table 5.2, in which both independent variables X_1 and X_2 are equally associated with X_3 to the extent that both differences of proportions have the numerical value of .40. If the two independent variables are negatively correlated in the population, we see that the value of the *sample* difference of proportions relating X_2 and X_3 will be considerably larger than the population value of .40. For example, if the population association between X_1 and X_2 is −.40, the sample value of d_{32} will be approximately .67. On the other hand, if X_1 and X_2 are positively linked in the population, the comparable figure may be considerably below the true value of .40. In the admittedly extreme case where the population difference of proportions for X_1 and X_2 is .60, the resulting predicted figure for d_{32} is .19.

The major point, of course, is that the association between the dependent variable X_3 and independent variables such as X_2 will depend upon the latter variables' association with the matching variable X_1. Assuming without loss of generality that increases in each independent variable will increase X_3, then variables that are strongly positively related to X_1 will appear to be weakly related to the dependent variable. In effect, when one forces X_1 and X_3 to be unrelated, one inadvertently weakens associations with other variables highly related to X_1 (unless these happen to involve an odd number of minus signs). It would be a mistake, then, to simply examine relationships with each independent variable without taking into consideration their relationships with the independent variables used in the matching process. These relationships, of course, cannot be estimated from the sample data unless the weights are known and properly used.

X_2 AND X_3 UNCORRELATED IN THE POPULATION[3]

To illustrate the general point that, properly interpreted, matching designs will not necessarily lead one astray, let us consider the case in which X_2 and X_3 are completely unrelated in the population. It might be thought that

---

[3] I am indebted to David Gold for calling my attention to this important special case.

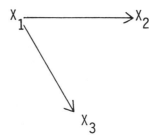

Figure 5.2

if matching by X_1 were to produce a correlation between X_2 and X_3, then this would automatically mean that the investigator would reach erroneous conclusions. But this all depends on the linkage between X_1 and X_2 and the investigator's theoretical interpretation of this linkage.

Suppose, first, that X_2 is unrelated to *both* X_1 and X_3 in the population. Then in the case of random sampling, the expected values of both r_{23} and $r_{23 \cdot 1}$ will be zero, and controlling for X_1, therefore, will not change the investigator's interpretations. It can also be shown that matching by X_1 will not change this relationship.[4] Thus, in this extreme case, matching will not affect one's conclusion that there is no (casual) connection between X_1 and X_3.

Now, consider the more general case where X_1 and X_2 are related in the population. The immediate theoretical question this should raise is that of *why* this should be, and the investigator should formulate some explanation, which might be more or less complex. The simplest possibilities would be that X_1 causes X_2, that X_2 causes X_1, that there is reciprocal causation, or that a single variable X_4 is producing a spurious relationship. For simplicity, consider the model of Figure 5.2, in which it is assumed that X_1 causes X_2 with only random disturbances. Without loss of generality, suppose that the relationship is positive and that X_1 and X_3 are also positively related in the population.

If this model is correct, why should there be *no* correlation between X_2 and X_3? These two variables should be spuriously related with a positive correlation. If r_{23} is zero, we can only conclude that something is wrong with the model. One plausible alternative is that there is, in fact, either a direct or an indirect linkage between X_2 and X_3, and that this relationship would be *negative* if X_1 could be controlled. An examination of the numerator of $r_{23 \cdot 1}$ indicates that this will be the case, since we will have zero minus the product of two positive correlations.

---

[4] Following the notation given in footnote 2, in this situation $W = Z = .25$ and therefore $X = Y/2$, and the numerator of d_{32} becomes

$$X - 2WY = Y/2 - Y/2 = 0$$

A control for X_1 by matching will give this same result, as can again be seen from the procedure outlined in footnote 2. In the case of our dichotomized variables, if we take the true value of d_{32} to be zero, and if $d_{21} = .6$ and $d_{31} = .4$, then the expected value of d_{32} for the matching design is $-.29$. Had we applied the random sample formulas for $r_{23 \cdot 1}$ and $b_{32 \cdot 1}$ to these dichotomized data, the results would have been $-.33$ and $-.38$, respectively. These results could be interpreted in terms of a negative linkage between X_2 and X_3 compensating for the positive (spurious) linkage produced by X_1.

Thus, the investigator would not be led astray provided that he took into consideration the linkage between X_1 and X_2. If it could be assumed that all "independent" variables appearing in the position of X_2 had the same causal relationship to X_1 (e.g., all spuriously related to X_3 because of X_1), then the investigator could compare these variables in a meaningful way. But to interpret these relationships between the various X_2's and the dependent variable X_3 requires a theory as to how and why the several independent variables are related. This fact might not be recognized if it were thought that the matching variable could be eliminated from consideration once the design had been executed. Furthermore, it might be difficult to obtain the true correlations of the matching variable with each of the X_2 variables unless supplementary data were collected.

THE CONFOUNDING OF VARIABLES IN AGGREGATING BY GEOGRAPHIC PROXIMITY[5]

The literature on aggregation and disaggregation is both technical and discouraging in its implications, if one takes seriously the goal of integrating microlevel analyses, based on the individual as unit of analysis, with macrolevel studies where groups are the focus of concern.[6] Ideally, theories on the one level should be consistent, in some sense, with those on the other (Hannan, 1971:18–23). Furthermore, since some groups are nested within larger ones, and since in many instances group boundaries are fuzzy and therefore arbitrarily defined, it is also desirable to pass systematically from one aggregate level to another, as for example from counties to states.

In discussions of aggregation in the econometrics literature, it is assumed that those who do the aggregating have a theoretical rationale for grouping individuals into behaviorally homogeneous aggregates. In most instances

---

[5] This section is excerpted from Blalock (1979) with the permission of the publisher. Copyright 1979, the American Sociological Association.

[6] For three very different, though complementary, perspectives on the aggregation problem, the reader is referred to the works of Firebaugh (1978, 1979); Hannan (1971), and Hannan and Burstein (1974); and Irwin and Lichtman (1976) and Langbein and Lichtman (1978). These sources also contain numerous additional references.

where sociologists use aggregated data, however, the grouping operation has already been done, usually with another purpose in mind. In these instances, aggregation can hopelessly complicate one's analysis unless the criterion for aggregation can be fitted rather simply into one's theory. For instance, whenever we are dealing with a corporate group as a unit of analysis it makes good sense to aggregate over individual members to obtain measures of group properties. Presumably, our interest will center on this group and other comparable groups as actors, as for example whenever business firms produce tangible products or state legislatures enact laws or allocate budgets.

In many other situations, the picture is not this simple, however. Sometimes we may aggregate over a territorial unit that for certain purposes may be considered a corporate group (e.g., a state or county) but where the corporateness may not be an essential feature of the theory in question. For example, we may be studying crime rates in various counties, where county-level policies have virtually no impact upon these rates. Or we may have segregation indices based on block data that are available only for a central city, whereas the SMSA extends far beyond these arbitrary political boundaries. Or our theoretical interest may be on the microlevel, say, in understanding why individuals commit suicide or tend to avoid members of another group. Yet the data may be available only in aggregated form (e.g., census tract data). In no sense can these territorial units be said to constitute true groups, nor is there any pretense that we are interested in highly coordinated behaviors.

In such instances, we use the aggregated data because they are the only ones available. What can we say about the problems created when individuals are aggregated by spatial criteria? The answer depends upon the causal connections between the criteria used in grouping and the variables that appear in our theories (Blalock, 1964; Hannan, 1971).

The usual assumption is that the aggregation criterion, which we shall call A, is an independent variable in the model and that it is not operating to confound the effects of the independent variables under study. When we acknowledge the myriad ways in which spatial location may be linked to the variables of interest to sociologists, we can anticipate the complications that such aggregation may produce. People are influenced by what goes on around them not only in the immediate present but also in the past. They may have moved from one community to another, carrying with them those effects in the former residence that we refer to as "background influences." Furthermore, not all individuals are affected in the same ways by the variables in their immediate environment. Some might have lived in the area all their lives. Others might have moved into the area because of its local traditions, whereas others might have entered and resisted them.

To come to grips with the problems that such complexities create, it will be helpful to examine several models that are themselves oversimplifications of the actual processes at work. We begin with a model in which it is presumed that the territorial units are closed to migration and that contextual effects operate entirely within the boundaries that have been operationally defined.

A CLOSED-SYSTEM EXAMPLE

Suppose we are willing to assume that our criterion for aggregation, here a spatial one, operates only as an independent variable. Of course we do not imagine that location, *per se*, affects the variables of interest. Instead, one's spatial position may be taken as a cause indicator of the unmeasured variables that are presumed to be the true causes of the variables in question. Take the model of Figure 5.3 as an illustration. Perhaps X_1 represents educational achievement, assumed to be a constant property of the individual once the process has been completed. Suppose X_2 represents a relatively constant type of personal value (say, egalitarianism) that has been developed over time as a result of socialization experiences linked closely with one's spatial location. Let X_3 represent another kind of attitudinal variable (say, one's attitude toward a specific minority) that is readily modifiable and therefore subject to changes in one's immediate environment. Finally, suppose X_4 represents a contextual variable (such as a set of sanctions) that operates in the immediate locale.

Now suppose that all these X_i affect a certain form of behavior Y. To simplify, we shall assume that the effects are additive, so that the behavior Y may be represented by the equation

$$Y = \alpha + \beta_1 X_1 + \beta_2 X_2 + \beta_3 X_3 + \beta_4 X_4 + \epsilon \tag{5.1}$$

In the model of Figure 5.3 we have drawn causal arrows from A to each of

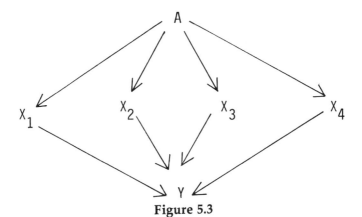

Figure 5.3

the X_i representing the argument that one's location in space in part determines the levels of these X_i as intervening variables.

In any realistic situation, an investigator will be unaware of or unable to measure many of the X_i that affect Y. Suppose, for example, that only X_1 and X_4 have been measured and used in an incorrectly specified equation for Y. The least-squares estimates b_1 and b_4 of the parameters β_1 and β_4 will then be biased to the degree that the omitted intervening variables are correlated with X_1 and X_4. In the model of Fig. 5.3, the intercorrelations among the X_i are due solely to A, implying that a control for A (if perfectly measured) would wipe out these interrelationships. Thus, if we were to examine the data *within* a single territorial unit, we would find no association among the X_i, implying that even in the incorrectly specified equation

$$Y = a + b_1X_1 + b_4X_4 + e \tag{5.2}$$

the estimates b_1 and b_4 would be unbiased estimates of β_1 and β_4.

Of course this is a highly oversimplified model in which there are no other arrows connecting the X_i, whereas in actuality we would expect intercorrelations within each area. But this prototype model is presumably illustrative of more complex ones and involves the kind of assumption needed to justify controlling for residential area. The essential notion is that many causal factors are generally confounded together because of common residence. Therefore, a control for residence is expected to weaken these associations, if not do away with them altogether.

What is less obvious is that when we aggregate by location, we do the very opposite of controlling for A. In grouping by A, we put together people who are similar in their X_1 levels. But they will also be similar with respect to their X_2, X_3, and X_4 values. Suppose the X_i are labeled so that the relationships with A are all in the same direction, so that we may represent them by positive signs. Then persons who reside in a location where the X_1 values tend to be high will also have high X_2, X_3, and X_4 values. If we shift our analysis to the macrolevel, using the estimating equation

$$\overline{Y} = a^* + b_1^*\overline{X}_1 + b_2^*\overline{X}_2 + b_3^*\overline{X}_3 + b_4^*\overline{X}_4 + e^* \tag{5.3}$$

where the $\overline{X}_i$ represent mean values for the same X_i as represented in Fig. 5.3, we may ask how the new least-squares estimates b_i^* may be expected to compare with estimates that would have been computed on the basis of individual-level data.

What happens in this case is that the $\overline{X}_i$ will be more highly intercorrelated than the microlevel counterparts X_i. If we have specified the model perfectly and if there is absolutely no measurement error in any variable, this will not lead to any systematic biases in the macrolevel estimates of the

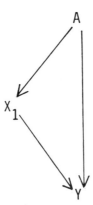

Figure 5.4

parameters. But because of the increased intercorrelations we encounter a multicollinearity problem that tends to increase sampling errors.

It is more important, however, to consider the implications of this confounding of intervening variables in instances where there are specification errors. Suppose we do not know all the X_i that cause Y and that are intercorrelated because of location. To be specific, suppose we have included only $\bar{X}_1$ and $\bar{X}_4$ in the equation for $\bar{Y}$. Our biases in parameter estimates will now be much more serious than in the micromodel discussed earlier. In effect, if we shift to group means but ignore certain of the causes of $\bar{Y}$, the effects of these omitted variables are even more confounded with those of the intervening variables we have been able to include. Put another way, our aggregated model is more sensitive to at least these types of specification errors than is the micromodel, even where the location variable A has been ignored.[7]

For the model of Fig. 5.3, we thus have three analysis possibilities. Our best option is to use microdata and to control for A. Our second best bet is to use microdata and to ignore A. In doing so, if we happen to leave out any of the intervening X_i, we will confound their effects with the remaining X's. The third option is to obtain between-area data by aggregating, in which case we increase the intercorrelations among the intervening variables, thereby confounding to an even greater degree the effects of the omitted $\bar{X}_i$ with the causal variables in which we are explicitly interested.

We cannot say that aggregation will always have this effect, but to the degree that reality approximates the model of Fig. 5.3 this will hold. In the extreme case where we have measured only X_1, the original model could be replaced by Fig. 5.4 in which the arrow from A to Y has been drawn as direct.

[7] Irwin and Lichtman (1976) stress that the essential criterion in deciding between a micro- and a macromodel is the relative degree of specification errors involved. Here, this criterion implies that the micromodel is to be preferred.

Here A is creating a partly spurious relationship between X_1 and Y and should be controlled. But if we aggregate by A, we are grouping by a cause of Y, and as I have shown elsewhere (Blalock, 1964), this produces a systematic bias in our slope estimate linking X_1 and Y, a bias that may be interpreted as resulting from the confounding with X_1 of all other effects of A that are also causes of Y.[8]

AN OPEN-SYSTEM EXAMPLE

Now consider the somewhat more complicated but also more realistic situation in which persons are immigrating into and emigrating from each of the areal units. Here we must take A as a dependent as well as an independent variable. Of course the area is not "dependent" upon its residents. What we mean is that since our microunits of analysis are individuals or families, the particular area in which they are located is dependent upon their decisions. To study this kind of situation, we now must bring in the time dimension and try to distinguish between contemporary and past influences as well as internal states that we are willing to assume are stable over time as contrasted with those that may change as a result of immediate stimuli.

Consider the model of Fig. 5.5. Here, we distinguish between an individual's location at time 1, namely A_{t_1}, and his or her location at time 2. Migration may or may not have occurred in the interim. Following Stinchcombe's (1968) discussion of historical explanations, we may draw an arrow linking A_{t_1} to A_{t_2}. What one does today, or where one is, influences tomorrow's behavior or location, if only in the sense that once a given pattern of behavior has been learned, there is a vested interest in not changing it unless there are specific pressures to do so. For those who have not migrated, A_{t_1} and A_{t_2} will be identical. The degree of association between these two variables will depend on the proportion of migrants and, although not indicated in the diagram, this proportion itself could be one of the contextual variables that affect behavior Y, perhaps through the sanction system represented by X_4.

Suppose X_1 and X_2 represent variables that do not change over time. Therefore, the change in location has not affected either of these variables. I have represented this by drawing in double lines without arrowheads to indicate that X_1 and X_2 remain identical at the two points in time. Suppose, however, that X_3 and X_4 may be affected by the new location as well as the

---

[8] Firebaugh (1978) discusses this kind of situation in terms of a general criterion for avoiding aggregation bias, namely that the association between Y and X, controlling for $\bar{X}$, must be zero if bias is to be avoided. In other words, $\bar{X}$ must not belong in the equation for Y, a criterion that will not be satisfied if $\bar{X}$ is a surrogate for other variables that have been omitted from the equation because of specification errors.

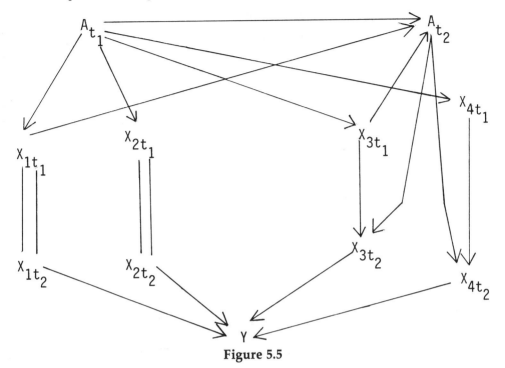

Figure 5.5

old. Therefore, I have drawn arrows to X_{3t_2} from both X_{3t_1} and A_{t_2} (and similarly for X_{4t_2}), making the assumption that the changes produced by the change in location are almost immediate. Finally, the behavior Y at time 2 is taken as dependent upon the contemporary values of the X_i, as was also true in Fig. 5.3.

Now suppose both migrants and nonmigrants are lumped together, as is often the case in microlevel analyses and as is practically always necessary for aggregated data. Again, if we have perfect measures of the contemporary values of all the X_i, we may estimate their separate effects without bias, though if they are too highly intercorrelated we shall have large sampling errors. But suppose there are specification errors, either in the form of poor measurement of some of the X_i or their omission from the equation. Previously, we noted in Fig. 5.3 that a control for A would remove all the intercorrelations among the X_i, so that if some were inadvertently omitted, the estimates of the structural parameters for the others would remain unbiased. This will not be true, however, for the more complex model of Fig. 5.5 unless both A_{t_1} and A_{t_2} are simultaneously controlled. If we looked only within A_{t_2} we would expect to find a correlation between X_1 and X_2 that would be some function of the proportion of immigrants, since these variables depend only on the factors operating during the earlier period. Presumably, X_1's correlation with X_3 and X_4 would be somewhat weaker, because of the contemporary factors affecting the latter two variables. The correlation between X_{3t_2} and X_{4t_2}, assuming we are dealing with within-area data, will depend on the relative importance of contemporary influences as compared with earlier ones.

What happens when we aggregate using only the present location A_{t_2}? Once again, we do the very opposite of controlling for location and thereby tend to confound the effects of the four X_i. But we now also are grouping by a variable that may be dependent upon certain of the X_i. In Fig. 5.5, I have drawn arrows from X_{1t_1} (say, education) and X_{3t_1} (say, attitude toward a minority) to A_{t_2}, presuming that these two X_i have influenced the decision to migrate. But if we aggregate by A (at time 2), we are manipulating a dependent variable in terms of the relationship between X_1 and X_3, and this will distort their relationship in an unknown way.

The models with which we have been concerned are grossly oversimplified and merely illustrative of the problems one encounters when aggregation operations are poorly understood. In a sense, aggregation by spatial units is understood in that the criteria for aggregation are clearly operationalized. But what we generally lack is a theoretical model connecting spatial location with the other variables in the system. Thus, we achieve operational simplicity at the expense of theoretical clarity. The result is that we are unable to link our macrolevel aggregated data with the microlevel causal processes that might have produced these data. Put another way, if we wanted to insert the aggregation criterion into the causal model, we would find that the model would have to be highly complex because one's spatial location is not simply related to the other variables in these models.

CONCLUDING REMARKS

All of the models and situations we have discussed in this chapter may be characterized in the following way: because of the very practical design considerations, it is often convenient to select or to aggregate individuals in such a way that variances or covariances involving dependent variables become manipulated in some manner. Such manipulations are often inadvertent and unrecognized as such, but this of course does not mean that their implications can be ignored for purposes of causal analyses. As long as controls are made for the other variables whose influences are being confounded with those in which the investigator is primarily interested, all is well and good. The fundamental difficulty, however, is that many such variables are likely to be omitted from one's data analysis altogether, perhaps because they have been unmeasured but also because it is manifestly impossible to anticipate the effects of all such variables even in the most careful of analyses.

Several very practical and important implications follow from these rather discouraging facts. First, one should be wary of advice from design specialists if they dwell almost exclusively on cost and convenience considerations without also inquiring about one's theoretical assumptions or the form of the data analysis that is to follow. Thus, the mere fact that a simple list of prison inmates or hospital patients is readily available does not absolve one of the necessity of thinking through the implications for one's causal models if individuals are then selected on the basis of behaviors that will be taken as dependent variables in one's subsequent analysis. As we also have seen, if one were to match such inmates or patients with "normal" individuals who are similar to them with respect to certain background characteristics, one must be cautious about inferring relationships to other independent variables that may be correlated with the matching variable(s) in some larger population. Furthermore, although aggregating individuals according to their spatial locations may be convenient or even necessary, it does not follow that one may then safely ignore this aggregating criterion in the subsequent analysis. The more general point is that cutting corners at the design stage, although perhaps a practical necessity, may prove costly in terms of the untested assumptions one may then have to make at the analysis stage. Most certainly, a failure to state such assumptions will not produce a correct interpretation, though perhaps it may help to preserve one's sense of sanity or lead to a published paper.

Second, where feasible it may make sense to expand the initial population so as to make it easier to justify one's simplifying assumptions. If, for example, one were to select workers at 10 to 15 plants or children throughout an entire school district, it may be more plausible to assume that truncation produced by self-selection does not occur and to avoid the oversampling of extreme cases in instances where there is insufficient variation in one's dependent variable(s). Rather than having to oversample executives, professionals, and unskilled workers, for example, one would initially begin with a far more heterogeneous population.

The main point is that questions such as these should be thought through *before* one's design has been determined, so that cost and convenience considerations can be balanced by concerns that the adequacy of one's data analysis not be sacrificed in the bargain. Design specialists, in particular, need to be alerted to these interpretive problems so that they make the effort to inform unsuspecting investigators to these tradeoffs. Simplifying design aspects of the research may help one submit what appears to be a highly efficient proposal for a research grant, but it may not enhance the quality of the overall research effort. Similarly, sponsors of research projects need to be made aware of the likely possibility that relatively cheap and convenient designs, although seemingly attractive, are also more likely to result in incomplete, noninformative, or even misleading data analyses.

Finally, all of our illustrations point to the need for relatively more complete and realistic causal models that include as many of the potentially confounding factors as feasible, along with their measures. This will undoubtedly increase the cost of the research project and in many instances also require the collection of information about the past. Retrospective data obviously involve considerable measurement errors, and it will also be difficult to track down individuals who are no longer in the relevant population but who might have self-selected themselves out for reasons that pertain to some of the other variables in the model. Obviously, no single empirical study can be "complete" in all these respects. The more information that is missing from one's study, however, the larger the number of untested assumptions that must be made and the more difficult it becomes to convince one's readers of the validity of one's practical or theoretical conclusions.

REFERENCES

Blalock, Hubert M. *Causal Inferences in Nonexperimental Research.* Chapel Hill: North Carolina Press, 1964.

Blalock, Hubert M. "Causal Inferences in Natural Experiments: Some Complications in Matching Designs." *Sociometry* 30(1967): 300–315.

Blalock, Hubert M. "Measurement and Conceptualization Problems: The Major Obstacle to Integrating Theory and Research." *American Sociological Review* 44(1979): 881–894.

Firebaugh, Glenn. "A Rule for Inferring Individual-Level Relationships from Aggregate Data." *American Sociological Review* 43(1978): 557–572.

Firebaugh, Glenn. "Assessing Group Effects: A Comparison of Two Methods." *Sociological Methods and Research* 4(1979): 384–395.

Hannan, Michael T. *Aggregation and Disaggregation in Sociology.* Lexington, Mass.: Heath-Lexington, 1971.

Hannan, Michael T., and Burstein, Leigh. "Estimation from Grouped Observations." *American Sociological Review* 39(1974): 374–392.

Irwin, Laura, and Lichtman, Allan J. "Across the Great Divide: Inferring Individual Level Behavior from Aggregate Data." *Political Methodology* 3(1976): 411–439.

Kish, Leslie. *Survey Sampling.* New York: John Wiley, 1965.

Langbein, Laura Irwin, and Lichtman, Allan J. *Ecological Inference.* Beverly Hills, Calif.: Sage, 1978.

Simon, Herbert A. "Spurious Correlation: A Causal Interpretation." *Journal of the American Statistical Association* 49(1959): 467–479.

Stinchcombe, Arthur L. *Constructing Social Theories.* New York: Harcourt, Brace, 1968.

Wold, Herman O. A., and Juréen, Lars. *Demand Analysis.* New York: John Wiley, 1953.

II

THE USE OF
CAUSAL MODELS IN
PANEL DESIGNS

Change data afford special opportunities to disentangle causes and effects and to distinguish the relative magnitude of the effect of X upon Y from that of Y upon X. They also permit one to assess the stabilities of different variables over time and thereby to gain greater insights as to the exogenous factors producing social change. But all of this depends upon several crucial assumptions, especially those relating to measurement errors and the correct specification of lag periods in relation to intervals of observation. Frequently, for example, the observed "changes" in a given period are relatively small as compared with presumed measurement-error variances, so that it becomes difficult to separate out real change from apparent change due to measurement error. Furthermore, unless one has a good theory regarding lag intervals, the superimposition of measurement errors on improperly specified lag models may create an extremely ambiguous situation, or even one of underidentification.

As the chapters in Part II indicate, there are a host of potential complications, the implications of which are just beginning to be understood even in the case of models involving only one or two theoretical variables. For example, as Heise notes in Chapter 6, if one allows for random measurement errors and only a single measure of a given variable, then observations at three time points will be necessary to achieve identification unless some very strong assumptions can be made. Chapter 7 by Wiley and Wiley and Chapter 8 by Werts, Jöreskog, and Linn both elaborate on this relatively simple type of model but point to further complications in its implementation. As soon as one moves to multiple indicators that may be utilized at two or more points in time, one may begin to allow for sources of nonrandom measurement errors as well, provided that certain kinds of simplifications are allowed. Chapter 10 by Blalock suggests some of the tradeoffs that exist in this connection in instances where one has either three measures at two points in time or two measures at three points in time.

Unless one is willing to assume either no measurement errors or strictly random ones, analyses of panel data must confront the question of how one allows for nonrandom sources of measurement errors in instances of repeated measurements. Clearly, this requires a *theory* of measurement errors that is sufficiently realistic to allow for very different sources of error. Strictly constant errors, as for example the addition of 10 units to every score, can be cancelled out rather simply by taking change or difference scores. Indeed, if such constant errors were the only major sources of error, this would suggest the clear-cut superiority of panel designs over those that rely on comparative data for which one were unwilling to assume such constant errors across all observations.

As measurements are repeated, however, several things begin to happen with human subjects. Respondents may become increasingly accurate as they gain experience, in which case measurement-error *variances* may become smaller over time. But perhaps the measurement-error variances remain constant, whereas the variances in the true scores are diminishing (or increasing) over time. Since it is the *ratio* of the two kinds of variances that matters, if one utilizes standardized measures — such as correlations or path coefficients — one may be misled if these ratios were to shift. Since both the true scores and the measurement-error components will be unobserved, however, these shifts in the unknown variances may remain undetected and thereby lead one astray. This point is specifically noted by Wiley and Wiley in Chapter 7.

If there are artifacts or biases produced by specific measurement techniques, it may be convenient to assume that such biases remain constant over time or that their distorting effects are constant across a certain set of variables at each time point, though they may shift at a later point in time, perhaps because of the increased sophistication of the respondents. If these measurement-instrument effects shift in unknown ways across variables and across time, however, the measurement-error model is likely to become underidentified, which means that empirical estimation will be impossible. Thus, there will inevitably be tradeoffs between, on the one hand, the need for simplifications and, on the other, the objective of building in necessary complications to allow for different types of sources of bias. The larger the number of measures of each variable and the more time points, the more such complications one can handle while still achieving an estimable model. As can be imagined, however, there are many reasons why this very simple generalization must be qualified in particular instances, as will become clear from the discussions in the remainder of the volume.

There must also be a concern about the correct specification of lag periods, particularly if one wishes to use panel designs to sort out the direction of causation between two or more variables. If one allows for both simultaneous and lagged effects and also for reciprocal causation between X and Y, one's model will become underidentified unless other kinds of restrictions are placed on the model. In Chapter 12, Greenberg and Kessler discuss the feasibility of making certain assumptions about the constancy of parameter values across adjacent time periods, if there are at least three such periods. They note that this approach can be utilized only under certain restricted conditions that are somewhat similar to those discussed by Blalock in Chapter 10.

An extensive but rather confusing body of literature now exists on the subject of "cross-lagged" analyses in panel data. Although it is not feasible to include sample papers from this literature, while still doing justice to other discussions of causal modeling in panel designs, the expository chapter by Shingles (Chapter 13) highlights the essential features of several approaches in this vein as well as the advantages and drawbacks of each. Although this particular body of literature has developed primarily out of psychology and social psychology and involves a somewhat different way of looking at the issues involved, it does not seem to lead to fundamentally different conclusions. Put most generally, one must handle panel data with care unless one is willing to assume away virtually all of the complications with extremely simplistic assumptions about measurement errors and lag periods.

The clear implication is that there is no substitute for the combination of very careful measurement—so as to reduce measurement errors to a minimum in the first place—and a set of explicit assumptions about the sources of those errors that may remain. In addition, there is the implication that, other things being equal, it is preferable to deal with situations in which true changes are substantial and in which there are a sufficient number of data-collection periods so that time intervals may be pinned down. Ideally, of course, one would like to be in a position to observe at least some of the changes as they are occurring so as to reduce the number of ambiguities in the system.

Substantive applications of any methodological procedures not only provide useful reality checks but sometimes also lead to important new insights as to further complications that may arise in practice. Chapters 9, 11, and 14 are primarily oriented to substantive topics in very different areas. Chapter 9 by Hargens, Reskin, and Allison focuses on the explanation of stability in scientific productivity and introduces some important notes of caution concerning the approaches suggested by Heise, Wiley, and Wiley and by Werts, Jöreskog, and Linn. Chapter 11 by McPherson, Welch, and Clark is concerned with the assessment of reliability and stability of an attitudinal variable of interest to political scientists, namely perceptions of political efficacy. This chapter also addresses the common problem of deciding whether or not to discard measures for which reasonably simple models provide poor fits to one's data. The final chapter in the volume, Chapter 14 by Kohn and Schooler, deals with the reciprocal relationship between two variables, complexity of work and intellectual flexibility, and how panel data may be used to assess their relative importance, even in the presence of measurement errors.

6

Separating Reliability and Stability in Test-Retest Correlation

David R. Heise*

The theory of measurements traditionally has been the province of psychometricians. Sociologists certainly can benefit from the large and excellent literature in that field (e.g., Lord and Novick, 1968). However, the problems in psychological and sociological measurement are not always the same, and psychometric solutions sometimes may be less useful than techniques tailored more directly to sociometric dilemmas. Measuring reliability appears to be a case in point. The psychometricians have grounded much of their reliability theory on the idea of a test in which there are multiple items and for which there may be equivalent forms. The resulting techniques of assessing reliability (internal consistency measures, crossform correlations) may be only of peripheral interest when key variables can be measured practically only by a single question. In this case, which is a frequent sociological situation, it is more appropriate to turn to test–retest correlations to assess reliabilities.

Unfortunately, a simple test–retest correlation may not measure true reliability because it is affected by temporal instability in a variable as well as by errors of measurement. Consider the hypothetical case of a test that

* Reprinted by permission of the author and publisher from the *American Sociological Review* 34: 93–101. Copyright 1969, The American Sociological Association.

measures without error and whose true reliability, therefore, is 1.00. Suppose persons are evaluated with the test at time 1 and time 2, and the measurement interval is sufficiently long so that some shifts in the measured attribute occur during the measurement interval. Then, because of the shifts in true scores (i.e., because some persons increase in value and others decrease) the distribution of individuals at time 2 will not coincide exactly with the distribution at time 1. It follows that the correlation between the two testings will be less than 1.00, and we would conclude that we have a test with reliability less than 1.00 even though this is contrary to the initial assumption.

One may attempt to reduce the effect of temporal instability on test–retest correlations by reducing the time interval between measurements, thereby reducing the amount of shifting that can occur in true scores. However, an immediate test–retest may not be practical with many measures. Further, this procedure often raises the problem of respondents recalling their first answer so that the second assessment is not independent of the first.

It would be desirable, therefore, to have a general procedure for analyzing test–retest correlations so that the effects of measurement errors and true-score instability could be separated analytically. Coleman (1968) has demonstrated that such a separation is possible if one gathers data at three points in time rather than two. This chapter interprets Coleman's insight in terms of traditional statistics used in tests and measurements.

The analysis below is carried out using path analysis, a quantitative procedure for analyzing relations between variables, developed by the biologist, Sewall Wright (1934). The rules of path analysis are not presented since a number of expository articles on the topic are available elsewhere (Boudon, 1968; Duncan, 1966; Heise, 1968; Turner and Stevens, 1959). Path analysis has been applied previously to reliability problems by Wright (1934) and by Siegel and Hodge (1968), and Blalock (1963) has employed a similar approach. Part of the discussion here is drawn from these sources.

PATH ANALYSIS OF MEASUREMENTS

Suppose we have a test or index that measures a variable x. Conceptually, we can distinguish between the true variable x and the obtained measurement x' as two different variables related by the fact that the value on x determines to some degree the value we find on the measurement, x'. In this case, we are making the customary assumption that $x' = x + e$, where e is a random variable representing errors of measurement and the correlation between errors and true values (i.e., between x and e) is zero. The relationship between x and x' can be represented in a path diagram as illustrated in Fig. 6.1. This diagram indicates that x' is determined both by x and by the random variable e. The parameter, $p_{x'x}$, is a number that indicates the

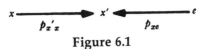

Figure 6.1

amount of relationship between x and x'. It is related to the traditional reliability coefficient, as will be seen below. The coefficient, p_{xe}, indicates the extent to which variations in x' are a function of errors. It is not an independent unknown since, once p_{xx} is known, we can determine how much variance in x' is *not* determined by x, and the value of p_{xe} is set accordingly.

Let us first consider how path analysis can be applied to analyze reliability coefficients based on parallel forms, a traditional psychometric topic. Because we now have two tests, we have a total of three substantive variables to consider: x and observed-score variables x_1' and x_2'. In addition, of course, there are two random variables, e_1 and e_2, which are assumed to be uncorrelated. The path diagram for this situation is given in Fig. 6.2. Notice that the amount of determination of test scores by x is represented as identical for both tests (p_{xx}). This follows from the customary assumption that the parallel forms are completely equivalent.

From Fig. 6.2 and the rules of path analysis, one finds that the relationship between p_{xx} and the reliability coefficient, r_{12}, is $r_{12} = p_{xx}^2$. Thus, the reliability measure, p_{xx}, which appears in the path analysis, is the square root of the traditional reliability coefficient.

Wright (1934) has shown how the correction for attenuation can be derived from a path analysis of measurements, and this demonstration is

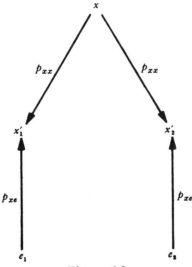

Figure 6.2

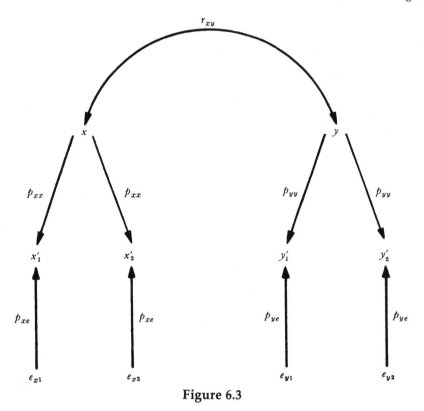

Figure 6.3

reproduced here to further illustrate the meaningfulness of path analysis in measurement problems.

We now have two true variables, x and y, plus two tests for measuring each of these, x'_1 and x'_2, and y'_1 and y'_2. The variables x and y are correlated, and our goal is to estimate the true correlation, r_{xy}, from correlations among the test variables. The path diagram for this situation is given in Fig. 6.3.

As empirical information, we have the reliabilities of the tests, $r_{x'_1x'_2}$ and $r_{y'_1y'_2}$, and the correlations between one of the x' forms with one of the y' forms, say, $r_{x'_1y'_1}$. Following the rules of path analysis, we can write:

$$r_{x'_1y'_1} = p_{xx}r_{xy}p_{yy}$$

$$r_{x'_1x'_2} = p_{xx}^2 \qquad (6.1)$$

$$r_{y'_1y'_2} = p_{yy}^2$$

These equations can be algebraically manipulated to:

$$r_{xy} = \frac{r_{x_1'y_1'}}{p_{xx}p_{yy}}$$

$$p_{xx} = \sqrt{r_{x_1'x_2'}} \qquad\qquad (6.2)$$

$$p_{yy} = \sqrt{r_{y_1'y_2'}}$$

Substituting, we obtain:

$$r_{xy} = \frac{r_{x_1'y_1'}}{\sqrt{r_{x_1'x_2'}}\sqrt{r_{y_1'y_2'}}} \qquad\qquad (6.3)$$

which is the traditional correction-for-attenuation formula.

THE TEST-RETEST SITUATION

Suppose we measure x imperfectly at time 1. Following the convention established above, we then have two substantive variables of interest: x_1, the true scores at time 1, and x_1', the empirical measurements with errors. Now suppose we measure again with the same test or index at time 2. Again, we have two variables, x_2 and x_2'. Here x_1 and x_2 are distinguished as separate variables since the distribution of individuals at the two times generally is not the same: Some changes have occurred during the measurement interval. However, x_1 and x_2 are correlated, and, in addition, we know that x_1 preceded x_2; hence, it is reasonable to say that x_1 in part determines x_2, but x_2 does not determine x_1. The path analysis for this situation is indicated in Fig. 6.4. The new variable, u_2, in this diagram represents the aggregation of variables that have affected or disturbed x during the interval from 1 to 2. The coefficient, p_{xu_2}, indicates the extent of such disturbances; p_{xu_2} is like p_{xe} in that it is defined as a residual and so does not constitute an independent unknown in the system. The path coefficient, p_{21}, is a measure of the stability of x over time, since it indicates the degree to which x_1 determines x_2 over the given interval.

A careful examination of the diagram reveals the several assumptions that are being made at this point. First, we are assuming the relationship between the true variable and the index is constant over time: Both paths, $x_1 \rightarrow x_1'$ and $x_2 \rightarrow x_2'$, are labeled p_{xx}. Second, the assumption that errors are uncorrelated with true scores is indicated by the absence of curved lines connecting e's with x's. Third, it is assumed that measurement errors at different times are uncorrelated: A curved line does not connect e_1 and e_2. Fourth, it is assumed that disturbances in x that develop between times 1 and 2 are uncorrelated with the initial values of x so that no curved line

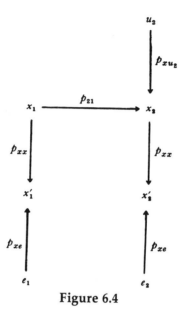

Figure 6.4

connects x_1 and u_2. Also, it may be noted that the rate of change in the true scores is presumed to be approximately constant within the measurement interval.

Following the rules of path analysis, the test–retest correlation can be analyzed as follows (where r_{12} indicates the true correlation between the *measured* variables, x_1' and x_2'):

$$r_{12} = p_{xx}p_{21}p_{xx} = p_{xx}^2 p_{21} \qquad (6.4)$$

The relationship between reliability coefficient and path coefficient, that was mentioned above (i.e., $r_{xx} = p_{xx}^2$) can be true in this case only if $p_{21} = 1.00$. But this would imply that the variable x remains completely stable over time. Allowing that this is not so (i.e., p_{21} is less than 1.00), we see that the test–retest correlation is not simply the square of the reliability parameter, p_{xx}.

What we would like to do, then, is to find the actual value of p_{xx}. Then we could square it, obtaining a reliability coefficient that is comparable to other reliability coefficients in that it is uncontaminated by the temporal instability of variable x. This reliability coefficient would have the value we theoretically would obtain by a test–retest correlation in which the retest came instantly after the first test.

Equation (6.4) expresses an observed correlation as a function of two unknowns, p_{xx} and p_{21}. Because there are *two* unknowns, we cannot turn this equation around and solve for p_{xx}. So, if we are to estimate the value of

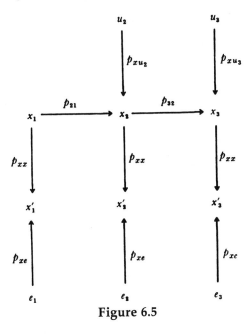

Figure 6.5

p_{xx}, we need more information, that is, another equation. This can be obtained by making another retest at a time 3. The path diagram for the three-wave testing is given in Fig. 6.5.

From the diagram, it can be seen that a third unknown (p_{32}) arises by adding another retest, if we maintain the assumptions stated above, and further require that disturbances at times 2 and 3 are uncorrelated. Now, however, the additional testing allows us to write two new equations so that we have three equations and three unknowns. (Again, the r's represent the true correlations between *measured* variables.)

$$r_{12} = p_{xx}p_{21}p_{xx} = p_{xx}^2 p_{21}$$

$$r_{23} = p_{xx}p_{32}p_{xx} = p_{xx}^2 p_{32} \qquad (6.5)$$

$$r_{13} = p_{xx}p_{21}p_{32}p_{xx} = p_{xx}^2 p_{21}p_{32}$$

The first two of these equations can be manipulated as follows:

$$p_{21} = \frac{r_{12}}{p_{xx}^2}$$

$$\qquad (6.6)$$

$$p_{32} = \frac{r_{23}}{p_{xx}^2}$$

Substituting these results into the last of Eqs. (6.5):

$$r_{13} = p_{xx}^2 \frac{r_{12}}{p_{xx}^2} \frac{r_{23}}{p_{xx}^2} = \frac{r_{12}r_{23}}{p_{xx}^2} \qquad (6.7)$$

or

$$p_{xx}^2 = \frac{r_{12}r_{23}}{r_{13}} \qquad (6.8)$$

It is the square of p_{xx} that corresponds to a customary reliability coefficient, so that Eq. (6.8) indicates the formula for a new measure of reliability based on test–retest data but free of temporal change effects.

$$r_{xx} = \frac{r_{12}r_{23}}{r_{13}} \qquad (6.9)$$

The symbols in formula (6.9) are meant to designate true correlations in the population of interest. When one substitutes empirical correlations based on samples, an estimate of the true reliability is obtained, and the estimate, of course, is subject to sampling variability.

STABILITY COEFFICIENTS

Once the reliability coefficient is available, it is possible to correct the test–retest correlations for attenuation and thereby obtain stability coefficients measuring the amount of change that occurred during a given interval. In fact, if interest centers on the stability coefficients, they can be obtained without calculating r_{xx} first. Let the stability coefficient for a given interval be s; this is the correlation between true scores at one time with true scores at another time. From Fig. 6.5 and the rules of path analysis, it follows that:

$$s_{12} = p_{21}$$

$$s_{23} = p_{32} \qquad (6.10)$$

$$s_{13} = p_{21}p_{32}$$

Now, Eqs. (6.6) and (6.8) can be solved directly for p_{21} and p_{32}.

$$p_{21} = r_{12}/p_{xx}^2 = r_{12}r_{13}/r_{12}r_{23} = r_{13}/r_{23}$$

$$p_{32} = r_{23}/p_{xx}^2 = r_{23}r_{13}/r_{12}r_{23} = r_{13}/r_{12}$$

(6.11)

Hence:

$$s_{12} = r_{13}/r_{23}$$

$$s_{23} = r_{13}/r_{12}$$

(6.12)

$$s_{13} = r_{13}^2/r_{12}r_{23}$$

EMPIRICAL EXAMPLES

Correlations between IQ measures of children passing through third, sixth, and ninth grades have been presented by Crowther (1965). At each level, the instrument employed was the California Test of Mental Maturity, and a measurement was the total score over all subscales. The test involves different forms for different levels, but this does not affect the analysis if it is assumed that the reliabilities and validities are the same for all forms.

Observed correlations between testings were as follows:

$$r_{12} = .56; \quad r_{23} = .65; \quad r_{13} = .52$$

Then, by formula (6.9):

$$r_{xx} = .70$$

By formulas (6.12):

$$s_{12} = .80; \quad s_{23} = .93; \quad s_{13} = .74$$

The corrected coefficient, r_{xx}, is considerably higher than the test–retest correlations computed over a 3-year interval. The r_{xx} compares well with, but is slightly lower than, the reported reliability based on parallel forms: The test–publisher reports that between-form correlations range from .72 to .81 at different age levels (Stanley, 1965). The values of the stability coefficients indicate that IQ is less stable between third and sixth grades than between sixth and ninth; further, only a little more than one-half of the ninth grade IQ variance is shared with the third grade variance. Although these values may seem low for what often is thought of as a "permanent" trait, notice that the stability coefficients are substantially higher than the raw test – retest correlations. If one were to overlook measurement error, he might seriously underestimate the stability of IQ.

A longitudinal study of college students (unpublished) by Edgar F. Borgatta provides another illustration. In this study, measurement 1 was made when the students were first semester freshmen; measurement 2, when they were second semester freshmen; and measurement 3, when they were second semester sophomores. The question of interest asked students how often they attended religious services. The test – retest correlations for males and females, respectively, were:

$$r_{12} = .71, .73$$

$$r_{23} = .80, .78$$

$$r_{13} = .60, .62$$

from which it follows that:

$$r_{xx} = .95 \text{ (males)}$$

$$r_{xx} = .92 \text{ (females)}$$

Again, the corrected reliabilities are substantially above the raw test – retest values, indicating the importance of making the correction.

The stability coefficients for these data are:

$$s_{12} = .75; .79$$

$$s_{23} = .85; .85$$

$$s_{13} = .64; .67$$

These figures indicate that patterns of church attendance change at a relatively rapid rate during the first few months on campus.

Freedman, Coombs, and Bumpass (1965) reported the following test – retest correlations obtained in a longitudinal study in which the key variable was expectations about family size.

$$r_{12} = .81$$

$$r_{23} = .85$$

$$r_{13} = .78$$

From these figures, one can estimate the reliability of their measure as .88 and the stability coefficients as:

$$s_{12} = .92$$

$$s_{23} = .96$$

$$s_{13} = .88$$

These reliability and stability coefficients suggest that a sizeable proportion of the flux in family-size expectations is a matter of ambiguity in measurement rather than due to actual changes of mind.

RESTRICTIONS

Formulas (6.9) and (6.12) provide estimates of the reliability and stability coefficients under the following assumptions: (a) determination of the index by the underlying variable is constant over time; (b) the rate of instability in the underlying variable is constant between adjacent measurement times; (c) measurement errors are uncorrelated with true scores; (d) measurement errors at different times are uncorrelated with each other; and (e) disturbances at times 2 and 3 are uncorrelated with each other or with the true scores at time 1. Both (a) and (c) are standard metric assumptions, and (b) can usually be managed by adjusting the test–retest intervals. The problems posed by (d) and (e) are discussed below.

Assumption (d) requires that errors be serially uncorrelated. The assumption may be violated when respondents recall earlier answers and try to be consistent in their responses. In such a case, distortions occurring in early measurements will tend to be reproduced over time. If errors are serially correlated, the model in Fig. 6.5 must be replaced by the one in Fig. 6.6. In this model, the error terms are connected by curved lines indicating they are correlated.

With three waves of testing, there are three empirical correlations available for defining equations. However, it can be seen from Fig. 6.6 that the model now has six independent unknowns (p_{xx}, p_{21}, p_{32}, $r_{e_1e_2}$, $r_{e_2e_3}$, $r_{e_1e_3}$), and

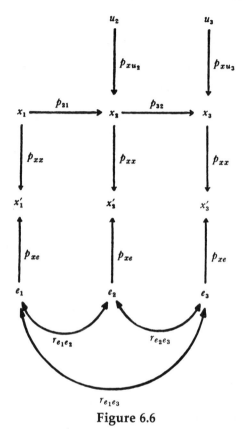

Figure 6.6

so there is not enough information to identify the parameters. Furthermore, adding additional waves of observations does not solve this problem since every new wave continues to add new unknowns. For example, obtaining a fourth wave would yield six test–retest correlations, but there would be a total of 10 unknowns to identify (those in Fig. 6.6 plus p_{43}, $r_{e_3e_4}$, $r_{e_2e_4}$, and $r_{e_1e_4}$). One might suppose that a different solution to this problem could be obtained by equalizing the measurement intervals and then assuming that the stability coefficients and the serial correlations in errors do not change over time. This would reduce the number of unknowns in Fig. 6.6 to four (p_{xx}, p_x, $r_{e_1e_2}$, and $r_{e_1e_3}$, where $p_x = p_{21} = p_{32}$ and $r_{e_1e_2} = r_{e_2e_3}$). Although it is impossible to identify these four unknowns from three waves of testing, it might seem that now additional retests could help, since each retest will add only one new unknown (i.e., the correlation between errors at time 1 and at the last testing). This is not so, however, since with the constant-parameters model each additional testing adds only one *new* empirical piece of information—the correlation between the first and last tests. All of the

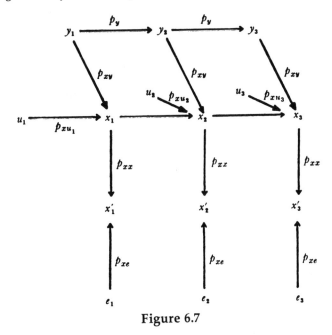

Figure 6.7

other additional correlations are merely replications of those already obtained. For example, the correlation r_{34} would be only another estimate of the true correlation between two adjacent testings, thus serving as a replication on r_{12} and r_{23}. With each additional retest adding a new unknown and only one new piece of information, it is clear that a constant-parameters model also is unsolvable, whatever the number of retests. In general, then, when measurement errors are serially correlated, it is impossible to obtain enough information to solve for reliability and stability coefficients.

Assumption (e) requires that disturbances in the underlying variable, x, are uncorrelated over time and that these disturbances are uncorrelated with the initial values of x. This assumption would be violated if there is some unmeasured variable, y, that has stability over time and unilaterally affects x, as indicated in Fig. 6.7.

This situation would necessitate the model in Fig. 6.8. This model has six unknowns (p_{xx}, p_{21}, p_{32}, r_{1u_2}, r_{1u_3}, $r_{u_2u_3}$) and is unsolvable. Adding a fourth wave of observations adds three test–retest correlations, but the required model also has three more unknowns (r_{1u_4}, $r_{u_2u_4}$, $r_{u_3u_4}$). Obviously, the situation is parallel to that discussed above for serially correlated errors, and, in general, accurate reliability and stability coefficients cannot be obtained when some unmeasured variable is having a continuous effect on the variable of interest during the period of measurements. Of course, the problem becomes serious only when the unmeasured variable has a substantial impact and when it is stable (i.e., p_{xy} and p_y are not small in value).

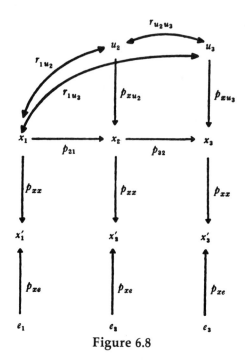

Figure 6.8

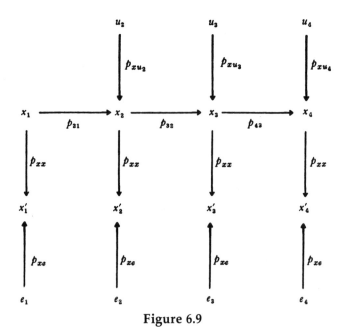

Figure 6.9

There is no way to analyze test–retest correlations on a single variable so as to eliminate the problems of correlated errors and correlated disturbances. However, if a fourth wave of measurements can be obtained, an analysis can be conducted that reveals whether correlated errors or correlated disturbances are interfering with reliability and stability estimates. To derive this procedure, we assume that the model in Fig. 6.9 holds; then the following equations would be appropriate according to formulas (6.8) and (6.11) (we obtain p_{43} by treating measurements 2 through 4 as a separate set of test–retests).

$$p_{xx}^2 = \frac{r_{12}r_{23}}{r_{13}}$$

$$(6.13)$$

$$p_{21} = \frac{r_{13}}{r_{23}} \qquad p_{32} = \frac{r_{13}}{r_{12}} \qquad p_{43} = \frac{r_{24}}{r_{23}}$$

The correlation r_{14} then can be predicted as follows:

$$r_{14} = p_{xx}^2 p_{21} p_{32} p_{43}$$

$$r_{14} = \left(\frac{r_{12}r_{23}}{r_{13}}\right)\left(\frac{r_{13}}{r_{23}}\right)\left(\frac{r_{13}}{r_{12}}\right)\left(\frac{r_{24}}{r_{23}}\right)$$

$$(6.14)$$

$$r_{14} = \frac{r_{13}r_{24}}{r_{23}}$$

or

$$r_{14}r_{23} = r_{13}r_{24} \qquad\qquad (6.15)$$

In actual practice, it is unlikely that the left and right terms of Eq. (6.15) will be exactly equal. However, if the model in Fig. 6.5 is appropriate and one is working with a large sample, then the two products should differ very little. If the left and right terms of Eq. (6.15) are distinctly different, one has evidence that required assumptions are not met, and the model is inappropriate for the data.

SUMMARY

Following Coleman's lead and using path analysis, formulas have been derived for estimating a measure's reliability and a variable's stability from test–retest correlations. The reliability estimate does not require a test with multiple items or two equivalent measures; hence, the reliability of a single question or observation can be determined. Furthermore, the reliability coefficient, unlike a simple test–retest correlation, is not attenuated in size because of changes that occur during the testing interval. The formulas depend on these assumptions: Measurement errors are not serially correlated, and no unmeasured variable has a significant continuous impact on the measured variable during the measurement period. The legitimacy of these assumptions can be examined if a fourth wave of measurements is obtained.

ACKNOWLEDGMENTS

The author is grateful to George Bohrnstedt and to the *Review's* referees for their helpful comments on earlier drafts of this chapter. Edgar F. Borgatta kindly provided data from a study in progress for one of the empirical examples.

REFERENCES

Blalock, H. M., Jr. "Making Causal Inferences for Unmeasured Variables from Correlations among Indicators." *American Journal of Sociology* 69(1963): 53–62.

Boudon, R. "A New Look at Correlation Analysis." In *Methodology in Social Research,* edited by H. M. Blalock, Jr. and A. B. Blalock. New York: McGraw-Hill, 1968.

Coleman, J. S. "The Mathematical Study of Change." In *Methodology in Social Research,* edited by H. M. Blalock Jr. and A. B. Blalock. New York: McGraw-Hill, 1968.

Crowther, Betty. "A Sociological Analysis of Academic Achievement Correlates." Ph.D. dissertation, University of Wisconsin, Madison, 1965.

Duncan, O. D. "Path Analysis: Sociological Examples." *American Journal of Sociology* 72(1966): 1–16.

Freedman, R., Coombs, L. G., and Bumpass, L. "Stability and Change in Expectations about Family Size: A Longitudinal Study." *Demography* 2(1965): 250–275.

Heise, D. R. "Problems in Path Analysis and Causal Inference." In *Sociological Methodology 1969,* edited by E. F. Borgatta. Jossey-Bass, 1969.

Lord, F. M., and Novick, M. R. *Statistical Theories of Mental Test Scores.* Reading, Mass.: Addison-Wesley, 1968.

Siegel, P. M., and Hodge, R. W. "A Causal Approach to the Study of Measurement Error." In *Methodology in Social Research,* edited by H. M. Blalock Jr. and A. B. Blalock. New York: McGraw-Hill, 1968.

Stanley, J. C. "Review of California Short-Form Test of Mental Maturity, 1963 revision." In *The Sixth Mental Measurements Yearbook,* edited by O. K. Buros. Highland Park, N.J.: Gryphon Press, 1965.

Turner, M. E., and Stevens, C. D. "The Regression Analysis of Causal Paths." *Biometrics* 15(1959): 236–258.

Wright, S. "The Method of Path Coefficients." *Annals of Mathematical Statistics* 5(1934): 161–215.

7

The Estimation of Measurement Error in Panel Data*

David E. Wiley

James A. Wiley

In general, there are three ways of dealing with the problem of measurement error in path analyses of social and psychological data. Correction of parameter estimates for the attenuating effects of random error of measurement may be accomplished (1) by the use of *a priori* estimates of measurement error, (2) by designing into studies alternate measures of the same construct, or (3) by repeated measurements on the same population over time. This chapter considers models for the estimation of measurement error in the latter case.

Taking his lead from Coleman (1968), Heise (1969) has formulated a path analysis model for the assessment of reliability when a variable is observed at three or more points in time. A consequence of this model is a simple formula for reliability uncontaminated by instability in the true scores. One of the several assumptions necessary to the empirical validity of Heise's model (i.e., the assumption that the reliability of the measured scores is stable over time) is argued to be doubtful.

* Reprinted by permission of the authors and publisher from the *American Sociological Review* 35: 112–117. Copyright 1970, The American Sociological Association.

MEASUREMENT MODELS

It is useful to distinguish between a *causal model*, describing the structure of causal relations between "true scores," and a *measurement model*, which describes the relationship between measured scores and true scores (Blalock, 1968). Models for empirical phenomena may be evaluated with respect to their formal mathematical properties or with respect to their correspondence with the phenomenon. The argument in support of the measurement model proposed in this chapter is based on the assumption that it is a more adequate representation of the empirical conditions of measurement than models heretofore proposed.

Consider the usual linear decomposition of a measured score into true score and error components.

$$x = \xi + \epsilon \tag{7.1}$$

Here, x is the measured score, ξ the true score, and ϵ the error of measurement. If the true score and error components are independent, the variance of the measured scores (i.e., the total variance) is simply the sum of the true-score variance and the measurement-error variance.[1]

$$V(x) = V(\xi) + V(\epsilon) \tag{7.2}$$

The reliability of the measured score x, here denoted ρ^2, is defined as the ratio of the true-score variance to total variance.

$$\rho^2 = \frac{V(\xi)}{V(\xi) + V(\epsilon)} \tag{7.3}$$

The classical definition of reliability is the square of the correlation between the observed and true scores (Lord and Novick, 1968:61). Equation (7.3) is equivalent to this definition under the stated assumptions.

Error variance is best conceived as a property of the measuring instrument itself and not of the population to which it is administered. On the other hand, the true-score variance is more realistically considered as a property of the population. Thus, the specification of stable reliability will

---

[1] We adopt the following notational convention: $V(x_i)$ denotes the population variance of x_i; $C(x_i x_j)$ denotes the population covariance of x_i and x_j; and $\rho(x_i x_j)$, the population correlation of x_i and x_j. The symbol $\text{``} \hat{} \text{''}$ over any of these symbols denotes an estimate of a population quantity based on a sample.

normally require assumptions about populations as well as assumptions about the measuring instrument.

Reliability will remain constant under two different conditions. Both true-score variance and error variance may change such that the ratio given in Eq. (7.3) remains constant. This appears to be unlikely. Second, both true-score and error variance may be constant. In this case, in addition to the assumption of constant-error variance, the specification of constant reliability requires either the measurement of a stable trait or some form of aggregate equilibrium for the true-score distribution. In Heise's paper, "the rate of change in the true scores is presumed to be approximately constant within the measurement interval" (Heise, 1969:96). If the rate of change in the true scores is *absolutely* constant in the interval $(0, t)$, that is, if $d\xi_i/dt = k$ where ξ_i represents the true score of individual i, then $\xi_{it} = kt + \xi_{io}$ for all i. Hence, the true score at time t is equal to the true score at time 0 plus a constant function of the time interval. Such a change process does produce constant true-score variance. However, it would require that the path coefficient relating pairs of times be unity and that there be no differential changes for individuals. Thus, the stability coefficient, defined as the correlation between the true scores at two points in time, will always be unity. In this case, there would be no need to formulate a model that separates stability and reliability in panel data.

Given the implausibility of stable true-score variance for most cases of practical interest, we are forced to conclude that most indicators cannot be characterized by a unique reliability. For example, any social process that tends to increase concensus (e.g., selective migration, increased interaction) results in a reduction of the true variability in attitudes without necessarily affecting the characteristics of the measuring instrument. Thus, the reliability of the instrument will tend to decrease. Even in completely stable situations, where reliability information, together with the total variance, is equivalent to information concerning the variance of the measurement error, this variance is probably a better index of the accuracy of the instrument's characterization of an individual's score, since the standard error of measurement is proportional to the width of the confidence interval for an individual's true score.

Similarly, comparisons across populations can be expected to yield widely varying reliabilities for the same indicator. An increase in reliability can always be obtained by conducting measurements on a more heterogeneous population (Lord and Novick, 1968:199).

It is clear that the specification of constant-error variance avoids excessively strong assumptions about populations inherent in the specification of constant reliability. In the most general case, neither assumption is valid. However, stable-error variance will hold approximately while reliability is subject to considerable fluctuation. And if the characterization of stable-error variance is faulty, then the characterization of stable reliability will almost always be in error.

A LAG-1 MODEL WITH CONSTANT ERROR VARIANCE

A path diagram for a lag-1 model in three waves of observation is given in Fig. 7.1. Here, x_i is the measured score at time i, ξ_i is the true score, θ_i is the random shock, ϵ_i is the measurement error, and the α_{ji} are lagged causal parameters linking the true scores at times j and i. It is assumed that (1) the measurement errors are uncorrelated with the true scores, (2) the measurement errors are serially uncorrelated, (3) the random shocks are serially uncorrelated, (4) the error variance is homogeneous $[V(\epsilon_1) = V(\epsilon_2) = V(\epsilon_3) = V(\epsilon)]$, and (5) the system is lag-1 (i.e., α_{31} is identically equal to zero). Two sets of equations describe the model. First, we write a set of structural equations specifying the causal relations among the true scores.

$$\xi_1 = \theta_1$$

$$\xi_2 = \alpha_{21}\theta_1 + \theta_2 \tag{7.4}$$

$$\xi_3 = \alpha_{32}(\alpha_{21}\theta_1 + \theta_2) + \theta_3$$

A set of measurement equations linking the measured and true scores is given in Eq. (7.5):

$$x_1 = \xi_1 + \epsilon_1$$

$$x_2 = \xi_2 + \epsilon_2 \tag{7.5}$$

$$x_3 = \xi_3 + \epsilon_3$$

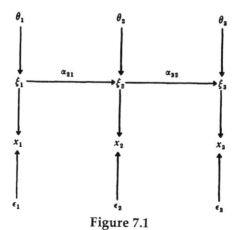

Figure 7.1

Substitution of the expressions for the true scores given in Eq. (7.4) into (7.5) generates a new set of equations (7.6) from which the structure of the covariances between the measured variables can be deduced.

$$x_1 = \theta_1 + \epsilon_1$$

$$x_2 = \alpha_{21}\theta_1 + \theta_2 + \epsilon_2 \tag{7.6}$$

$$x_3 = \alpha_{32}(\alpha_{21}\theta_1 + \theta_2) + \theta_3 + \epsilon_3$$

The matrix of covariances between the observed variables is given in Table 7.1. Note that there are six parameters to be estimated: $V(\theta_1)$, the variance of the true scores at time 1; α_{21} and α_{32}, the lag-1 path regressions linking the true scores; $V(\theta_2)$ and $V(\theta_3)$, the variances of the shocks at times 2 and 3; and finally $V(\epsilon)$, the error variance of the measuring instrument. The model is *just identified* since there are precisely six distinct entries in the covariance matrix, and the Jacobian of the transformation relating the parameters to be estimated to the population variances and covariances is non-zero for non-zero values of the relevant parameters (Wald, 1950).

Estimators for the parameters of this model are presented in Table 7.2. In this case, estimators are obtained by recursive solution of the six equations given in Table 7.1. Expressions for these estimators solely in terms of observed variances and covariances can be obtained by successive substitution.

Under reasonable distributional assumptions, the estimators specified above will be consistent. Under the assumption of normality, since the estimates will reproduce the sample covariance matrix exactly, they will thus maximize the likelihood function. Therefore, under these conditions the estimators will be efficient.

Table 7.1. Population covariance matrix for lag-1 model assuming constant-error variance for three waves of observations

$$V(x_1) = V(\theta_1) + V(\epsilon)$$
$$C(x_1x_2) = \alpha_{21}V(\theta_1)$$
$$C(x_1x_3) = \alpha_{21}\alpha_{32}V(\theta_1)$$
$$V(x_2) = \alpha_{21}^2 V(\theta_1) + V(\theta_2) + V(\epsilon)$$
$$C(x_2x_3) = \alpha_{32}[\alpha_{21}^2 V(\theta_1) + V(\theta_2)]$$
$$V(x_3) = \alpha_{32}^2[\alpha_{21}^2 V(\theta_1) + V(\theta_2)] + V(\theta_3) + V(\epsilon)$$

Table 7.2. Parameters and estimators
for lag-1 model assuming
constant-error variance[a]

Parameter	Estimator
α_{32}	$\hat{C}(x_1x_3)/\hat{C}(x_1x_2)$
$V(\epsilon)$	$\hat{V}(x_2) - [\hat{C}(x_2x_3)/\hat{\alpha}_{32}]$
$V(\theta_1)$	$\hat{V}(x_1) - \hat{V}(\epsilon)$
α_{21}	$\hat{C}(x_1x_2)/\hat{V}(\theta_1)$
$V(\theta_2)$	$\hat{V}(x_2) - [\hat{\alpha}_{21}\hat{C}(x_1x_2) + \hat{V}(\epsilon)]$
$V(\theta_3)$	$\hat{V}(x_3) - [\hat{\alpha}_{32}\hat{C}(x_2x_3) + \hat{V}(\epsilon)]$

[a] The estimators are given in the appropriate recursive order.

RELIABILITY AND STABILITY

Since this model imposes no restrictions on the variance of the true scores, for three waves of observations there are three reliabilities to be estimated, not one. The expressions for the reliabilities below are derived directly from the definition of reliability given previously.

$$\rho_1^2 = V(\theta_1)/[V(\theta_1) + V(\epsilon)]$$

$$\rho_2^2 = [\alpha_{21}^2 V(\theta_1) + V(\theta_2)]/[\alpha_{21}^2 V(\theta_1) + V(\theta_2) + V(\epsilon)]$$ (7.7)

$$\rho_3^2 = \{\alpha_{32}^2[\alpha_{21}^2 V(\theta_1) + V(\theta_2)] + V(\theta_3)\}/\{\alpha_{32}^2[\alpha_{21}^2 V(\theta_1) + V(\theta_2)] + V(\theta_3) + V(\epsilon)\}$$

It may be demonstrated that Heise's formula for reliability

$$\frac{\rho(x_1x_2)\rho(x_2x_3)}{\rho(x_1x_3)}$$

is, given the assumptions of the present model, the reliability of the instrument at time 2.

We define the stability coefficient γ_{ij} as the correlation between the true scores at times i and j. For the three-wave model, the three stability coefficients are given as follows:

$$\gamma_{12} = \alpha_{21} \frac{\sqrt{V(\theta_1)}}{\sqrt{\alpha_{21}^2 V(\theta_1) + V(\theta_2)}}$$

$$\gamma_{23} = \alpha_{32} \frac{\sqrt{\alpha_{21}^2 V(\theta_1) + V(\theta_2)}}{\sqrt{\alpha_{32}^2 [\alpha_{21}^2 V(\theta_1) + V(\theta_2)] + V(\theta_3)}} \qquad (7.8)$$

$$\gamma_{13} = \alpha_{21}\alpha_{32} \frac{\sqrt{V(\theta_1)}}{\sqrt{\alpha_{32}^2 [\alpha_{21}^2 V(\theta_1) + V(\theta_2)] + V(\theta_3)}}$$

Note that $\gamma_{13} = \gamma_{12}\gamma_{23}$.

It can be shown that Heise's measures of stability, S_{ij}, have the structure:

$$S_{12} = \rho_{13}/\rho_{23} = \gamma_{12} \frac{\rho_1}{\rho_2}$$

$$S_{23} = \rho_{13}/\rho_{12} = \gamma_{23} \frac{\rho_3}{\rho_2} \qquad (7.9)$$

$$S_{13} = \rho_{13}^2/\rho_{12}\rho_{23} = \gamma_{13} \frac{\rho_1 \rho_3}{\rho_2^2}$$

where ρ_i is the square root of the reliability at time i.

It is clear from this result that $S_{ij} = \gamma_{ij}$ for all i, j, if, and only if, the reliabilities are homogeneous. Since this is an implausible assumption, we conclude that the S_{ij} are contaminated by heterogeneity in the reliabilities.

The γ_{ij} may be regarded as path coefficients relating the true scores across time. However, in this case, they cannot be derived directly from the correlations between the observed variables, since under the stable-error variance model the standardization of the observed variables results in a loss of relevant information.

AN APPLICATION OF THE MODEL

As an illustration we apply the lag-1 model, assuming homogeneous-error variance, to repeated observations on reported earnings. Covariances between reported earnings for 3 successive years are given in Cutright (1969). These covariances are based on reported earnings from a sample of 6,222 white males for the years 1962–1964. The sample covariance and

Table 7.3. Sample covariances and correlations for reported earnings in three successive years

	Covariance matrix with correlations in parenthesis[a]		
Earnings	X_1	X_2	X_3
X_1:1962	11.495	—	—
X_2:1963	10.106 (.827)	12.995	—
X_3:1964	10.455 (.778)	11.808 (.827)	15.708

[a] Multiply entries by 10^6 to obtain sample covariances.

correlation matrices are presented in Table 7.3. Estimates of the six parameters of the model are given below:

$$\hat{\alpha}_{32} = 1.035$$

$$\hat{\alpha}_{21} = 1.019$$

$$\hat{V}(\epsilon) = 1.581 \times 10^6$$

$$\hat{V}(\theta_1) = 9.914 \times 10^6$$

$$\hat{V}(\theta_2) = 1.116 \times 10^6$$

$$\hat{V}(\theta_3) = 1.906 \times 10^6$$

The estimated reliability and stability coefficients under Heise's model and the model formulated in this chapter are presented in Table 7.4.

Table 7.4. Estimated reliability and stability coefficients under assumptions of stable reliability versus stable-error variance

	Stable reliability	Stable-error variance
Reliability		
Time 1	.878	.862
Time 2	.878	.878
Time 3	.878	.899
Stability		
Times 1 and 2	.941	.950
Times 2 and 3	.941	.930
Times 1 and 3	.886	.884

Note that the reliabilities under the second model increase regularly with time; this is a necessary consequence of the increasing variability of true income. For these data, Heise's measures underestimate the stability of true income between 1962 and 1963 and overestimate the stability of true income between 1963 and 1964. The small differences between the two models are due to the relatively close spacing of the observations. An increase in the time interval between measurements should lead to more dramatic differences between the models.

THE EFFECTS OF STANDARDIZATION

An important implication of the previous discussion is that the choice between standardized and unstandardized forms of a model is not trivial. In fact, the difference between the two models considered herein is strongly related to the distinction between path coefficients and path regressions.

Each standardized parameter is a function of more than one unstandardized parameter. In general, *if two or more of the unstandardized parameters of a model are equal, the corresponding standardized parameters will be unequal because they are not related to the unstandardized parameters by an equivalent transformation.*

For example, while it is possible to impose the condition of equal reliability in a standardized model (as Heise does), this model cannot, in general, satisfy the constraint of equal-error variance in the corresponding unstandardized model. Similarly, stability in the path coefficients of a standardized model is not, in general, compatible with stability in the path-regression coefficients of an unstandardized model. This is the reason that quantitatively different results (see above) are obtained when the two models are applied to the same data.

The distinction between path analysis and path-regression analysis is crucial where one is attempting to compare the parameters of several populations. This case is fully discussed by Blalock (1967a). The distinction is equally important for models characterizing stable processes or where stability is assumed in order to achieve identifiability. In this case, it will generally be more appropriate to assume stability in the unstandardized parameters.

DISCUSSION

The preceding discussion has assumed that the system is lag-1. This assumption is not a trivial one. If, in fact, the degree of lag is higher than that, the parameters are not identifiable for only three time points. Under the assumption of stability of measurement-error variance, it is possible to fit a model with a lag degree 2 less than the number of time points. Since the degree of lag is unlikely to be too high for most systems, it seems possible to fit a reasonable model if enough time points are available. It is then possible to test empirically the assumption of homogeneous-error variance if the degree of lag in the model is small in comparison to the number of time points. We have argued that homogeneity of error variance is a more plausible assumption than homogeneous reliability.

Despite repeated warnings (Blalock, 1967a, 1967b; Tukey, 1954; Turner and Stevens, 1959) most sociological applications of linear models are confined to standardized systems (e.g., Blau and Duncan, 1967; Duncan, 1966; Duncan, Haller, and Portes, 1968; Sewell, Haller, and Portes, 1969). The convenience of path analysis algorithms and the apparent ease of translation from standardized to unstandardized systems (Wright, 1960) probably accounts for this tendency. We have demonstrated above that the structure of the model considered in this chapter is *not* invariant under standardization. In particular, homogeneity of error variance is not preserved under transformation to a standardized system. These considerations are also relevant for more complex longitudinal models, where it may be desirable to assume *a priori* that certain causal parameters are stable. The corresponding standardized parameters will generally be heterogeneous.

ACKNOWLEDGMENTS

The authors would like to acknowledge the helpful comments of the referee.

REFERENCES

Blalock, H. M., Jr. "Causal Inference, Closed Populations, and Measures of Association." *American Political Science Review* 61 (1967): 130–136.

Blalock, H. M., Jr. "Path Coefficients versus Regression Coefficients." *American Journal of Sociology* 72(1967): 675–676.

Blalock, H. M., Jr. "The Measurement Problem: A Gap between the Languages of Theory and Research." In *Methodology in Social Research*, edited by H. M. Blalock, Jr. and A. B. Blalock. New York: McGraw-Hill, 1968.

Blau, Peter M., and Duncan, Otis Dudley. *The American Occupational Structure.* New York: Wiley, 1967.

Coleman, J. S."The Mathematical Study of Change." In *Methodology in Social Research*, edited by H. M. Blalock, Jr., and A. B. Blalock. New York: McGraw-Hill, 1968.

Cutright, Phillips. *Achievement, Military Service, and Earnings*, 1969.

Duncan, Otis Dudley. "Path Analysis: Sociological Examples." *American Journal of Sociology* 72 (1966): 1–16.

Duncan, Otis Dudley, Haller, Archibald O., and Portes, Alejandro. "Peer Influences on Aspirations: A Reinterpretation." *American Journal of Sociology* 74 (1968): 119–137.

Heise, David R. "Separating Reliability and Stability in Test–Retest Correlation." *American Sociological Review* 34 (1969): 93–101.

Lord, Frederick M., and Novick, Melvin R. *Statistical Theories of Mental Test Scores.* Reading, Mass.: Addison-Wesley, 1968.

Sewell, William H., Haller, Archibald O., and Portes, Alejandro. "The Educational and Early Occupational Attainment Process." *American Sociological Review* 34 (1969): 82–91.

Tukey, John W. "Causation, Regression, and Path Analysis." In *Statistics and Mathematics in Biology*, edited by O. Kempthorne *et al.* Ames: Iowa State College Press, 1954.

Turner, M. E., and Stevens, C. D. "The Regression Analysis of Causal Paths." *Biometrics* 15 (1959): 236–258.

Wald, A. "Note on the Identification of Economic Relations." In *Cowles Commission Monograph No. 10*, edited by T. C. Koopmans. New York: Wiley, 1950.

Wright, Sewall, "Path Coefficients and Regression Coefficients: Alternative or Complementary Concepts?" *Biometrics* 16 (1960): 189–202.

8

Comment on "The Estimation of Measurement Error in Panel Data"*

Charles E. Werts

Karl G. Jöreskog

Robert L. Linn

Wiley and Wiley (1970) have made a contribution to the literature on dealing with errors of measurement by showing how to build a model employing the assumption of homogeneity of error variance in panel data. They argue that this assumption is more plausible than the assumption that the reliability remains constant over time (Heise, 1969). Since we have available data that allow a statistical test of which assumption is the most plausible, this note was written to give the results of this test and to demonstrate how such tests can be performed when at least four sequential measurements are available.

The model employed by Wiley and Wiley (1970) is shown in Fig. 8.1. In this model, the reliability of a measure (x_i) is the square of the correlation (ρ_i) between that measure and its underlying true score (ξ_i). Denoting a_{21}^* and a_{32}^* as the standardized path coefficients corresponding to a_{21} and a_{32}, respectively, path analysis indicates that the correlations generated by the model are:

* The research reported herein was performed pursuant to Grant No. OEG-2-700033(509) with the United States Department of Health, Education, and Welfare and the Office of Education. Reprinted by permission of the authors and publisher from the *American Sociological Review* 36:110–113. Copyright 1971, the American Sociological Association.

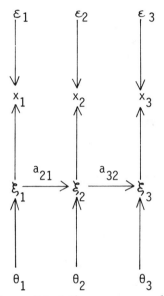

Figure 8.1. A three-wave model.

$$\rho(x_1 x_2) = \rho_1 a_{21}^* \rho_2$$

$$\rho(x_1 x_3) = \rho_1 a_{21}^* a_{32}^* \rho_3 \qquad (8.1)$$

$$\rho(x_2 x_3) = \rho_2 a_{32}^* \rho_3$$

It follows from Eq. (8.1) that

$$\rho_2^2 = \frac{\rho(x_1 x_2)\rho(x_2 x_3)}{\rho(x_1 x_3)} \qquad (8.2)$$

$$[\rho_1 a_{21}^*]^2 = \frac{\rho(x_1 x_2)\rho(x_1 x_3)}{\rho(x_2 x_3)} \qquad (8.3)$$

$$[\rho_3 a_{32}^*]^2 = \frac{\rho(x_1 x_3)\rho(x_2 x_3)}{\rho(x_1 x_2)} \qquad (8.4)$$

Thus, without making any assumptions about homogeneity of error variances or reliabilities, it has been demonstrated that the reliability of $x_2(\rho_2{}^2)$ is identifiable, and hence also that the corresponding error variance $V(\epsilon_2) = V(x_2)[1 - \rho_2^2]$ and true-score variance $V(\xi_2) = V(x_2) - V(\epsilon_2)$ is identifiable. For the two outer measures x_1 and x_3, only the products $[\rho_1 a_{21}^*]$ and $[\rho_3 a_{32}^*]$ are identifiable.

Now consider the case in which four sequential measurements are available. Making the same assumptions about the fourth measure that Wiley and Wiley (1970) made about the first three, the model in Fig. 8.2 is obtained. Generalizing the results of Eqs. (8.2), (8.3), and (8.4), we see that in Fig. 8.2:

1. ρ_2, $V(\epsilon_2)$, $V(\xi_2)$, and the product $[\rho_1 a_{21}^*]$ may be identified using either x_1, x_2, and x_3 or x_1, x_2, and x_4
2. ρ_3, $V(\epsilon_3)$, $V(\xi_3)$, and the product $[\rho_4 a_{43}^*]$ may be identified using either x_1, x_3, and x_4 or x_2, x_3, and x_4.

Path analysis of Figure 8.2 also indicates that $\rho(x_2 x_3) = \rho_2 a_{32}^* \rho_3$ and $\rho(x_1 x_4) = \rho_1 a_{21}^* a_{32}^* a_{43}^* \rho_4$, which means that a_{32}^* is overidentified. Therefore, $a_{32} = a_{32}^* \sqrt{V(\xi_3)} \div V(\xi_2)$ is identifiable. Generalizing to multiple-wave panel studies, we may state that, when the assumptions of the Wiley and Wiley structural model are given, error variances, true-score variances, and unstandardized regression weights between corresponding true scores are identified for all but the first and last measures. For this reason, it appears unnecessary to make either the equal reliability or the equal error variance assumption for inner measures. However, one might wish to know which is the better assumption to make about the first and last measures in order to identify the corresponding true and error variances and regression weights among true scores. Given at least four-wave data, suggestive, but not con-

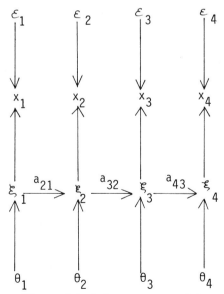

Figure 8.2. A four-wave model.

clusive, evidence about which (if either) assumption is better may be obtained by comparing the estimated error variances and reliabilities for the inner measures.

The four-wave data to be analyzed using the model in Figure 8.2 were collected in a longitudinal study (Anderson and Maier, 1963), which included a group of students tested in the fifth, seventh, ninth, and eleventh grades with the School and College Ability Tests (SCAT), which yields a Quantitative (Q) and a Verbal (V) score. Table 8.1 gives (previously unreported) correlations and standard deviations on these tests for a sample of 703 males with complete data.

As Goldberger (1970) notes, the path analysis literature offers no guidance in systematic estimation of overidentified models, such as that depicted in Fig. 8.2. To obtain estimates, we used Jöreskog's (1970b) general method for the analysis of covariance structures with its associated computer program (Jöreskog, Gruvaeus, and van Thillo, 1970). The four-wave model in Fig. 8.2 is of the *quasi Markov simplex* type, the analysis and programming of which is discussed in detail by Jöreskog (1970a). Under the assumption that the observed distributions are normal (reasonable for these data), Jöreskog's procedure yields maximum likelihood estimates of model parameters, and a large sample chi-squared test is computed for testing the fit of the model to the data. Furthermore, the program allows certain model parameters to be specified as equal to other parameters or to some constant. This is useful for the present problem because the chi-square fit before imposing a restriction (e.g., equal-error variances) can be compared to the chi-square fit for the more restricted model as a measure of the tenability of that restriction. The analysis proceeded in four steps:

1. The model in Fig. 8.2 was analyzed without assumptions about equal-error variances or reliabilities.
2. To test whether it is reasonable to believe that ξ_2 and ξ_3 are perfectly

Table 8.1. Correlations for quantitative (below unities) and verbal (above unities) test scores[a]

Grade	5	7	9	11
5	1.000	.849	.795	.779
7	.742	1.000	.868	.838
9	.718	.747	1.000	.860
11	.687	.686	.791	1.000

[a] Standard deviations for quantitative scores are 8.986, 13.771, 16.986, and 17.699, respectively; standard deviations for verbal scores are 11.748, 12.704, 13.756, and 14.379, respectively.

correlated, the *a priori* restriction that $a_{32}^* = 1.0$ was imposed. The chi square for this condition less the chi square for the first condition is the chi square with 1 degree of freedom for testing the restriction.

3. To test the equal-reliability assumption, the *a priori* specification was made that $\rho_2 = \rho_3$. The chi square in this condition less the chi square in the first condition yields a chi square with 1 degree of freedom for this hypothesis. This assumption is equivalent to the assertion that the error variances are a fixed proportion of the corresponding test variances.

4. To test the equal-error variance assumption, the specification was made that $V(\epsilon_2) = V(\epsilon_3)$. The chi-square test of this hypothesis is the difference between the chi square for this condition and the one for the first condition and also has 1 degree of freedom.

The results of the above analysis are shown in Table 8.2. In step one, for both SCAT-V and SCAT-Q, the χ^2 is small, indicating a good fit. The pattern of the estimates is reasonable in that $\hat{\rho}_2$ and $\hat{\rho}_3$ are approximately equal (published test reliabilities are equal and of the same order of magnitude as these estimates), whereas $[\hat{\rho}_1 \hat{a}_{21}^*]$ and $[\hat{\rho}_4 \hat{a}_{43}^*]$ are lower, as expected since they are the product of a reliability and a true-factor correlation. When the assumption that $a_{32}^* = 1$ is inserted, the χ^2 increased significantly (> 40) for both SCAT-V and SCAT-Q. The third step testing the equal-reliability assumption yielded a fairly good fit and the difference χ^2 does not suggest that this hypothesis should be rejected; however $[\hat{\rho}_4 \hat{a}_{43}^*]$ appears unreasonable since it is approximately equal to $\hat{\rho}_2$ and $\hat{\rho}_3$. For SCAT-V, $[\hat{\rho}_4 \hat{a}_{43}^*]$ is slightly larger than $\hat{\rho}_2$ and $\hat{\rho}_3$, which would require $\hat{a}_{43}^*$ to be greater than 1.0 for $\hat{\rho}_4$ to equal $\hat{\rho}_2$ and $\hat{\rho}_3$. In step 4, the difference χ^2 for SCAT-V is statistically

Table 8.2. Model parameter estimates and goodness of fit tests

| Model | Estimates[a] | | | | | Fit | | |
	$[\hat{\rho}_1 \hat{a}_{21}^*]$	$\hat{\rho}_2$	$\hat{\rho}_3$	$[\hat{\rho}_4 \hat{a}_{43}^*]$	$\hat{a}_{32}^*$	χ^2	d.f.	p
SCAT-V Data								
Fig. 8.2	.884	.960	.942	.912	.959	1.38	1	.240
$a_{32}^* = 1$	.877	.941	.927	.903	1.000	42.61	2	.000
$\rho_2 = \rho_3$	.816	.952	.952	.956	.959	2.17	2	.338
$V(\epsilon_2) = V(\epsilon_3)$	.887	.950	.952	.908	.960	12.18	2	.002
SCAT-Q Data								
Fig. 8.2	.851	.872	.919	.860	.925	2.78	1	.095
$a_{32}^* = 1$	.823	.840	.899	.852	1.000	42.77	2	.000
$\rho_2 = \rho_3$	.557	.899	.899	.894	.924	5.40	2	.067
$V(\epsilon_2) = V(\epsilon_3)$	.851	.873	.918	.861	.925	2.80	2	.247

[a] The symbol, "^", denotes an estimate of a population parameter based on sample data.

significant ($\chi_1^2 = 12.18 - 1.38 = 10.8$) although the absolute magnitude of the difference may not be too important. The step 4 results are more sensible than the step 3 results since $[\hat{\rho}_1 \hat{a}_{21}^*]$ and $[\hat{\rho}_4 \hat{a}_{43}^*]$ are both less than $\hat{\rho}_2$ and $\hat{\rho}_3$. The step 4 difference χ^2 for SCAT-Q (like step 3) is not statistically significant. Overall, these results suggest that the equal-reliability assumption gives a good statistical fit but yields theoretically unreasonable results; whereas the equal-error variance assumption may yield poorer fit but estimates that are like the original model of step 1.

REFERENCES

Anderson, S. B., and Maier, M. H. "34,000 Pupils and How They Grew." *Journal of Teacher Education* 14(1963):212–216.

Goldberger, A. S. "Econometrics and Psychometrics: A Survey of Communalities." *Social Systems Research Institute Workshop Series*, EME 7013, University of Wisconsin, 1970.

Heise, D. R. "Separating Reliability and Stability in Test–Retest Correlation." *American Sociological Review* 34(1969):93–101.

Jöreskog K. G. "Estimation and Testing of Simplex Models." *Research Bulletin* 70-42. Princeton, N. J. Educational Testing Service, 1970(a).

Jöreskog, K. G. "A General Method for Analysis of Covariance Structures." *Biometrika* 57(1970):239–251(b).

Jöreskog, K. G., Gruvaeus, G. T., and van Thillo, M. "ACOVS, A General Computer Program for Analysis of Covariance Structures. *Research Bulletin* 70-15. Princeton, N.J. Educational Testing Service, 1970.

Wiley, D.E., and Wiley, J. A. "The Estimation of Measurement Error in Panel Data." *American Sociological Review* 35(1970):112–117.

9

Problems in Estimating Measurement Error from Panel Data: An Example Involving the Measurement of Scientific Productivity*

Lowell L. Hargens
Barbara F. Reskin
Paul D. Allison

Several recent papers (Heise, 1969; Werts, Jöreskog, and Linn, 1971; Wiley and Wiley, 1970; 1974) have presented closely related models for the estimation of reliability coefficients and the measurement-error variances from univariate panel data collected at three or more time points. The principal innovation of these models is the introduction of a disturbance in the true scores at successive time points. They thus represent a considerable advance over the direct use of test–retest correlations as reliability estimators, since the latter method assumes that true scores are perfectly stable over time. Despite this wider applicability, the panel models still have some restrictive assumptions, notably that the errors of measurement and the disturbances in the true scores must be auto-uncorrelated over time (Heise, 1969: 98–101; Wiley and Wiley, 1974). Nevertheless, for the four-wave model, Heise (1969: 101) and Werts et al. (1971) have suggested that the violation of these assumptions may be detected by testing the single overidentifying restriction implied by the model.

Here we present an instance in which the four-wave model fits the data

* Reprinted by permission of the authors and publisher from *Sociological Methods and Research*, Vol 4, No. 4 (May 1976): 439–458. Copyright © 1976 by Sage Publications, Inc.

very well; yet, when it is elaborated with a tau-equivalent measure at one of the time points, the fit is very poor. We discuss possible violations of the assumptions of the model, propose an alternative model that resolves the apparent difficulty, and conclude that some types of correlated disturbances cannot be detected by the goodness-of-fit test for the basic four-wave model.

ESTIMATING THE RELIABILITY OF SCI ARTICLE COUNTS

In a study of the properties of several measures of scientific productivity, we sought to estimate the reliability and error variance of article counts taken from the *Science Citation Index* (SCI) as a measure of the true article production of individual scientists. Our study was based on a sample of 240 chemists who were members of the population of chemists who obtained their Ph.D. in chemistry during the period from 1955 to 1961.[1] We counted the number of articles attributed to each of the chemists in the Source Index of the SCI for each of the 4 years from 1965 through 1968. Since the collection of these data was part of a larger study of the career patterns of the cohort of chemists, we had a large amount of information concerning the areas of specialization, past publications, and institutional affiliations of the chemists. This information helped us obtain correct article counts in cases where SCI listings combined information for two or more scientists with the same surname and initials. In ambiguous cases, we consulted the

Table 9.1. Correlations, variances, and covariances among article counts in four one-year intervals, 240 chemists[a]

	Science citation index (SCI)				Chemical abstracts
	1965 (x_1)	1966 (x_2)	1967 (x_3)	1968 (x_4)	1967 (x_3')
1965	2.59	.515	.469	.436	.484
1966	1.21	2.15	.613	.520	.585
1967	1.26	1.49	2.73	.552	.937
1968	1.11	1.21	1.45	2.51	.586
1967	1.30	1.43	2.58	1.55	2.77

[a] Correlations above the diagonal, variances and covariances on and below the diagonal.

[1] The sampling frame was the population of all chemists reported in the 1957, 1959, and 1961 editions of the *Directory of Graduate Research* (American Chemical Society, 1957, 1959, 1961) as having completed the Ph.D. between 1955 and 1961. For a more detailed description of the sample, see Reskin (1973: 374–391).

publications listed by SCI in order to ensure that we were correctly attributing authorship. These steps were taken to minimize errors in our transcription of the data from the SCI, and we believe that remaining errors in the enumeration of articles for the members of our sample are largely the result of errors in the listing procedures of the SCI itself. Table 9.1 gives the correlations between the article counts for the members of our sample over the 4-year period above the diagonal, with the variances and covariances on and below the diagonal.

The basic four-wave model proposed by Heise (1969) and Werts et al. (1971) can be represented for a single individual by the following recursive system of equations in unstandardized form (Model Ia):

$$x_t = X_t + e_t \qquad t = 1, 2, 3, 4$$

$$X_1 = U_1$$

$$X_t = b_t X_{t-1} + U_t \qquad t = 2, 3, 4$$

In this application, t refers to a specific 1-year interval; X_t is the true number of articles published in t; x_t is the number of articles counted in SCI; e_t is random measurement error; U_t is a random disturbance; and b_t is a constant for each t. All variables are expressed as deviations about their respective means. The conditions on the disturbance terms are:

$$E(e_t U_s) = 0 \qquad t, s = 1, 2, 3, 4$$

$$E(e_t e_s) = E(U_t U_s) = 0 \qquad t, s = 1, 2, 3, 4 \qquad t \neq s$$

A path diagram of the model is shown in Fig. 9.1.

This model has 11 parameters—$b_t(t = 2, 3, 4)$, $V(e_t)$, and $V(U_t)$ ($t = 1, 2, 3, 4$)—but only 10 observed moments. Although it is therefore underidentified as a whole, 5 of the parameters are individually identified: b_3, b_4, $V(e_2)$, $V(e_4)$, and $V(U_3)$. For computational convenience, we reparameterized the model so that the remaining 6 underidentified parameters were combined into 4 parameters, all of which are identified. The structural equations for this reparameterized model (denoted Ia*) are:

$$x_1 = aX_2 + e_1^*$$

$$x_2 = X_2 + e_2$$

$$x_3 = X_3 + e_3$$

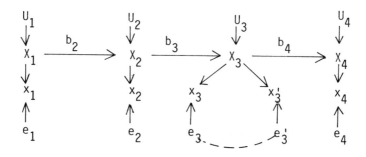

Model I

Model II
Figure 9.1. Path diagrams of Models I and II.

$$x_4 = b_4 X_3 + e_4^*$$

$$X_2 = U_2^*$$

$$X_3 = b_3 X_2 + U_3$$

where

$$a = \frac{b_2 V(U_1)}{b_2^2 V(U_1) + V(U_2)}$$

$$e_1^* = (1 - ab_2)U_1 - aU_2 + e_1$$

$$e_4^* = e_4 + U_4$$

$$U_2^* = b_2 U_1 + U_2$$

It can be shown that this set of equations implies that all the new disturbance and error terms are mutually uncorrelated. The four new parameters
are a, $V(e_1^*)$, $V(e_4^*)$, and $V(U_2^*)$.

It is then a straightforward procedure to derive expressions for observed
moments (see Wiley and Wiley, 1974: 179 for an example of how this is
done). The equations for the observed covariances are:

$$C_{12} = aV(U_2^*)$$

$$C_{13} = ab_3V(U_2^*)$$

$$C_{14} = ab_3b_4V(U_2^*)$$

$$C_{23} = b_3V(U_2^*)$$

$$C_{24} = b_3b_4V(U_2^*)$$

$$C_{34} = b_3^2b_4V(U_2^*) + b_4V(U_3)$$

where $C_{ij} = C(x_i, x_j)$. The equations for the observed variances are

$$V_1 = a^2V(U_2^*) + V(e_1^*)$$

$$V_2 = V(U_2^*) + V(e_2)$$

$$V_3 = b_3^2V(U_2^*) + V(U_3) + V(e_3)$$

$$V_4 = (b_4b_3)^2V(U_2^*) + b_4^2V(U_3) + V(e_4^*)$$

where $V_i = V(x_i)$. The above 10 equations contain 9 parameters. The 6
covariance equations yield the following parameter solutions:

$$a = C_{13}/C_{23} = C_{14}/C_{24}$$

$$b_3 = C_{13}/C_{12}$$

$$b_4 = C_{14}/C_{13}$$

$$V(U_2^*) = C_{23}C_{12}/C_{13}$$

$$V(U_3) = C_{34}C_{13}/C_{14} - C_{13}C_{23}/C_{12}$$

These expressions may be substituted into the four variance equations to solve for the four error variances. Notice the one overidentifying restriction that $C_{13}/C_{23} = C_{14}/C_{24}$.

To get efficient estimates of these parameters and to test the overidentifying restriction, we used the LISREL program (Jöreskog and Van Thillo, 1973) which provides maximum-likelihood estimators and a large-sample chi-square test under the assumption that the observation vector is multinormally distributed. In the first column of Table 9.2, we give estimates of the parameters of interest, b_3, b_4, $V(e_2)$ and $V(e_3)$. We also give derived estimates of ρ^2 (x_2, X_2) and ρ^2 (x_3, X_3), the reliability coefficients for the 2 middle years, and ρ (X_2, X_3), the stability coefficient (Heise, 1969) for the 1-year interval.[2] With a chi-square of .47, the model cannot be rejected at the .05 level.

Despite the excellent fit of the model, it seems implausible for two reasons. First, the stability coefficient of .947 seems too high. Given the many contingencies of scientific publication, it is difficult to believe that our sample members' relative article productivity would be almost perfectly stable in 2 consecutive years. Second, the reliability coefficients of .648 and .635 seem much too low. It is improbable that errors of enumeration and transcription within SCI's collection and publication of these data can amount to over one-third of the observed variance. (See Garfield, 1974, for a discussion of possible errors in SCI.)

To further test the model, we used *Chemical Abstracts* (CA) to get a separate count of articles published in 1967 by the members of the sample. CA abstracts articles from both foreign and United States journals and is

---

[2] For the population, the correlational measures may be derived from the basic parameters as follows:

$$\rho^2(x_2, X_2) = \frac{V(U_2^*)}{V(U_2^*) + V(e_2)}$$

$$\rho^2(x_3, X_3) = \frac{b_3^2 V(U_2^*) + V(U_3)}{b_3^2 V(U_2^*) + V(U_3) + V(e_3)}$$

$$\rho(X_2, X_3) = \left(\frac{b_3^2 V(U_2^*)}{b_3^2 V(U_2^*) + V(U_3)} \right)^{1/2}$$

These formulas also hold for models Ib*, IIa*, and IIb*, with $V(e_3')$ substituted for $V(e_3)$ in calculating $\rho^2(x_3', X_3)$. Since we have maximum-likelihood estimates of the basic parameters contained in these formulas, the formulas can be used to obtain maximum-likelihood estimates of the correlational measures.

Table 9.2. Parameter estimates and goodness-of-fit statistics for models Ia*, Ib*, IIa*, and IIb*

Parameter	Model			
	Ia*	Ib*	IIa*	IIb*
b_3	1.06	1.07	1.06	1.06
b_4	.833	.850	.588	.842
$V(e_2)$	.757	.821	.769	.789
$V(e_3)$	.996	—	.180	.949
$V(e_3')$	—	.951	.171	.951
$\rho^2(x_2, X_2)$	.648	.619	.643	.634
$\rho^2(x_3, X_3)$	.635	—	.935	.646
$\rho^2(x_3', X_3)$	—	.656	.938	.646
$\rho(X_2, X_3)$	.947	.917	.777	.932
$\rho(e_3, e_3')$	—	—	—	.822
Statistical fit				
χ^2	.475	.014	27.6	8.58
d.f.	1	1	5	4
p	.491	.907	.0000	.0725

similar to SCI in its coverage of chemistry publications.[3] We examined the 1967, 1968, and 1969 volumes of CA in order to include all the articles published in 1967.[4] Once again, we attempted to eliminate ambiguities in the entries so that the primary source of error would be the enumeration and transcription process of CA itself. The correlations and covariances of the 1967 CA counts with all the SCI counts are shown in Table 9.1.

Our first test was to substitute the 1967 CA counts for the 1967 SCI counts, or, formally, to substitute the equation

[3] There are some differences in coverage between CA and SCI. SCI covers a wide variety of disciplines in addition to chemistry, but CA covers articles in a greater number of chemistry journals than SCI. Thus, we sometimes found that our chemists published work in journals not classified as chemistry journals and that the work was therefore listed in SCI but not CA. Similarly, we sometimes found that the chemists published work in obscure chemistry journals that were not surveyed by SCI. Our experience suggests, however, that the major portion of the published work of chemists is included in both sources. Of the papers authored by members of our sample, 84% were included in both sources, 90% were in SCI, and 94% in CA.

[4] CA abstracts the articles that appear in a given year over a period that extends beyond the year itself. Thus, we examined the 1967 through 1969 volumes of CA to obtain article counts for the 1967 calendar year. We found no 1967 articles in the issues of CA for the last half of 1969 (Vol. 71 of CA). We chose 1967 as the year for which both SCI and CA article counts would be collected because the 1967–1969 volumes of CA are indexed in a single cumulative index.

$$x_3' = X_3 + e_3'$$

for

$$x_3 = X_3 + e_3$$

to produce Model Ib*. Estimates based on this model are shown in Table 9.2. Since the parameter estimates are quite similar for Ia* and Ib*, our reservations about the plausibility of the estimates for Model Ia* also apply to those for Model IB*. On the other hand, Model Ib* has a chi-square of only .014, which is a better fit than that shown by Ia*.

Our next step was to combine the two models into one by incorporating both the equations for x_3 and x_3', given above, into Model I with the same conditions on e_3' as on e_3. We also assume $E(e_3'e_3) = 0$. This is Model IIa, displayed as a path diagram in Fig. 9.1. The specification of an identical slope (unity) for both x_3 and x_3' on X_3 is an assumption of tau-equivalence (Lord and Novick, 1968). Given that CA and SCI attempt to enumerate the same items, there seems to be sufficient prior justification for imposing this constraint.

The reparameterization of Model I may also be employed for this model, giving IIa*. Adding x_3' to Model Ia* adds five observed moments but only one new parameter, $V(e_3')$, yielding a total of 5 degrees of freedom. These degrees of freedom correspond to five constraints on the observed covariances. Models Ia and Ib each contribute one degree of freedom by constraining $C_{14}/C_{24} = C_{13}/C_{23}$ and $C_{14}/C_{24} = C_{13'}/C_{23'}$, respectively. Combining the two models and assuming that x_3 and x_3' are congeneric tests (Jöreskog, 1971) imply that $C_{34}/C_{3'4} = C_{13}/C_{13'}$. A fourth constraint follows from the tau-equivalence assumption which implies that $C_{13} = C_{13'}$. The fifth comes from $C_{3'3}$ which is the only observed moment not included in either Ia or Ib. Specifically, the combined model requires that $C_{3'3} = C_{34}C_{13}/C_{14}$.

Estimates for Model IIa* are shown in Table 9.2. Some of the estimates are markedly different from those in the four-variable models and somewhat nearer our expectations. The reliability coefficients of approximately .94 for both x_3 and x_3' are substantially higher, while the stability coefficient of .78 is correspondingly lower. However, the reliability coefficient of x_2 is still only .643, whereas one would expect it to be in the same neighborhood as those for x_3 and x_3'. More important, however, is the chi-square of 27.6 (5 d.f., $p < .0001$), which surely calls for rejection of the model.

This poses a dilemma. The four-variable models, Ia and Ib, fit the data very well indeed but yield what we judge to be unreasonable estimates. Their natural extension into a five-variable model yields more reasonable estimates for some parameters but a very poor fit to the data. Is there any way to alter the five-variable model in order to resolve this inconsistency? We considered several possibilities. We first relaxed the tau-equivalence assumption to see if it were the source of the difficulty. Although the resulting estimates are not shown in Table 9.2, they are quite similar to those for Model IIa*, and the chi-square is still 27.3 (4 d.f.), indicating that this model is also unacceptable. Next, we reasoned that since $C_{3'3}$ is the only observed moment not included in Models Ia and Ib, it might be the source of the poor fit. One way to improve the fit is to allow a correlation between e_3 and e'_3. This model (IIb*) is identified, and estimates are given in Table 9.2. Allowing for the correlation results in a substantial improvement in fit. The chi-square drops to 8.58 (4 d.f.), and the model cannot be rejected at the .05 level. Unfortunately, the parameter estimates are still unreasonable, with a stability coefficient of .932 and reliability estimates of around .64 for x_2, x_3, and x'_3. Moreover, the estimated correlation of .822 between e_3 and e'_3 seems much too high. CA and SCI are completely distinct organizations, and we cannot imagine any mechanism that would produce so strong a relationship between their errors of enumeration and transcription.[5]

It is curious that the treatment of the 1967 CA and SCI article counts as measures of the true but unmeasured 1967 article counts leads to results for Models IIa* and IIb* which seem untenable on either statistical or theoretical grounds. Since it seemed unreasonable to abandon the assumption that the CA and SCI counts are in fact congeneric measures of the true counts, we decided to explore other possible models for representing the determinants of the true and observed article counts. One possible misspecification of these causal relations is the assumption, contained in all of the above models, that the disturbance terms, U_1 through U_4, are independent of each other. In the case of scientific productivity, there are strong reasons for expecting correlations among these disturbances. Specifically, we can expect the published output of the individual during each time interval to be determined by relatively stable personality or role traits such as ability, motivation, or professional socialization, as well as stable contexts and facilities (Allison and Stewart, 1974). A first approximation to this idea would be to relax the assumption that $E(U_t U_s) = 0$, $t \neq s$, and specify a first-order autoregressive process for the disturbances:

[5] We believe that the only possible source of a correlation between the errors of CA and SCI is the misspelling of authors' names on the original articles examined by the two organizations. If this occurred, both CA and SCI counts would be underestimates of the true article counts of affected authors and overestimates of the true article counts of any authors whose names matched the misspelled names. Since authors are especially sensitive to such misprints and usually review galley proofs before actual publication of their articles, the probability of this type of error should be negligible, and any resulting correlation between CA and SCI errors should be small.

$$U_1 = v_1$$

$$U_t = c_t U_{t-1} + v_t \qquad t = 2, 3, 4$$

$$E(v_t) = E(v_t e_s) = 0 \qquad t,s = 1, 2, 3, 4$$

$$E(v_t v_s) = 0 \qquad t,s = 1, 2, 3, 4 \qquad t \neq s$$

Added to Model IIa, these equations produce Model III which is shown diagrammatically in Fig. 9.2. A very similar model was considered by Heise (1969: Fig. 7).

There are two difficulties with the model. First, as Heise observes, none

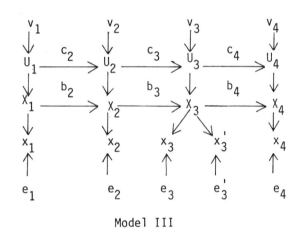

Model III

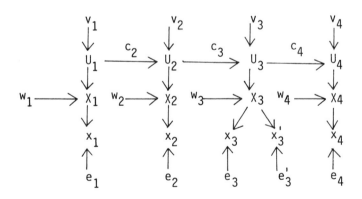

Model IV

Figure 9.2. Path diagrams of Models III and IV.

of the parameters is identified — which brings the analysis to a halt. Second, it is a straightforward but tedious exercise to show that, in general, this model does not imply the overidentifying restriction implied by Model I (and also by Model II). If III is the correct model, we should have expected large chi-square values in our estimation of Ia* and Ib*. That they were small suggests that we ought to look further.

Our solution to these difficulties is to choose a variant of Model III that does not violate the overidentifying restriction. Specifically, we set $b_t = 0$, $t = 2, 3, 4$, and incorporate an additional disturbance term into the determination of X_t, $t = 1, 2, 3, 4$. The complete structural equations for Model IV are:

$$U_1 = v_1$$

$$U_t = c_t U_{t-1} + v_t \qquad t = 2, 3, 4$$

$$X_t = U_t + w_t \qquad t = 1, 2, 3, 4$$

$$x_t = X_t + e_t \qquad t = 1, 2, 3, 4$$

$$x'_3 = X_3 + e'_3$$

The disturbance conditions are:

$$E(e_t w_s) = E(e_t v_s) = E(w_t v_s) = 0 \qquad t,s = 1, 2, 3, 4$$

$$E(e_t e_s) = E(v_t v_s) = E(w_t w_s) = 0 \qquad t,s = 1, 2, 3, 4 \qquad t \neq s$$

A path diagram of the model is shown in Fig. 9.2. Our rationale for setting the $b_t = 0$ is that, like many other variables, publications must be created anew in each time interval. Whatever correlation exists between X_t and X_{t+1} must, therefore, be due to a correlation among their determinants rather than to any direct effect. We have represented what are undoubtedly multiple determinants by a unitary trait, U_t, which might be interpreted as the propensity to publish. This may be doing some violence to our understanding of the determinants of scientific productivity over the long run, but, as we shall see, it does seem to be the most parsimonious model consistent with the data for the 4-year period of observation.

With 16 parameters and 15 observed moments, Model IV is underidentified. But again, several of the parameters are individually identified. To eliminate any unidentified parameters, we reparameterized the model as follows (Model IV*):

$$x_1 = dU_2 + e_1^*$$

$$x_2 = U_2 + e_2^*$$

$$x_3 = X_3 + e_3$$

$$x_3' = X_3 + e_3'$$

$$x_4 = c_4 U_3 + e_4^*$$

$$X_3 = U_3 + w_3$$

$$U_2 = v_2^*$$

$$U_3 = c_3 U_2 + v_3$$

Here,

$$d = \frac{c_2 V(v_1)}{c_2^2 V(v_1) + V(v_2)}$$

Table 9.3. Parameter estimates and goodness-of-fit statistics for model IV

Parameter	Value
c_3	1.06
c_4	.841
$V(e_2^*)$	.788
$V(e_3)$	.173
$V(e_3')$	.174
$V(w_3)$	.801
$\rho^2(x_2, U_2)$	.634
$\rho^2(x_3, X_3)$	.937
$\rho^2(x_3', X_3)$	.937
$\rho^2(X_3, U_3)$	.689
$\rho(U_2, U_3)$	.932
Statistical fit	
χ^2	8.5783
d.f.	4
p	.0725

| | Additional constraints | | |
	χ^2	d.f.	p
$c_3 = c_4$	1.81	1	.10
$V(e_3) = V(e_3')$	.0002	1	.99

$$e_1^* = (1 - dc_2)v_1 - dv_2 + e_1 + w_1$$

$$e_2^* = e_2 + w_2$$

$$e_4^* = e_4 + w_4 + v_4$$

$$v_2^* = c_2v_1 + v_2$$

Once again, the disturbances, v_i and w_i, and errors of the reparameterized model are all uncorrelated. This specification reduces the number of parameters to 11, leaving 4 degrees of freedom. The constraints corresponding to these 4 degrees of freedom are the same as those of Model IIb*.

Estimates of the parameters of interest, as well as several derived correlational statistics, are given in Table 9.3.[6] While not so good a fit as Models Ia and Ib, the chi-square of 8.58 (4 d.f.) for Model IV* is a substantial improvement over Model IIa*, and the model cannot be rejected at the .05 level. Moreover, all the parameter estimates are consistent with our expectations. The high reliability of .937 for counts from both CA and SCI in 1967 seems about right, and it is also plausible that the latent trait, U_t, has a stability coefficient as high as .932. If we assume that $\rho(X_3, U_3) = \rho(X_2, U_2)$, we get an estimate for $\rho(X_2, X_3)$ of .642, which seems more reasonable than the substantially larger values for the year-to-year correlation between the true numbers of articles given by models Ia*, Ib*, and IIb*. We also find that the correlation between x_2 and U_2 (.796) is about the same as $\hat{\rho}(x_3, U_3) = .803$. Thus, unlike Model IIa*, Model IV* yields estimates that are fairly stable for $t = 2, 3$.

[6] The correlational statistics derived from:

$$\rho^2(x_2, U_2) = \frac{V(v_2^*)}{V(v_2^*) + V(w_2) + V(e_2)}$$

$$\rho^2(x_3, X_3) = \frac{c_3^2 V(v_2^*) + V(v_3) + V(w_3)}{c_3^2 V(v_2^*) + V(v_3) + V(w_3) + V(e_3)}$$

$$\rho^2(X_3, U_3) = \frac{c_3^2 V(v_2^*) + V(v_3)}{c_3^2 V(v_2^*) + V(v_3) + V(w_3)}$$

$$\rho(U_2, U_3) = \left(\frac{c_3^2 V(v_2^*)}{c_3^2 V(v_2^*) + V(v_3)} \right)^{1/2}$$

The formula for $\rho^2(x_3, X_3)$ is the same as that for $\rho^2(x_3' X_3)$ except that $V(e_3')$ is substituted for $V(e_3)$.

It is important to note that in this model, the meanings of reliability and error variance depend on what one is trying to measure. If the object of measurement is X_t, the true number of articles, SCI counts have a reliability of about .94 and a measurement-error variance of about .17. On the other hand, if one wants to measure the latent trait U_t, which in this instance is interpreted as the propensity to publish, the reliability goes down to approximately .64 while the error variance increases to around .97. If Model IV is correct, then Models I and II yield incorrect interpretations of the nature of the derived reliability coefficients because they mistakenly hypothesize that the unmeasured variables, which meet the assumptions of a lag-1 autoregressive process, are the true scores of the yearly article counts when in fact they are, according to our interpretation, the yearly propensities of scholars to publish. As a result, Models I and II suggest that the squared correlation between true and observed article counts tends to be in the neighborhood of .64, while according to Model IV this figure should be interpreted as the squared correlation between observed scores and the propensity to publish.

There is an even more intimate relation between Models IV and IIb. As noted above, both imply the same four constraints on the observed variance – covariance matrix, which means that one model can be viewed as a reparameterization of the other. For this reason, our preference for Model IV can only be justified by our *a priori* beliefs about the causal process determining productivity and our expectations as to the magnitudes of the coefficients.

We also tested some additional restrictions on Model IV. Since the estimated error variances of e_3 and e_3' were almost identical, we constrained them equal and reestimated the model. Together with the restriction of tau-equivalence, this constraint is equivalent to assuming that 1967 SCI and CA counts are parallel measures (Lord and Novick, 1968). Since this additional constraint only increased the chi-square in the fourth decimal place, we conclude that counts from SCI and CA are functionally interchangeable — at least for 1967.

We also tested the hypothesis of constant autoregression for the latent trait in successive years, specifically that $c_3 = c_4$. Even though the estimates appear to be different (1.06 and .842), the test showed no significant difference ($\chi^2 = 1.81$, 1 d.f.). The constrained estimate was $c_3 = c_4 = .937$. In both the tests, estimates of other parameters hardly varied and so have not been reported.

CONCLUSION

Recent models for the estimation of measurement error from panel data assume a lag-1 autoregressive process in the true-score variable with uncorrelated disturbances. We believe that this assumption will usually be problematic for sociological variables that typically are determined by other variables having some stability over time. Although it has been suggested that such a violation of the assumptions can be tested when four or more waves of data are present, we have presented a model for which that is not the case. The model assumes a first-order autoregressive process among the *disturbances* and an absence of any lagged effects of the true-score variable. This model seems particularly appropriate for variables like scientific productivity, which must be created or produced anew for each time interval, in contrast to variables that have an internal principle of stability (i.e., which tend to remain the same unless acted upon from without).

For the case of scientific productivity, we showed how the two models could be distinguished by augmenting the data with another measure for one of the time points. While the four-variable model produced an excellent fit to the data, its natural extension to the five-variable model resulted in a very poor fit. On the other hand, our five-variable model incorporating correlated disturbances produced an acceptable fit. Estimates of reliability, stability, and measurement-error variance differed markedly for the two models, with the correlated-disturbance model giving much more plausible results. Unfortunately, the correlated-disturbance model cannot be distinguished statistically from a model that allows for correlated measurement errors for the equivalent measures at the same time point. However, the latter model gave parameter estimates that seemed quite unreasonable.

In general, we believe that the application of panel models that assume a first-order autoregressive process among true-score variables can often yield misleading results, even when such models show good statistical fits to the data. It therefore seems prudent to incorporate additional variables into such models so that a more effective test of this assumption can be carried out. This may be accomplished either with multiple indicators, as in the study reported here, or with measures of variables that are exogenous to the true-score variables of interest (Wheaton, Muthen, Alwin, and Summers (1977).

ACKNOWLEDGMENTS

We gratefully acknowledge the helpful suggestions of Hubert M. Blalock, George W. Bohrnstedt, Herbert L. Costner, Arthur S. Goldberger, Thomas A. Heberlein, Ronald Schoenberg, and H. H. Winsborough.

REFERENCES

Allison, P. D., and Stewart, J. A. "Productivity Differences among Scientists: Evidence for Accumulative Advantage." *American Sociological Review* 39 (1974): 596–606.

American Chemical Society. *Directory of Graduate Research.* Washington, D.C.: American Chemical Society, 1957, 1959, 1961.

Garfield, E. "Errors — Theirs, Ours and Yours." *Current Contents* 6 (1974): 5–6.

Heise, D. R. "Separating Reliability and Stability in Test–Retest Correlation." *American Sociological Review* 34 (1969): 93–101, and this volume.

Jöreskog, K. G. "Statistical Analysis of Sets of Congeneric Tests." *Psychometrika* 36 (1971): 109–133.

Jöreskog, K. G. and Van Thillo, M. "LISREL: A General Computer Program for Estimating a Linear Structural Equation System Involving Multiple Indicators of Unmeasured Variables." *Research Bulletin* 72–56. Princeton, N.J.: Educational Testing Service, 1973.

Lord, F. M. and Novick, M. R. *Statistical Theories of Mental Test Scores.* Reading, Mass.: Addison-Wesley, 1968.

Reskin, B. F. "Sex Differences in the Professional Life Chances of Chemists." Ph.D. dissertation, University of Washington, 1973.

Werts, C. E., Jöreskog, K. G. and Linn, R. L. "Comment on 'the Estimation of Measurement Error in Panel Data.'" *American Sociological Review* 36 (1971): 110–113.

Wheaton, B., Muthén, B., Alwin, D. F., and Summers, G. F. "Assessing Reliability and Stability in Panel Models." In *Sociological Methodology 1977,* edited by D. R. Heise. San Francisco: Jossey-Bass, 1977.

Wiley, D. E., and Wiley, J. A. "The Estimation of Measurement Error in Panel Data." *American Sociological Review* 35 (1970): 112–117, and this volume.

Wiley, J. A., and Wiley, M. G. "A Note on Correlated Errors in Repeated Measurements." *Sociological Methods and Research* 3 (1974): 172–188.

10

Estimating Measurement Error Using Multiple Indicators and Several Points in Time*

H. M. Blalock, Jr.

The successful application of reasonably sophisticated multivariate techniques, such as those involving the use of simultaneous equation systems, obviously depends on our ability either to reduce measurement errors to negligible proportions or to estimate and correct for their effects by statistical means. This is particularly the case whenever we wish to sort out the effects of a number of independent variables that are highly intercorrelated. (Gordon, 1968). Given the indirectness of measurement procedures in general, and the fact that in most sociological research the operational indicators are linked with the theoretical variables by rather poorly understood processes, it is clear that our analytic techniques must allow for substantial measurement errors. Therefore, it is very important to study the methodological implications of alternative ways of handling random and nonrandom measurement errors.

A number of recent papers have considered various approaches to measurement error by utilizing explicit causal models linking unmeasured variables to their measured indicators.[1] In general, we know that unless there

* Reprinted by permission of the publisher from the *American Sociological Review* 35:101–111. Copyright 1970, *The American Sociological Association.*
[1] See especially Blalock (1969); Blalock, Wells, and Carter (1970); Bohrnstedt (1969); Costner (1969); and Siegel and Hodge (1968).

are a large number of measured variables relative to unmeasured variables it will be difficult, if not impossible, to reach definite conclusions, since the existence of unmeasured variables in a causal system introduces a relatively large number of unknowns, thereby necessitating additional assumptions that are often rather implausible. This suggests that it is often desirable to utilize a combination of repeated measurements and multiple indicators so that indirect tests of the assumptions can be made.

In this chapter, I combine selected features of the arguments developed by Costner (1969) and Heise (1969) while emphasizing the flexibility of the general approach that is common to both papers. Costner is concerned with multiple indicators at a single point in time, whereas Heise deals with single indicators for panel data at three or more points in time. Both Costner and Heise discuss situations involving distortions producing nonrandom measurement error. Costner shows that the use of multiple indicators can help one infer the existence of relatively simple kinds of nonrandom errors, whereas Heise notes that it is difficult to handle such errors in the case of single indicators. We shall see that by combining features of both approaches, one can sometimes deal more effectively with such systematic disturbances.

In many situations, an investigator will find it necessary to improvise on these procedures according to the availability of his data. For example, in the case of Costner's procedure, it is advisable to have at least three indicators of each variable in order to analyze nonrandom errors. Where only a single indicator of each variable is available, Heise notes that it will be necessary to have data at three or more points in time. But perhaps the investigator will have data for only two points in time, though he may have two (or more) indicators of each variable. Of course, if studies have been planned with such analysis procedures in mind, problems of correcting for unreliability can be anticipated in advance. But with secondary analyses this is seldom possible; therefore, a flexible approach will be necessary.

THE COSTNER AND HEISE APPROACHES

Costner's basic approach can be illustrated in terms of the simple model of Fig. 10.1, in which X_1 and X_2 are two measures of the underlying variable X; Y_1 and Y_2 are measures of Y; and where a, b, c, d, and e are path coefficients. In this very simple model, all of the path coefficients happen to be total correlations, though of course none can be directly obtained since neither X nor Y are measured. If we make the assumption that all of the measurement errors are completely random, we may represent the sources of measurement error by u_i that are uncorrelated with X and Y and with each other. For the sake of completeness, I have represented the path coefficients connecting the u_i with the several indicators as a', b', d', and e'. As noted by

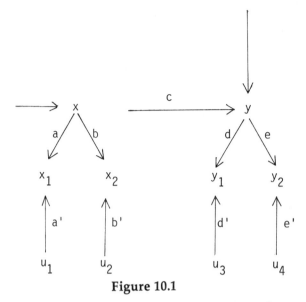

Figure 10.1

Heise (1969:94), these latter coefficients are not independent unknowns since they may be determined from the unexplained variances once a, b, d, and e are known.

Except for sampling error, the following should hold:

$$r_{X_1 X_2} = ab$$

$$r_{Y_1 Y_2} = de$$

$$r_{X_1 Y_1} = acd$$

$$r_{X_1 Y_2} = ace$$

$$r_{X_2 Y_1} = bcd$$

$$r_{X_2 Y_2} = bce$$

Since there are only five unknowns and six independent equations, one for each of the empirically obtained correlations among indicators, we will be able to solve for the path coefficients. For example:

$$c^2 = \frac{r_{X_1 Y_1} r_{X_2 Y_2}}{r_{X_1 X_2} r_{Y_1 Y_2}} = \frac{a b c^2 d e}{a b d e}$$

and

$$a^2 = r_{X_1X_2}(r_{X_1Y_2}/r_{X_2Y_2}) = ab(ace/bce)$$

Notice that, since there are six equations and five unknowns, there is one redundant equation that may be used as a test criterion. In other words, if the data satisfy the model, they should also (approximately) satisfy this sixth equation. Costner selects as this test condition the relationship:

$$r_{X_1Y_1}r_{X_2Y_2} = r_{X_1Y_2}r_{X_2Y_1} = abc^2de$$

This condition will generally not be satisfied unless the required assumptions about measurement error are met. However, there will always be a certain number of alternative models that also satisfy the condition. In particular, if there is a common source of measurement error linking X_1 and X_2 (or Y_1 and Y_2), but not linking any of the X_i with the Y_j, then this test criterion will also be satisfied.

If there were absolutely no specification or sampling errors, the data would fit the model exactly, and it would make no difference which equations were treated as redundant. However, in practice, no data will fit the model exactly; therefore, there is a certain arbitrariness in one's selection of the particular equations that will be used for estimation purposes and those that will be treated as excess equations used to test the model. This difficulty

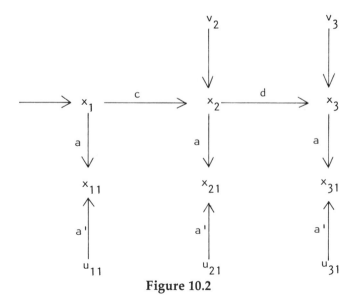

Figure 10.2

will be seen in all of the models I shall discuss and would seem to admit of no completely satisfactory solution. Boudon (1968) has suggested a least-squares procedure that, in effect, uses all of the equations in the estimation process, but Goldberger (1970) has shown that, if there is in fact no specification error, Boudon's procedure is actually less efficient than the simpler procedure of treating some of the equations as redundant. Perhaps the issue will reduce to the question of whether one assumes specification errors to be more serious than sampling errors, but in any event this topic is too complex to be dealt with in the present context.

Costner's approach can be extended in several ways. If we add more indicators of each variable, still assuming that all measurement error is random, then there will be additional test criteria that must be satisfied, since the number of equations (knowns) will exceed the number of unknowns by more than one. Therefore, if the data satisfy all such criteria simultaneously, we will have additional confidence in our model.[2] Also, if there are three or more indicators of each variable, it becomes possible to handle certain relatively simple kinds of nonrandom measurement error. This technique can be extended to any number of variables, provided the model is recursive (Blalock, 1969).

Heise's approach is basically similar except for notation and a focus on corrections for attenuation. He confines his attention, however, to single indicators of a variable measured at two or more points in time. His simplest model involving three points in time is given in Fig. 10.2, where I have modified his notation so as to emphasize the parallels with Costner's models. In Fig. 10.2, I have represented the unmeasured variable X at three time periods by X_1, X_2, and X_3, while using double subscripts for the indicators. Since there is only a single indicator at each point in time in this model, the indicators have been labeled X_{11}, X_{21}, and X_{31}, respectively.[3] Heise retains explicit labels for the sources of measurement error (here designated as the u_{ij}) and for the aggregate effect of variables that produce changes in X (here the v_i). Sources of stability in X are designated as c and d, thus allowing for possible differences in stability over time.

Notice that we are explicitly assuming that the path coefficient a linking X

---

[2] It is, of course, almost impossible to be very precise about how much additional confidence one has as he increases the degree to which a system is "overidentified" (i.e., the degree to which the numer of independent equations exceeds the number of unknowns). The essential reason for this difficulty is that one must evaluate a given model against competing alternatives that are reasonably plausible. In general, we know that the more predictions a theory makes that are rejectable, the smaller the number of alternative models that will also make these same predictions, but it is almost impossible to construct a list of all "plausible" alternatives in any given case.

[3] When we later introduce models with two or three indicators at each time period, the first subscript will refer to the time and the second to the indicator number.

to its indicator remains constant over time. This basic assumption permits important simplifications as compared with models in which the unmeasured variables are distinct, thereby reducing the number of unknowns and permitting the introduction of more complex assumptions regarding measurement errors. However, this kind of assumption can be disarmingly simple, as has been noted by Wiley and Wiley (1970). A path coefficient (or correlation) is a standardized measure that will not be invariant if there are changes in the variances of either variable. In this instance, the path coefficient a would not be expected to remain unchanged if there were changes in the measurement-error variances produced by the u_{ij} or in the variances of the true X_i over time. Wiley and Wiley note that although it may be reasonable to assume that measurement-error variances remain constant over time, we cannot so easily assume that the variances of the true (but unmeasured) X_i will remain constant. Therefore, one should attempt to assess the plausibility of this particular simplifying assumption as compared with others that might be made.[4] Unfortunately, it will always be necessary to make a certain number of not-too-realistic assumptions in order to obtain definite solutions. The important feature of causal models is that such assumptions are made explicit, so that they are open to challenge.

Heise calls our attention to the fact that if we have data for only two time periods, we will only be able to compute a single correlation, and it will be impossible to solve for the two unknowns: a and c. For example, if we lacked data at time 3, we would only have the equation

$$r_{X_{11}X_{21}} = a^2c$$

If it were reasonable to assume *no* change in the true value of X, so that $c = 1$, we could then obtain a^2, which is the square of the ordinary "correction for attenuation" discussed in connection with split-half reliability. Thus, if this single correction were used in test–retest situations, it would require the assumption that X had remained stable over time. But we encounter difficulties as soon as we allow for *both* real change and measurement error. However, if we also had data at time 3, we would be able to solve for the three unknowns: a, c, and d, using the three empirical correlations as follows:

[4] This will not be easy, though some sort of rough guess will always be necessary. In particular, if the variance of the *measured* value of X remains roughly constant over time, it may seem reasonable to assume that its components (the variance of the true value and the variance of the measurement-error term) are also both constant. Of course, one might be increasing and the other decreasing by exactly the same amount, but in the absence of a prediction to this effect, we might rule out this particular alternative possibility as being rather implausible.

$$r_{X_{11}X_{21}} = a^2c$$

$$r_{X_{11}X_{31}} = a^2cd$$

$$r_{X_{21}X_{31}} = a^2d$$

from which

$$a^2 = \frac{r_{X_{11}X_{21}} r_{X_{21}X_{31}}}{r_{X_{11}X_{31}}} = \frac{a^4cd}{a^2cd}$$

$$c = \frac{r_{X_{11}X_{31}}}{r_{X_{21}X_{31}}}$$

and

$$d = \frac{r_{X_{11}X_{31}}}{r_{X_{11}X_{21}}}$$

Heise goes on to note that if the sources u_{ij} of the measurement errors are serially correlated (say, due to memory of past responses), there will be too many unknowns for solution. This will remain true even if data are collected at later points in time, though in this latter instance there will be redundant equations available for testing the adequacy of the simpler model involving completely random errors. Heise also notes that there will again be too many unknowns if the v_i affecting the stability of the true values are related to the previous true values (necessitating our drawing in curved arrows connecting v_2 with X_1 and v_3 with X_2). Thus, if we confine ourselves to single indicators, we will not be able to handle nonrandom disturbances.

A COMPOSITE APPROACH

Now suppose we combine the essential features of both approaches, beginning with the very simple model of Fig. 10.3, assuming random measurement error and involving only two points in time and two indicators at each time. Formally, the model of Fig. 10.3 is the same as that of Fig. 10.1, except that X_1 has replaced X and X_2 has replaced Y. But we have reduced the number of unknowns by two by substituting a for d and b for e. Comparing this model with Fig. 10.1, we may use a pair of redundant testing equations such as

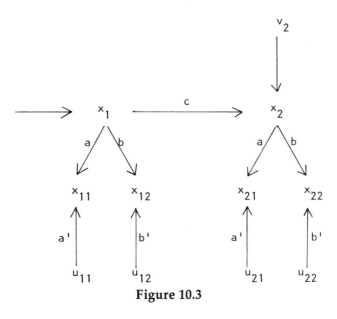

Figure 10.3

$$r_{X_{11}X_{22}} = r_{X_{12}X_{21}} = abc$$

$$r_{X_{11}X_{12}} = r_{X_{21}X_{22}} = ab$$

which should be approximately satisfied if the model is to be retained. This very simple model is relatively uninteresting except for noting that we can now estimate the unknown path coefficients with data at only two points in time.

Let us next examine the model of Fig. 10.4, which retains the assumption that the measurement errors are random but which admits an unknown correlation between v_2, the source of instability in X, and X_1, the initial true value of X. Heise has noted that this type of situation contains too many unknowns in the case of single indicators, even if there are three points in time. Writing down expressions for the six correlations that can be obtained empirically, we get

$$r_{X_{11}X_{12}} = ab$$

$$r_{X_{21}X_{22}} = ab$$

$$r_{X_{11}X_{21}} = a^2c + a^2de = a^2(c + de) = a^2c'$$

$$r_{X_{11}X_{22}} = ab(c + de) = abc'$$

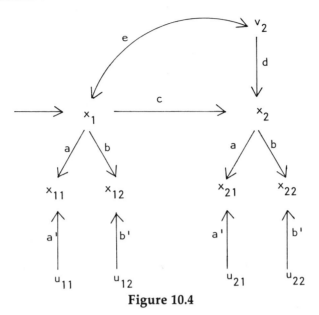

Figure 10.4

$$r_{x_{12}x_{21}} = ab(c + de) = abc'$$

$$r_{x_{12}x_{22}} = b^2(c + de) = b^2c'$$

Since the expression $(c + de)$ always appears together in the last four equations, we will not be able to isolate the stability coefficient c from the disturbance factor de. If, for convenience, we label this entire term c', we can nevertheless solve for a and b (and for c' as well, if we wish).[5] Thus, one set of solutions would be

$$a^2 = \frac{r_{x_{11}x_{21}}r_{x_{11}x_{12}}}{r_{x_{11}x_{22}}} = \frac{a^2c'(ab)}{abc'}$$

and

$$b^2 = \frac{r_{x_{11}x_{22}}r_{x_{11}x_{12}}}{r_{x_{11}x_{21}}} = \frac{abc'(ab)}{a^2c'}$$

[5] Again, since there is an excess of equations over the number of unknowns, there will ordinarily be several solutions that will be approximately equal only if the data satisfy the model. If these solutions turn out to be grossly unequal, then obviously the model must be modified. For further discussion of this point, see Costner (1969).

Also

$$c' = \frac{r_{X_{11}X_{22}}}{r_{X_{11}X_{12}}} = \frac{abc'}{ab}$$

Rewriting the expression for a^2 as

$$a^2 = r_{X_{11}X_{21}}(r_{X_{11}X_{12}}/r_{X_{11}X_{22}})$$

we see that the term in parentheses is just the reciprocal of c'.

MORE COMPLEX MODELS

If we allow for more than two points in time, more than two indicators of each variable, and various kinds of disturbances, it is not feasible to treat all of the various combinations. Nevertheless, it is instructive to compare a model involving two indicators of X at three points in time with one involving three indicators at only two time periods. In both instances, we shall allow for a reasonable number of disturbances in the measurement terms. Consider, first, the model of Fig. 10.5, where there are three time periods and two indicators.

In this particular model, we are allowing for two different stability coefficients, c' and d', with the primes indicating that we will again be unable to separate the effects of x at the previous time from those of v_2 and v_3 if the latter are correlated with these previous values of X. In other words, as might be expected, we cannot rely on multiple measures to help us make causal inferences about the sources of the variation in the true values of X. Indeed, if this were possible, it would mean that we would have available an almost magic solution to our inference problems.

In the model of Fig. 10.5, the single indicator f is used to represent the correlations connecting the sources of measurement error at the same point in time.[6] This means that we are assuming that whatever sources (e.g., the ordering of items) are producing spurious covariation between the indicators at time 1 are operating to the same extent at times 2 and 3, relative to the extent of covariation produced by X. As we shall see, it will be possible to test

---

[6] I have retained the u_{ij} and the path coefficients a' and b' in Figs. 10.5 and 10.6 in order to preserve the conventions of path analysis. Since these u_{ij} will be unmeasured and will often be extremely difficult to identify substantively, it will not be possible to decompose a compound expression such as $a'b'f$ into its three component parts. One therefore obtains the same practical results as those implied by Eqs. (10.1)–(10.15), by simply connecting the X_{ij} with curved arrows, thereby bypassing the exogenous u_{ij}.

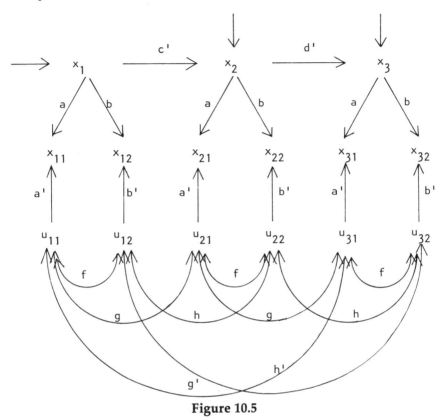

Figure 10.5

for this particular assumption of equal f's, provided one is willing to accept the correctness of the remaining assumptions.

We are also assuming that it is appropriate to use the same correlation coefficient g, linking the sources of measurement error in the first indicator during the interval between times 1 and 2 and between times 2 and 3. Such an assumption would seem reasonably plausible only if the two intervals are roughly comparable in duration. A different coefficient g' has been used for the first indicator between times 1 and 3, thus allowing for attenuation in nonrandom measurement error due to memory loss or other factors. If one were willing to assume some specific relationship between g and g' (say, $g' = g^2$), then it would be possible to reduce the number of unknowns by one. Similarly, we have introduced h and h' to represent the comparable sources of nonrandom errors for the second indicator between the three points in time.

It should be specifically noted that we are assuming *no* measurement error correlations connecting different indicators at different points in time. If such additional correlations were introduced, we would have too many unknowns for solution, unless our assumptions about these additional disturbances were unusually simplistic (e.g., all identical). As a general principle, we wish to keep the number of unknowns well below the number of equations so that we will have a substantial number of redundant equations for testing purposes.

Since there are a total of six measured values, we may write down the following 15 equations, one for each correlation:

$$r_{X_{11}X_{12}} = ab + a'b'f \tag{10.1}$$

$$r_{X_{21}X_{22}} = ab + a'b'f \text{ (redundant)} \tag{10.2}$$

$$r_{X_{31}X_{32}} = ab + a'b'f \text{ (redundant)} \tag{10.3}$$

$$r_{X_{11}X_{21}} = a^2c' + (a')^2g \tag{10.4}$$

$$r_{X_{21}X_{31}} = a^2d' + (a')^2g \tag{10.5}$$

$$r_{X_{11}X_{31}} = a^2c'd' + (a')^2g' \tag{10.6}$$

$$r_{X_{12}X_{22}} = b^2c' + (b')^2h \tag{10.7}$$

$$r_{X_{22}X_{32}} = b^2d' + (b')^2h \tag{10.8}$$

$$r_{X_{12}X_{32}} = b^2c'd' + (b')^2h' \tag{10.9}$$

$$r_{X_{11}X_{22}} = abc' \tag{10.10}$$

$$r_{X_{11}X_{32}} = abc'd' \tag{10.11}$$

$$r_{X_{12}X_{21}} = abc' \text{ (redundant)} \tag{10.12}$$

$$r_{X_{12}X_{31}} = abc'd' \text{ (redundant)} \tag{10.13}$$

$$r_{X_{21}X_{32}} = abd' \tag{10.14}$$

$$r_{X_{22}X_{31}} = abd' \text{ (redundant)} \tag{10.15}$$

Looking first at the simplest of these equations, (10.10)–(10.15), we see that three of these can be taken as redundant and can therefore be used as conditions that the data must satisfy if the model is to be retained. For example, from (10.10) and (10.12) we have the implied result that $r_{X_{11}X_{22}} = r_{X_{12}X_{21}}$, which should hold within the limits of sampling error. The three equations of this set that have been taken as nonredundant yield the following:

$$c' = \frac{r_{X_{11}X_{32}}}{r_{X_{21}X_{32}}} = \frac{abc'd'}{abd'}$$

$$d' = \frac{r_{X_{11}X_{32}}}{r_{X_{11}X_{22}}} = \frac{abc'd'}{abc'}$$

$$ab = \frac{r_{X_{11}X_{22}}r_{X_{21}X_{32}}}{r_{X_{11}X_{32}}} = \frac{(abc')(abd')}{abc'd'}$$

If we now subtract Eq. (10.5) from (10.4), we can eliminate $(a')^2 g$ as follows:

$$a^2(c' - d') = r_{X_{11}X_{21}} - r_{X_{21}X_{31}} = \delta_1$$

and similarly, subtracting Eq. (10.8) from (10.7):

$$b^2(c' - d') = r_{X_{12}X_{22}} - r_{X_{22}X_{32}} = \delta_2$$

Provided that $(c' - d') \neq 0$, we can divide the first of these equations by the second, getting

$$a^2/b^2 = \delta_1/\delta_2 = \frac{r_{X_{11}X_{21}} - r_{X_{21}X_{31}}}{r_{X_{12}X_{22}} - r_{X_{22}X_{32}}}$$

If we then multiply both sides by $(ab)^2$, we get

$$a^4 = (\delta_1/\delta_2)\left[\frac{r_{X_{11}X_{22}}r_{X_{21}X_{32}}}{r_{X_{11}X_{32}}}\right]^2$$

and therefore

$$a^2 = \pm\sqrt{\delta_1/\delta_2}\left[\frac{r_{X_{11}X_{22}}r_{X_{21}X_{32}}}{r_{X_{11}X_{32}}}\right]$$

Similarly,

$$b^2 = \pm \sqrt{\delta_2/\delta_1} \left[\frac{r_{X_{11}X_{22}} r_{X_{21}X_{32}}}{r_{X_{11}X_{32}}} \right]$$

where we would use either the plus or the minus sign so as to give positive values for a^2 and b^2. Finally, we may use these estimates of a^2, b^2, c', and d' to solve for the composite paths a' b' f, etc. Since Eqs. (10.1)–(10.3) involve only ab and a' b' f, we could have allowed for three different disturbance terms f_1, f_2, and f_3, although this would not permit our using Eqs. (10.2) and (10.3) for testing purposes.

The above procedure depends on the assumption that $c' \neq d'$. If, in fact, the two stability coefficients are nearly identical in the population, then even though their sample counterparts may be slightly different, there will be very large sampling errors for the estimates of the ratio a^2/b^2 and also for all of the estimates dependent upon this ratio. Therefore, for all practical purposes, the procedure will be useful only if the stability coefficients c' and d' are very different. Of course, if the three observations were unequally spaced temporally, we might expect this condition to hold, but then it would be unrealistic to assume that g and h remain constant from one interval to the next. Therefore, this procedure for estimating coefficients under conditions where nonrandom measurement errors are allowed depends on our finding situations of a rather peculiar nature, such as a pronounced curvilinear trend in the stability coefficients.

In experimental designs where an experimental variable has been introduced between times 1 and 2 and where individuals are measured under other conditions at time 3, it may be possible to create such situations. Or, in natural settings, where some major event has intervened between times 1 and 2 and where a third observation has been taken to infer more long-run consequences of this event, there may also be a sufficient difference between c' and d'. But if we merely have three observations taken during "normal" time periods, the stability coefficients may be too close together. Of course, Eqs. (10.10)–(10.15) may be used to estimate c' and d' so as to decide whether or not to proceed with the estimates of the remaining coefficients. It would be advantageous to know more about the sampling errors of these rather complex expressions.

As our final model, let us consider Fig. 10.6, in which we have three indicators at each of two points in time. If we wish to allow for the possibility that the three indicators are not equally "good" (by some criterion), we must not only use the three different symbols a, b, and c to represent their direct links with X, but we must also allow for different correlations among the sources of measurement error at the same points in time (e, f, and g) and across time (h, i, and j). We shall again assume no correlations connecting the sources of measurement error in one indicator at time 1 with a different indicator at time 2. Our equations are now as follows:

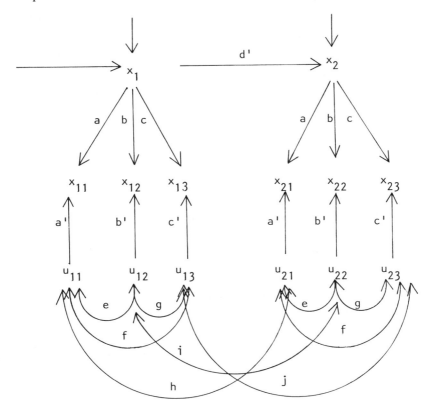

Figure 10.6

$$r_{X_{11}X_{12}} = ab + a'b'e \tag{10.1'}$$

$$r_{X_{11}X_{13}} = ac + a'c'f \tag{10.2'}$$

$$r_{X_{12}X_{13}} = bc + b'c'g \tag{10.3'}$$

$$r_{X_{21}X_{22}} = ab + a'b'e \text{ (redundant)} \tag{10.4'}$$

$$r_{X_{21}X_{23}} = ac + a'c'f \text{ (redundant)} \tag{10.5'}$$

$$r_{X_{22}X_{23}} = bc + b'c'g \text{ (redundant)} \tag{10.6'}$$

$$r_{X_{11}X_{21}} = a^2d' + (a')^2h \tag{10.7'}$$

$$r_{X_{12}X_{22}} = b^2d' + (b')^2i \tag{10.8'}$$

$$r_{X_{13}X_{23}} = c^2d' + (c')^2j \tag{10.9'}$$

$$r_{X_{11}X_{22}} = abd' \tag{10.10'}$$

$$r_{X_{11}X_{23}} = acd' \tag{10.11'}$$

$$r_{X_{12}X_{21}} = abd' \text{ (redundant)} \tag{10.12'}$$

$$r_{X_{12}X_{23}} = bcd' \tag{10.13'}$$

$$r_{X_{13}X_{21}} = acd' \text{ (redundant)} \tag{10.14'}$$

$$r_{X_{13}X_{22}} = bcd' \text{ (redundant)} \tag{10.15'}$$

We immediately see that since there are six equations that can be considered redundant, there are only nine independent equations that may be used to solve for the unknowns. Therefore, certain simplifications will be necessary. If we begin with Eqs. (10.10')–(10.15') (three of which are redundant), we find that we can no longer estimate the stability coefficient d' as was possible when we had three points in time. We can, however, use the three nonredundant equations of this set to obtain the following:

$$a/b = \frac{r_{X_{11}X_{23}}}{r_{X_{12}X_{23}}} \qquad a/c = \frac{r_{X_{11}X_{22}}}{r_{X_{12}X_{23}}} \qquad b/c = \frac{r_{X_{11}X_{22}}}{r_{X_{11}X_{23}}}$$

$$a^2d' = \frac{r_{X_{11}X_{22}}r_{X_{11}X_{23}}}{r_{X_{12}X_{23}}} \qquad b^2d' = \frac{r_{X_{11}X_{22}}r_{X_{12}X_{23}}}{r_{X_{11}X_{23}}}$$

$$c^2d' = \frac{r_{X_{11}X_{23}}r_{X_{12}X_{23}}}{r_{X_{11}X_{22}}}$$

We immediately see that the last three expressions may be used in conjunction with Eqs. (10.7')–(10.9') to solve for the three compound paths representing the over-time disturbances, $(a')^2h$, $(b')^2i$, and $(c')^2j$. However, since Eqs. (10.4')–(10.6') are redundant with Eqs. (10.1')–(10.3'), we cannot estimate a, b, and c if we know only the ratios a/b, a/c, and b/c.

If we assume that $(a')^2h = (b')^2i = (c')^2j$, we merely make two of the three Eqs. (10.7')–(10.9') redundant. Let us therefore examine the implications of the assumption that $a'b'e = a'c'f = b'c'g$. If this is the case, we may subtract (10.2') from (10.1'), obtaining an expression for $a(b - c)$. Utilizing the expressions for a/b and a/c, we obtain the result that

$$a^2 = \frac{r_{X_{11}X_{22}}r_{X_{11}X_{23}}}{r_{X_{12}X_{23}}}\left[\frac{r_{X_{11}X_{12}} - r_{X_{11}X_{13}}}{r_{X_{11}X_{22}} - r_{X_{11}X_{23}}}\right]$$

Similar expressions can of course be obtained for b^2 and c^2. Also we get

$$d' = \frac{r_{X_{11}X_{22}} - r_{X_{11}X_{23}}}{r_{X_{11}X_{12}} - r_{X_{11}X_{13}}}$$

It should be noted that each of these expressions contains a ratio of *differences* between two correlations, and we can therefore expect considerable sampling error whenever the comparable population differences are small. If we examine the nature of the pairs of correlations involved in these differences, we see that the estimating procedure depends rather heavily on our being able to find three indicators that are related rather differently to X. For example, if the second and third indicators are more or less interchangeable, it would seem rather unlikely that their correlations with the first indicator would be very different, and thus we would expect both pairs of differences among correlations to be rather small. This result is somewhat analogous to the practical restriction obtained in connection with three time periods, namely the requirement that the two stability coefficients be different in value.

CONCLUDING REMARKS

When we study the implications of nonrandom measurement errors, even where we have multiple indicators and several time periods, we begin to see the importance of careful measurement at the data *collection* stage, as well as working with large samples that have been carefully designed. Even so, since it will be difficult, if not impossible, to assess the extent and nature of measurement errors without utilizing multiple measures in addition to *a priori* assumptions about the causal structure, a major implication is that studies must be designed with measurement-error problems in mind.[7] For example, the foregoing analysis would imply that, whenever feasible, one should utilize at least 10 or 12 items for each attitudinal scale, so that split halves (and split thirds) may be used to assess the extent of measurement error.

With a single measure of each variable, one can remain blissfully unaware of the possibility of measurement error, but in no sense will this make his inferences more valid. Though there is always the danger of becoming so hypersensitive to the possibility of measurement error that one becomes immobilized in the process, present practice seems to err in the opposite

---

[7] Where there is only a single indicator of each variable, the method of instrumental variables may be used to take out random measurement errors. Basically, this approach requires one to find variables that can be assumed to be causes of the independent variables under consideration but which do not appear in the equation for the dependent variable. See Blalock *et al.* (1970) and Christ (1966:404–410).

direction. Methodological studies of the implications of measurement errors can help us see more clearly the nature of the steps we must take if we are to become increasingly precise. In the absence of better theory about our measurement procedures, I see no substitute for the use of multiple measures of our most important variables except, possibly, the use of instrumental variables that require *a priori* assumptions of a different sort.

REFERENCES

Blalock, H. M. "Multiple Indicators and the Causal Approach to Measurement Error." *American Journal of Sociology* 75 (1969):264–272.

Blalock, H. M., Wells, Caryll S., and Carter, Lewis F. "Statistical Estimation in the Presence of Random Measurement Error." In *Sociological Methodology 1970*, edited by Edgar Borgatta. San Francisco: Jossey-Bass, 1970.

Bohrnstedt, George W. "Observations on the Measurement of Change." In *Sociological Methodology 1969*, edited by Edgar Borgatta. San Francisco: Jossey-Bass, 1969.

Boudon, Raymond. "A New Look at Correlation Analysis." In *Methodology in Social Research*, edited by H. M. Blalock and Ann B. Blalock. New York: McGraw-Hill, 1968.

Christ, Carl. *Econometric Models and Methods.* New York: Wiley, 1966.

Coleman, James S. "The Mathematical Study of Change." In *Methodology in Social Research*, edited by H. M. Blalock and Ann B. Blalock. New York: McGraw-Hill, 1968.

Costner, Herbert L. "Theory, Deduction and Rules of Correspondence." *American Journal of Sociology* 75(1969):245–263.

Goldberger, Arthur S. "On Boudon's Method of Linear Causal Analysis." *American Sociological Review* 35(1970):97–101.

Gordon, Robert. "Issues in Multiple Regression." *American Journal of Sociology* 73(1968): 592–616.

Heise, David R. "Separating Reliability and Stability in Test–Retest Correlation." *American Sociological Review* 34(1969):93–101, and this volume.

Siegel, Paul M., and Hodge, Robert W. "A Causal Approach to the Study of Measurement Error." In *Methodology in Social Research*, edited by H. M. Blalock and Ann B. Blalock. New York: McGraw-Hill, 1968.

Wiley, David E., and Wiley, James A. "The Estimation of Measurement Error in Panel Data." *American Sociological Review* 35(1970):112–117, and this volume.

11

The Stability and Reliability of Political Efficacy: Using Path Analysis to Test Alternative Models*

J. Miller McPherson

Susan Welch

Cal Clark

Political efficacy is an important concept in the analysis of American political behavior, having been used to explain a wide variety of political activities
and attitudes.[1] Most of those who use the concept have assumed that efficacy is a relatively deep-seated, stable orientation rather than a superficial
and transient attitude (Campbell *et al.*, 1964:516; see also Lane, 1959:149–
151).[2] Recently, however, doubt has been cast on the stability of one com-

* Reprinted by permission of the authors and publisher from the *American Political Science Review*, 71:509–521. Copyright 1977, The American Political Science
Association.

[1] Most observers agree about the general nature of political efficacy. It is a feeling
that individual political action does have an impact upon the political process (see
Campbell, Gurin, and Miller, 1954:187). The authors of the *American Voter* used the
concept to explain voting rates, but efficacy has been used since to try to explain a
wide variety of kinds of political participation. Operationalizations have been di-
verse, but the four items developed by the Survey Research Center that are examined here are certainly the most widely used (see also Campbell, Converse, Miller,
and Stokes, 1964; Matthews and Prothro, 1966; Almond and Verba, 1963; Paige,
1971). For an extensive bibliography on political efficacy, see Easton and Dennis
(1967).

[2] The child socialization literature also contributes to this belief by suggesting that
attitudes about efficacy formed in childhood carry over into adult life (see Easton
and Dennis, 1967:33–38; Langton and Jennings, 1968). Some of the assumptions of

monly applied measure of efficacy — the SRC four-item index.[3] Cross-tabular and correlational analysis have indicated that over a period of months, an individual's level of efficacy is fairly unstable. The cross-time correlations of individual items fall between .30 and .44, while the total index is correlated with itself at approximately .50 (Welch and Clark, 1974). Furthermore, there is a lack of consensus about the dimensionality of the four efficacy items. Some have argued that the four items comprise two discrete two-item subscales distinguishing "subjective competence" from "governmental responsiveness" (Converse, 1972).[4] Others have found that three of the four items in the SRC index cluster together reasonably well to form a single subscale.[5] The discussion of the dimensionality of the component efficacy items raises the question of the reliability of each item in measuring

---

this kind of socialization research have been challenged on grounds relevant to the problems under consideration here. Searing, Schwartz, and Lind (1973) show, for example, that attitudes of political efficacy as well as other "political orientations" have hardly any relationship at all to issue beliefs in adults.

[3] Converse found that three of the four items in the SRC efficacy scale significantly increased during the 1950s then significantly decreased in the 1960s, while the other showed a continuous increase between 1952 and 1968. More detailed analysis indicated that these aggregate statistics substantially *understate* the instability of efficacy feelings because individual changes cancelled each other out to a significant degree (see Converse, 1972).

Using data from an SRC panel study, Asher found that for the 1956–1960 period, when only very marginal changes occurred in the aggregate efficacy scores, correlations between an individual's response to each question at the beginning and end of the study showed much greater inconsistencies as their temporal correlations averaged only .36. Even for the short period between the pre- and postelection survey of 1968, the temporal stability of efficacy feelings is hardly greater than for the 4-year span (see Asher, 1974). Welch and Clark, investigating the relationships among the efficacy items and their changes over time, found a multidimensionality as well as substantial instability. Stability was only slightly greater for scores on separate dimensions as for individual items (see Welch and Clark, 1974).

The high temporal variability of the efficacy items is underlined by a comparison with other political attitudinal sets and opinions about specific political issues. One would expect that deep-seated orientations should be more stable than positions on political issues. However, responses to the four efficacy items were on the average less consistent between 1956 and 1960 (Pearson's r averaging from .30 to .42) than attitudes toward a range of current issues (Pearson's r between .20 and .53) and much more variable than such a basic orientation as party identification ($r = .90$).

[4] Balch calls the dimensions "Internal" and "External" efficacy, as cited in Balch (1974).

[5] Welch and Clark (1974) factor analyzed the four conventional efficacy items along with four questions about the importance of voting and found that the three items that Converse retained defined one of the two factors that emerged. These three variables also tended to have similar correlations with several indicators of political participation that were somewhat stronger than the ones with "voting only political influence," but all four had approximately the same relationships to the political trust and cynicism questions.

the concept *efficacy*; the observed lack of stability casts some doubt on the validity of the efficacy construct.

For a variety of reasons, the arguments about the stability and reliability of efficacy have not been particularly fruitful. Different methodologies have yielded different results. Some believe that arguing about the stability and reliability of the SRC efficacy items is like arguing over the number of angels dancing on the heads of pins. On the other hand, serious questions have been raised about one of the important and widely used concepts in political behavior. Questions raised about efficacy are, furthermore, probably applicable to most concepts used in the study of political behavior. Evaluating the stability and reliability of the most common measure of efficacy more accurately should have consequences for researchers using indices not only of efficacy but of other political attitudes as well.

The difficulties in evaluating and extending research on stability and reliability of efficacy lie partly with the methods used to examine these characteristics. In addition to examining change in aggregate responses to individual items, simple over-time correlations have been most widely used to examine stability (Asher, 1974; Welch and Clark, 1974). Aside from the question of what constitutes a "high" over-time correlation, there exists the more basic problem that relatively low over-time correlations may be due to causes other than stability. Simple cross-time correlations may be diminished by random or systematic measurement error or other sources of unreliability. None of these possibilities, however, reflects on the true stability of the concept. Real change (instability) in individual efficacy may also depress the over-time correlation, but it, in turn, does not reflect inadequacy of the measures themselves. Neither correlational nor cross-tabular analysis is adequate to measure stability, since in interpreting low over-time associations, one cannot untangle the effects of item unreliability and measurement error from true change.

The measurement of the reliability of the items in the efficacy scale has been approached in at least three ways: external validation (i.e., comparing the variables's relationships with other items) (Balch, 1974), factor analysis (Welch and Clark, 1974), and analysis of differences in over-time change in aggregate responses to each of the four items (Converse, 1972). External validation of items is, of course, a useful approach, but it cannot give precise measures of reliability and unidimensionality. The same holds for the analysis of aggregate response to the items. One item may move in a direction independent of the other items, but this gives no measure of reliability. Factor analysis does give an indication of dimensionality, but traditional factor analysis is subject to the same limitations as simple correlation analysis with respect to measurement error. What is needed, then, is a method of separating reliability of the items from their over-time stability and estimating the extent of measurement error in index items.

Techniques for handling this problem by path analysis have been developed in the sociological literature within the past 5 years, but with one exception these methods have not been used in political science (see Blalock, 1970).[6] And, the application of these techniques to substantive problems has been rare. Generally, the technique allows the separation of construct stability and indicator reliability in over-time analysis; specification of nonrandom error is also possible.

First, we shall outline two forms of the causal approach to separating stability and reliability. The earlier form of the approach can be performed by hand for simple models. The more sophisticated covariance structure approach gives efficient estimates and allows one to work with a large number of items but requires a computer. Second, we will show how this approach can give answers to important questions concerning the measurement of political efficacy. Our analysis will have both substantive and methodological interest; many variables used in political science have indicators similar to those sketched above, so that path analysis may be useful in other substantive problems.

THE CAUSAL APPROACH TO MEASUREMENT ERROR

In simple path analysis, regression coefficients are used to describe the relationships among variables in a causal model. The basic theorem assumes that the correlation between any two variables is equal to the product of the paths linking the variables. This fact allows the zero-order correlation between two variables to be decomposed into direct and indirect effects. Costner (1969) shows that path analysis can be used with unmeasured variables and their indicators to estimate item reliability.[7]

The approach can be explained most easily by reference to Fig. 11.1. Let us assume that X_1 is the "true" efficacy score at time 1, X_2, the "true" efficacy score at time 2.[8] The actual indicators of efficacy at time 1 are denoted as x_1 to x_4, and at time 2 are labeled x_5 to x_8. Paths $a-d$ estimate the relationship of the true variable efficacy to each indicator at time 1, and paths $f-i$ are similar estimators for time 2. Obviously, if each indicator was a perfect reflection of the "true" efficacy score, paths $a-d$ and $f-i$ (the epistemic coefficients) would be equal to 1. Unreliability caused by measurement error would produce diminished path coefficients $a-d$ and $f-i$. Thus, the

[6] The major discussions of the use of causal modeling for this purpose include Costner (1969); Heise (1969); Wiley and Wiley (1970); and Blalock (1969).

[7] Here we will use standardized regression coefficients (beta weights); unstandardized coefficients can also be used. At this point in the chapter, we make no distinction between sources of error variance in the items due to specification error and sources in error variance due to measurement error.

[8] "True" in this sense meaning an efficacy score that could be perfectly measured. The following discussion is drawn largely from Heise (1969) and from Costner (1969).

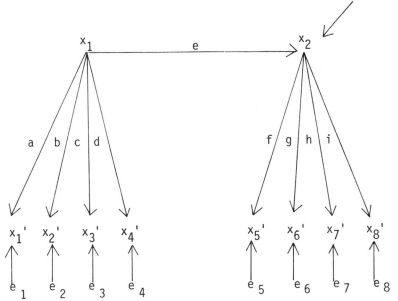

Figure 11.1. Causal model for a four-item scale at the two points in time.

observed score is a combination of the true value and the error in measurement, which is assumed to be random.[9] The assumption is made in the model of Fig. 11.1 that error terms are randomly distributed and uncorrelated with each other and the unmeasured variables either at one point in time or over time.

Path e reflects the assumption of the model that "true" efficacy at time 2 is caused by "true" efficacy at time 1. If efficacy were perfectly stable from time 1 to time 2, path e would be unity. To the extent that path e is less than unity, efficacy at time 2 is being caused by factors other than efficacy at time 1.

The rules of path analysis (Duncan, 1966; Wright, 1934) allow estimates of all paths in the model of Fig. 11.1, provided that the number of known correlations exceeds the number of paths to be estimated. In this case, we have 28 known correlations ($8 \times 7/2$) from which path estimates can be

[9] The assumption that the error terms are uncorrelated is equivalent to the assumption that no major omitted variables cause common variation in the items except through the efficacy construct or other explicit unmeasured variables. This assertion is the *ceteris paribus* assumption for causal models. It should be emphasized that this method does not deal with the semantic aspects of indicator validity. "True" efficacy may or may not be what most observers mean by efficacy. High reliabilities of the indicators of efficacy with the efficacy construct mean only that the indicators are validated for that particular model; different models might yield different indicator reliabilities.

made. Since we have only 9 unknowns, the model is overidentified,[10] and several estimates can be made for each path. The "Costner" procedure consists of taking the mean of these estimates for the summary estimate. For example, seven equations involving path a can be derived:

$$r_{x_1'x_2'} = ab \qquad r_{x_1'x_6'} = aeg$$

$$r_{x_1'x_3'} = ac \qquad r_{x_1'x_7'} = aeh$$

$$r_{x_1'x_4'} = ad \qquad r_{x_1'x_8'} = aei$$

$$r_{x_1'x_5'} = aef$$

Solving these equations for the paths in terms of the correlations produces many distinct estimates for each path. Two of these derivations are illustrated below:

Estimate 1:

$$b = \frac{r_{x_1'x_2'}}{a} \qquad b = \frac{r_{x_2'x_3'}}{c}$$

(since $r_{x_2'x_3'} = bc$)

$$c = \frac{r_{x_1'x_3'}}{a}$$

thus

$$b = \frac{r_{x_1'x_2'}}{a} \quad \text{and} \quad b = \frac{r_{x_2'x_3'}}{r_{x_1'x_3'}/a} = \frac{(r_{x_2'x_3'})(a)}{r_{x_1'x_3'}} \qquad \frac{r_{x_1'x_2'}}{a} = \frac{(r_{x_2'x_3'})(a)}{r_{x_1'x_3'}}$$

$$a^2 = \frac{(r_{x_1'x_2'})(r_{x_1'x_3'})}{r_{x_2'x_3'}} \quad \text{and} \quad a = \sqrt{\frac{(r_{x_1'x_2'})(r_{x_1'x_3'})}{r_{x_2'x_3'}}}$$

Estimate 2:

$$b = \frac{r_{x_1'x_2'}}{a} \qquad b = \frac{r_{x_2'x_4'}}{d}$$

[10] Overidentification in general denotes an excess of known quantities in relation to the number of unknowns to be estimated (see Duncan, 1966).

(since $r_{x_2' x_4'} = bd$)

$$d = \frac{r_{x_1' x_4'}}{a}$$

thus

$$b = \frac{r_{x_1' x_2'}}{a} \quad \text{and} \quad b = \frac{r_{x_2' x_4'}}{r_{x_1' x_4'}/a} \quad \frac{r_{x_1' x_2'}}{a} = \frac{r_{x_2' x_4'}}{r_{x_1' x_4'}/a} = \frac{(a)(r_{x_2' x_4'})}{r_{x_1' x_4'}}$$

$$a^2 = \frac{(r_{x_1' x_2'})(r_{x_1' x_4'})}{r_{x_2' x_4'}} \qquad a = \sqrt{\frac{(r_{x_1' x_2'})(r_{x_1' x_4'})}{r_{x_2' x_4'}}}$$

For these examples, it is obvious that if the quotient

$$\frac{r_{x_1' x_4'}}{r_{x_2' x_4'}}$$

is unequal to the quotient

$$\frac{r_{x_1' x_3'}}{r_{x_2' x_3'}}$$

the two estimates will be unequal.

Given the abundance of estimates that can be made, three problems arise. First, there is no obvious way to choose among the various estimates computed for each path. Each estimate of a particular path is as "good" as any other. When these estimates disagree, as they almost invariably will, it is very difficult to interpret the results. Thus, it is desirable to have a summary measure for each path instead of a large number of possibly conflicting estimates. Second, the procedure offers no way to test the model as a whole, since the path coefficients are computed individually; no overall goodness-of-fit measure is produced. On a more mechanical level, while the calculations involved in this procedure are individually simple, the sheer number of them is overwhelming if the model contains many variables. Furthermore, if the researcher finds that one item appears to be very unreliable, a whole new set of calculations is necessary for a slightly modified model. While this would not be too much trouble for a two- or three-indicator model, recalculating estimates based on larger models would be a major project.

A solution to these problems has been found by Jöreskog (1970) and Jöreskog, Gruvaeus, and van Thillo (1970).[11] This solution may be interpreted as a weighted average of the conflicting estimates in the Costner solution. The estimates produced by the Jöreskog procedure give more weight to those Costner estimates with the smallest sampling variability (and covariability).[12] Thus, the Jöreskog procedure averages the Costner estimates in such a way as to produce the most efficient summary estimate. Alternatively, the Jöreskog procedure may be thought of as a confirmatory factor analysis model, in which certain factor loadings are known in advance to equal zero.[13] In essence, the approach selects estimates for each path that most accurately reproduce the correlations among the observed variables.[14] The Jöreskog procedure not only gives unique, efficient estimates of the parameters, but it provides a chi-square statistic that allows hypothesis tests to be made.[15] Finally, the Jöreskog procedure has been formalized in a computer program that overcomes the difficulty of calculation mentioned previously (see Jöreskog et al., 1970). In the next section, we will use the causal approach to test the three major hypotheses concerning the efficacy measures.

HYPOTHESES

A first hypothesis is that the four-item efficacy scale is a highly stable and reliable measure of efficacy. Since much of previous research has shown that the scale is not stable and reliable, this hypothesis can serve as a starting point for the analysis. Positing this assumption, this allows us to examine the whole scale before testing specific hypotheses about the nature of the four items, the complete wording of which may be found in Table 11.1.

---

[11] The computer program designed to analyze data according to this covariance structure procedure is documented in Jöreskog et al. (1970). A technical appendix outlining the application of the Jöreskog procedure to the four-item two-wave model considered here may be obtained from the authors by request.

[12] See Hauser and Goldberger (1971); for a more technical discussion, see Goldberger (1973).

[13] Note that this a priori knowledge (for instance, that certain factor loadings are zero) is what distinguishes confirmatory factor analysis from the more generally known exploratory factor analysis. As its name suggests, confirmatory factor analysis is designed to test hypotheses rather than suggest them.

[14] More precisely, the method minimizes a scalar function of the differences between the variance–covariance matrix of the sample and that matrix produced by the causal structure of the model and the estimates of the parameters. For a more technical discussion, see Jöreskog (1970); for extensions of the technique, see Jöreskog (1973).

[15] The assumptions are essentially those of correlation analysis, including the assumption of multivariate normality. See references cited in the previous footnote.

Table 11.1. Correlation matrix for eight items[a]

	1	2	3	4	5	6	7	8
1. No say (1956)[b]	1.0							
2. Voting (1956)	.24	1.0						
3. Complex (1956)	.31	.15	1.0					
4. No care (1956)	.41	.14	.29	1.0				
5. No say (1960)	.32	.15	.16	.23	1.0			
6. Voting (1960)	.20	.34	.19	.18	.23	1.0		
7. Complex (1960)	.18	.08	.44	.21	.26	.14	1.0	
8. No care (1960)	.24	.07	.21	.32	.39	.12	.29	1.0

[a] All correlations are Pearson's r; $N = 978$.

[b] Complete wording of each item is as follows: (1) Sometimes politics and government seem so complicated that a person like me can't really understand what's going on (Complex); (2) voting is the only way that people like me can have a say about how the government runs things (Voting); (3) I don't think public officials care much what people like me think (No Care); (4) people like me don't have any say about what the government does (No Say).

The second hypothesis about the four-item scale is that three of the four items form a relatively cohesive scale, while the fourth item, "voting is the only way people like me can have a say about who runs things" (VOTING) is logically and empirically distinct. In a factor analytic study, Welch and Clark found support for this hypothesis in the fact that only the VOTING item did not load strongly on one dimension with the other items (Welch and Clark, 1974). Independently, House and Mason found that the VOTING item correlated with demographic variables differently from the other three items (House and Mason, 1973). And, Converse has shown that the trend in aggregate responses to the VOTING item has moved in a different direction from the other three items in recent years (Converse, 1972).

A third hypothesis is that the four-item efficacy scale is composed of two distinctive subscales. Converse first argued that the COMPLEX item ("Sometimes politics and government seem so complicated that a person like me can't understand what's going on") represented a subjective competence dimension of efficacy, while beliefs that "I don't think public officials care much about what people like me think" (NO CARE) and "people like me don't have any say about what government does" (NO SAY) are indicative of a dimension of belief in governmental responsiveness. The VOTING item he felt was difficult to place empirically in only one dimension (Converse, 1972). Balch later provided "external validation" for a two-dimensional division by showing that the governmental responsiveness items, on one hand, and the VOTING and COMPLEX items, on the other, manifested consistently different relationships with other theoretically relevant variables (Balch, 1974). The relationship between the two dimensions was unspecified, but one can infer that the dimensions could be correlated.

We used the SRC panel study of 1956–1958–1960 as the data base for our analysis. The efficacy questions were asked in 1956 and 1960, providing a 4-year period for possible attitudinal change. Only those respondents who completed both the 1956 and 1960 interviews were included in the analysis. The Costner method was used to estimate the stability and reliability of the basic four-item scale; then we moved to the covariance procedure to test other hypotheses about the scale. A matrix of the correlations used for the following computations is presented in Table 11.1.

FINDINGS

Estimated-mean path coefficients calculated from the Costner method are presented in Fig. 11.2a. The reliabilities of the items range from .32 for the VOTING item in 1956 to .64 for the NO SAY item in the same year; one-half of the items had mean estimates of reliability less than .50. The estimated stability coefficient was over 1.0, an unrealistic estimate. Table 11.2 provides more information about the estimates for each path; the reliability estimates are fairly stable, with a low standard deviation, while the standard deviation of the estimates of the stability coefficient is larger.

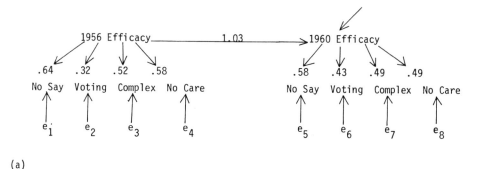

(a)

(b)

Figure 11.2. The four-item efficacy scale with uncorrelated error terms. (a) Mean Costner estimates; (b) Jöreskog estimates ($\chi^2 = 248.7$, 19 df).

Table 11.2. Summary of estimates made using Costner method[a]

Path	Estimate			
	Maximum	Minimum	Mean	S.D.
a No Say (1956)	.90	.35	.64	.14
b Voting (1956)	.64	.16	.32	.13
c Complex (1956)	.91	.29	.52	.18
d No Care (1956)	.80	.27	.58	.14
e Path	2.66	.19	1.03	.64
f No Say (1960)	.91	.31	.58	.15
g Voting (1960)	.77	.25	.43	.16
h Complex (1960)	.85	.18	.49	.17
i No Care (1960)	.74	.16	.49	.15

[a] Fourteen estimates were made for Paths a, b, c, d, f, g, h, i, and 72 estimates for e.

At this point, the difficulties with the Costner method become more apparent. The model of Fig. 11.2a is obviously defective in some way, but it is difficult to pinpoint the problem. The solutions as presented require an unlikely conclusion — that the measures are more than perfectly stable.[16] In terms of item reliability, the VOTING item is weakest, but in 1960, at least, it was not substantially weaker than two of the other items.

Estimating the same model with the Jöreskog method provides a slightly different picture. A comparison of the Costner estimates in Fig. 11.2a with the Jöreskog estimates in Fig. 11.2b reveals that the mean reliability coefficients using the Costner method are very similar to those computed using the covariance structure approach. The stability coefficients, however, are quite different. The Jöreskog method calculations show a stability coefficient of .79 between efficacy at time 1 and time 2, compared with that of 1.03 computed by the Costner method. This stability coefficient is still much higher than the Pearson's correlation of .48 found between the four-item scale at the two points in time; this difference represents a gain in estimated variance explained in efficacy in 1960 by the 1956 score from less than 25% to more than 60%. Thus, the conclusion is that the four-item scale is more stable than previously thought. Yet a closer examination of Fig. 11.2b re-

[16] In fact, if the analogy of the interpretation of the estimate e as a path coefficient can be maintained, the fact that e is 1.03 would simply mean that a score in 1956 which is one standard deviation above the mean becomes a score in 1960 which is 1.03 standard deviations above the mean. This finding is still rather unlikely. We note also that one could formulate the problem in unstandardized terms (i.e., use covariances instead of correlations, and examine unstandardized coefficients instead of path coefficients); however, a parallel unstandardized analysis using Jöreskog's procedure revealed no substantively different conclusions from the ones presented here. We present the standardized results for the purposes of clarity and simplicity.

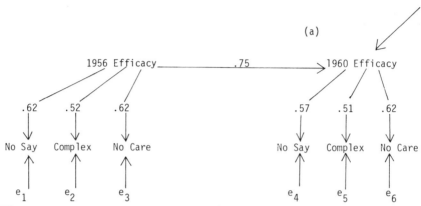

Figure 11.3. Two alternative models. (a) Three-item scale ($\chi^2 = 141.4, 8$ df); (b) four-item scale with two correlated dimensions ($\chi^2 = 129.4$, 14 df) (*see opposite page*).

veals some problems with the simple four-item model. The VOTING item is less reliable than even in the Costner estimates, and the COMPLEX item is not particularly strong. Overall, the fit of the model is resoundingly poor, with a χ^2 of over 248 with 19 degrees of freedom.[17] A correlation matrix reconstructed from the computed path coefficients reveals a particularly large difference between the actual and reconstructed over-time correlations of VOTING and COMPLEX. This suggests that the causal structure of the model in Figure 11.2 does not accurately describe the relationships among the four items in general; VOTING fits particularly poorly.

Since the least reliable indicator according to the estimates of Figure 11.2 is the VOTING item and since hypothesis two suggests that this item is logically distinct, a conceivable alternative to the four-item model is a three-item model that excludes the VOTING item. Such a model is presented in Fig. 11.3a. The estimates of Fig. 11.3a suggest that such a three-item model is plausible. The reduction in χ^2 is quite pronounced,[18] ($\chi^2 = 107.3$) while the reliabilities of the items are almost identical; the estimated stability of the construct differs by only .04 units. This fact and the observation that the VOTING item is consistently the least reliable indicator suggest that the three-item hypothesis is more viable than the hypothesis that all four items best represent the construct. Notice, however, that even the "reduced" model

[17] In general, we expect to find relatively large χ^2 values with large samples such as the present one. The χ^2 statistic will be most useful in such cases to compare different models, rather than to evaluate the absolute fit of any single model. We will use the χ^2 values produced by the different models generated in this section for this comparative purpose.

[18] The use of chi square in this case is heuristic, since the model of Fig. 11.3 is not an exact statistical alternative to the model of Fig. 11.2.

(b)

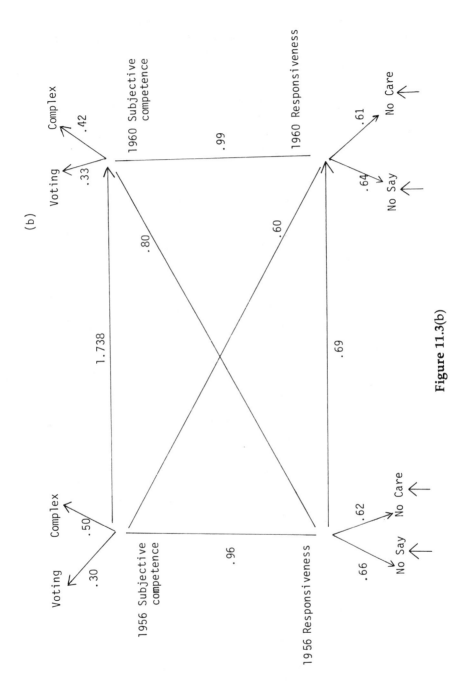

Figure 11.3(b)

does not fit the data very well. With a chi square of 141 and 8 degrees of freedom, it is clear that the three-item model does not provide a perfect representation of the causal structure in the data.

Turning to hypothesis three, we find that the notion of two correlated dimensions is totally unrealistic for these data. The intercorrelations among the constructs of "subjective competence" and "responsiveness" are nonsense. The third hypothesis produces unreasonable estimates for the relationships among the constructs. For instance, the "responsiveness" construct is almost perfectly correlated with the "subjective competence" construct, while the former is less than one-half as stable as the latter. Practically everything about Fig. 11.3b suggests that the notion of two correlated dimensions is not supported by the data; the hypothesis of two correlated dimensions must be rejected.

The most troublesome aspect of Fig. 11.3b is the extreme variation in the estimated stabilities of the two constructs. This variability suggests that there may be sources of stability in the four items over time that are independent of the efficacy construct. That is, the "unique" components of the individual items seem to produce different amounts of stability in each item. This fact can be seen more clearly in Fig. 11.4a, which allows each item to be correlated with itself over time independently of the efficacy construct. We will call this type of correlation "autocorrelation." In support of the impressionistic evidence offered in Fig. 11.3b, this model strongly suggests that the COMPLEX and VOTING items have sources of autocorrelation unrelated to the political efficacy construct.[19] These two items are consistently the least reliable of the four and demonstrate substantially different stabilities in Fig. 11.3. The obvious conclusion is that there are strong influences on each of these items that are unrelated to efficacy and to the other two items. The COMPLEX item shows the highest level of autocorrelation at .30; approximately 9% of the variation in COMPLEX in 1960 is attributable to COMPLEX in 1956 independently of the efficacy construct and the other items. While small in absolute terms, this amount is nearly one-half of the total common variance in COMPLEX 1956–1960. This finding constitutes very strong evidence that the COMPLEX item does not measure the same thing as the other items and should not be combined with them. The situation is even clearer with the VOTING item; even though the estimated autocorrelation is smaller, it is a greater proportion of the total common variance. While the common variance is less than 12%, the common variance due to sources other than efficacy is well over 55% of that amount.

---

[19] Others may prefer to call the COMPLEX or VOTING items the "real" efficacy while giving a different name to NO CARE and NO SAY. Since all four items were initially designed to measure efficacy and since we have discovered that only two of them measure substantially the same thing, we think it is most reasonable to call what the two items measure in common "efficacy."

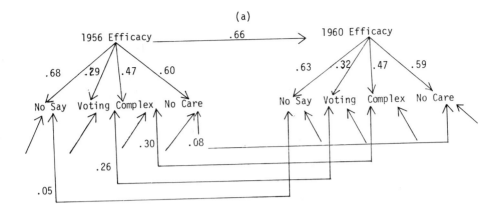

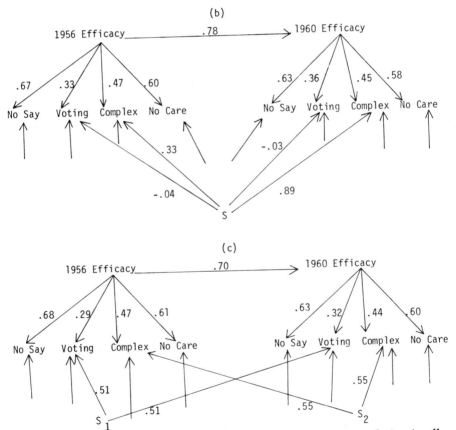

Figure 11.4. Three alternative four-item models. (a) Autocorrelation in all four items ($\chi^2 = 40.7$, 15 df); (b) four-item scale with single source of autocorrelation in "VOTING" and "COMPLEX" items ($\chi^2 = 130.9$, 15 df); (c) four-item scale with two independent sources of correlation in "VOTING" and "COMPLEX" items (the estimates for S_1 and S_2 are constrained to be equal to allow estimation of the model; $\chi^2 = 55.3$, 17 df).

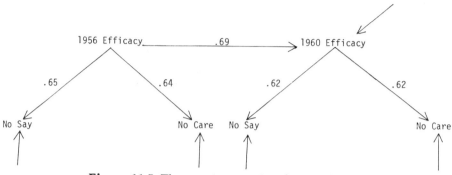

Figure 11.5. The two-item scale ($\chi^2 = 18.0$, 1 df).

The data indicate that the VOTING and COMPLEX items do not have the same sources of stability as the other two items. A formal test of the hypothesis that VOTING and COMPLEX themselves have the same sources of autocorrelation is provided by Fig. 11.4b. This figure shows that VOTING and COMPLEX do not have identical sources of autocorrelation. In fact, the hypothesized single source is actually inversely (if at all) correlated with the VOTING item.[20] The implausibility of this model is further amplified by the χ^2 fit of over 130. When this model is compared with that of Fig. 11.4c, which actually uses fewer degrees of freedom, it is easily seen that VOTING and COMPLEX have different sources of stability. This means that it is very unlikely that VOTING and COMPLEX are indicators of the same dimension.

Figure 11.4c itself presents what seems to be the most plausible model. The model allows independent sources of autocorrelation in VOTING and COMPLEX (S_1 and S_2, respectively) and assumes no autocorrelation in the other items. This assumption of no autocorrelation in NO SAY and NO CARE is the only substantive difference between the models in Fig. 11.4a and c. A comparison of χ^2 values of the two models shows that this constraint increases the χ^2 fit only 14.6 units, which is quite a small difference for a sample of nearly 1000. Thus, the autocorrelation in NO SAY and NO CARE is negligible, whereas that in VOTING and COMPLEX is substantial and comes from different sources. VOTING and COMPLEX do not belong with the other items of the scale, and they show no evidence of fitting with each other.

Throughout the analysis, the two hypothesized governmental responsiveness items have been high in reliability, and their uncorrelated error terms suggest that this stability results from their relationship to the political efficacy construct. Figure 11.5 illustrates a model incorporating only these

[20] The hypothesized single source of autocorrelation for VOTING and COMPLEX is simply a third unmeasured variable which is constrained to have a zero correlation with the two efficacy constructs. The paths linking this construct with the measured items are estimated in the same manner as the paths linking efficacy to the items.

two items. The recomputed correlation matrix is very similar to the actual one, and the chi-square value is 18 with 1 degree of freedom, which is substantially less than the initial model's chi square of 248. This suggests a reasonably good fit of the two-item model with the data, given the extremely large number of cases in the analysis.[21] Thus, the two-item scale appears to maximize reliability and stability, while minimizing the contamination of the scale by extraneous sources of autocorrelation.

DISCUSSION

What does the use of path analytic techniques to examine reliability and stability in efficacy tell us about the construct that we did not know before? Before answering this question, we again emphasize that we have not dealt with the semantics of indicator validity. We have measured the reliability and validity of four items that have been widely used to measure efficacy. While it is impossible to say which, if any, measures "real" efficacy, we can say that two of the items seem to us to represent best the efficacy construct. With this caveat, we can make the following conclusions. First, the use of the technique allows us to discard as implausible the models suggested by all three of our original hypotheses. Neither the four-item, the three-item, nor the two-dimensional model is strongly supported by the data.

Second, the procedure allowed us to pinpoint two of the four items (NO SAY and NO CARE) which did have high reliabilities. These findings led us to the conclusion that the two "governmental responsiveness" items are highly reliable indicators of the efficacy construct, which is more stable than previously thought. Efficacy in 1956 explains barely less than 50% of the variance in efficacy in 1960 (models 11.4c and 11.5); over a 4-year period this represents substantial stability.

The use of this measurement model also showed that the other two items (VOTING and COMPLEX) were relatively unreliable and had substantial sources of stability unrelated to the efficacy construct. In other words, some type of systematic error in both 1956 and 1960 inflated the over-time stability of these items independently of their relationship to efficacy. Further, the fit of model 11.4c to the data suggests that VOTING and COMPLEX are themselves indicators of two different constructs since they have different sources of autocorrelation. Thus, an alternative hypothesis concerning the composition of the efficacy index can be shown to be supported by the data: that efficacy is most reliably measured by two items and the other two items each reflect a separate construct. Converse's tentative speculation is supported. These findings also suggest that external validation does not substitute for

---

[21] The chi-square statistic is, of course, directly proportional to the sample size. Note that the two values have different degrees of freedom.

tests of internal validity. The subjective competence items appeared homogeneous in the former tests but proved to be quite distinct here.

There are concrete applications of these results. Those working with efficacy indices in survey research would probably be wise to consider using NO CARE and NO SAY items without the VOTING and COMPLEX items. The former two items are reliable, reasonably stable, and almost uncontaminated by systematic measurement error, whereas the latter items are relatively unreliable, unstable, and display systematic differences from each other and the NO SAY and NO CARE items.

The next step may be to examine further the different error sources of the COMPLEX and VOTING questions. The case of VOTING is perhaps the more clear-cut. The very wording of the item suggests ambiguity: "Voting is the *only way* people like me can have a say. . . ." (emphasis ours). One assumes that an individual who felt highly efficacious would respond "no," believing he or she had a variety of other effective ways to influence government. But an individual quite low in efficacy could respond negatively as well, believing that he or she had no means at all to influence government. At best, such a person would be confused by the question. This indicates a possible curvilinear relationship between efficacy and responses to the VOTING item, with only those who are rather moderately efficacious responding "yes." Likewise, the VOTING item may also display a curvilinear relationship to participation. Those who participate in no activities and those who participate in many would likely respond "no," whereas voting specialists (see Verba and Nie, 1972)[22] may be most likely to respond affirmatively.

The wording of the COMPLEX item is less ambiguous. Yet, since a "yes" response admits ignorance, the question wording suggests the possibility of contamination by a social desirability response set, which may in turn be linked to social class. The testing of these hypotheses with an extension of the measurement model presented here will be the next step in the examination of the efficacy construct.

For the moment, however, the use of this measurement model has allowed us to advance knowledge about the operationalization of efficacy. Its stability has been more precisely measured, and its potential indicators narrowed to those that show the strongest relationship to the efficacy construct. Finally, the techniques used here have broader applications than just

---

[22] The evidence on the curvilinearity based on a simple analysis of variance is mixed. The eta^2 between the voting item and the responsiveness dimension is 6% in 1956 and 4% in 1960, surely a small relationship. Of that, the linear relationship accounts for an R^2 of 5% and 3%, respectively. The simple relationship between voting and degrees of political participation is practically nil, although those who participate in a wide variety of political acts are slightly more likely to respond "no" to the item than either voting specialists or nonparticipants.

to political efficacy, since questions of indicator reliability, stability, and dimensionality arise for many political constructs.[23]

ACKNOWLEDGMENTS

The data for this chapter were provided by the Inter-University Consortium for Political and Social Research. Neither the Consortium nor the original collectors of the data are responsible for the analysis and conclusions presented here.

REFERENCES

Almond, Gabriel, and Verba, Sidney. *The Civic Culture.* Princeton: Princeton University Press, 1963.

Asher, Herbert B. "The Reliability of the Political Efficacy Items." *Political Methodology* 1 (1974):45–72.

Balch, George. "Multiple Indicators in Survey Research: The Concept 'Sense of Political Efficacy.'" *Political Methodology* 1 (1974):1–43.

Blalock, H. M., Jr. "Multiple Indicators and the Causal Approach to Measurement Error." *American Journal of Sociology* 75 (1969):264–272.

Blalock, H. M., Jr. "A Causal Approach to Nonrandom Measurement Error." *American Political Science Review* 64 (1970):1099–1111.

Campbell, Angus, Converse, Philip E., Miller, Warren, and Stokes, Donald. *The American Voter.* New York: John Wiley & Sons, 1964.

Campbell, Angus, Gurin, Gerald, and Miller, Warren. *The Voter Decides.* Evanston, Ill.: Row, Peterson, 1954.

Converse, Philip E. "Change in the American Electorate." In *The Human Meaning of Social Change,* edited by Angus Campbell and Philip E. Converse. New York: Russell Sage Foundation, 1972.

Costner, Herbert L. "Theory, Deduction, and Rules of Correspondence." *American Journal of Sociology* 75 (1969):245–263.

Duncan, O. D. "Path Analysis: Sociological Examples." *American Journal of Sociology* 72 (1966):1–16.

Easton, David, and Dennis, Jack. "The Child's Acquisition of Regime Norms: Political Efficacy." *American Political Science Review* 61 (1967):25–38.

Goldberger, A. S. "Efficient Estimation in Overidentified Models: An Interpretive Analysis." In *Structural Equation Models in the Social Sciences,* edited by A. S. Goldberger and O. D. Duncan. New York: Seminar Press, 1973.

---

[23] In fact, the full generality of the Jöreskog procedures has not even been hinted at in this chapter. For instance, in the context of a more elaborate analysis, additional variables representing outside influences upon efficacy or individual items could be introduced. The technique can also be used to address more sophisticated measurement issues such as whether tests are parallel, congeneric, or tau-equivalent (Jöreskog, 1971). For a fuller discussion of the flexibility of the technique, see especially Jöreskog (1970, 1973).

Hauser, R. M., and Goldberger, A. S. "The Treatment of Unobservable Variables in Path Analysis. "In *Sociological Methodology,* edited by H. L. Costner. San Francisco: Jossey-Bass, 1971.

Heise, David R. "Separating Reliability and Stability in Test–Retest Correlations." *American Sociological Review* 34 (1969):93–101, and this volume.

House, James S., and Mason, William. "Trends in Some Survey Measures of Political Alienation in America." Paper presented at the meeting of the American Sociological Association, New York, August 1973.

Jöreskog, K. G. "A General Method for the Analysis of Covariance Structures." *Biometrika* 57 (1970):239–251.

Jöreskog, K. G. "Statistical Analysis of Sets of Congeneric Tests." *Psychometrika* 36 (1971):109–133.

Jöreskog, K. G. "A General Model for Estimating a Linear Structural Equation System." In *Structural Equation Models in the Social Sciences,* edited by A. S. Goldberger and O. D. Duncan. New York: Seminar Press, 1973.

Jöreskog, K. G., Gruvaeus, Gunnar T., and van Thillo, Marielle. *ACOVS: A General Computer Program for the Analysis of Covariance Structures.* Princeton: Educational Testing Service, 1970.

Lane, Robert E. *Political Life.* New York: The Free Press, 1959.

Langton, Kenneth, and Jennings, M. Kent. "Political Socialization and the High School Civics Curriculum in the United States." *American Political Science Review* 62 (1968):852–867.

Matthews, Donald, and Prothro, James. *Negroes and the New Southern Politics.* New York: Harcourt, Brace, and World, 1966.

Paige, Jeffery M. "Political Orientation and Riot Participation." *American Sociological Review* 36 (1971):810–820.

Searing, Donald D., Schwartz, Joel J., and Lind, Alden E. "The Structuring Principle: Political Socialization and Belief Systems." *American Political Science Review* 67 (1973):415–432.

Verba, Sidney, and Nie, Norman. *Participation in America.* New York: Harper and Row, 1972.

Welch, Susan, and Clark, Cal. "Political Efficacy as an Underlying Political Orientation: The Problem of Attitudinal Instability." Paper presented at the Midwest Political Science Association Meeting, April 1974.

Wiley, David E., and Wiley, James A. "The Estimation of Measurement Error in Panel Data." *American Sociological Review* 35 (1970):112–117, and this volume.

Wright, Sewall. "The Method of Path Coefficients." *Annals of Mathematical Statistics* 5 (1934):161–215.

12

Equilibrium and Identification in Linear Panel Models*

David F. Greenberg
Ronald C. Kessler

Social scientists have been turning with increasing frequency to the analysis of nonrecursive linear models to study complex causal relationships among a set of variables. Yet the stringent identification requirements of these models have sometimes been troublesome. To identify an equation for one of a set of reciprocally related endogenous variables, say X, on the basis of cross-sectional data, one introduces instrumental variables and specifies the partial regression coefficients for the effects of these instruments on X (see, for example, Duncan, 1975; Hanushek and Jackson, 1977; Namboodiri, Carter, and Blalock, 1975). The source of the trouble is that the analyst may lack the grounds for specifying the values of these coefficients.

Duncan (1969) demonstrated that the identification problem also arises in two-wave panel models by showing that the most general two-way, two-variable panel model is not identified. Assuming perfect measurement, ignoring common causes of the observed scores X_t and Y_t (where t represents time), and expressing the latter as deviations from their means, this model is

$$X_2 = b_1X_1 + b_2Y_1 + b_3Y_2 + u \qquad (12.1a)$$

* Reprinted by permission of the authors and publisher from *Sociological Methods and Research*, Vol. 10, No. 4 (May 1982):435–451. Copyright © 1982 by Sage Publications, Inc.

$$Y_2 = d_1 Y_1 + d_2 X_1 + d_3 X_2 + v \qquad (12.1b)$$

where u and v are, respectively, the residuals of X_2 and Y_2. The six covariances among the observed scores can be expressed in terms of the eight model parameters: three b_i, three d_i, the covariance of X_1 and Y_1, here denoted by $(X_1 Y_1)$, and the residual covariance (uv). It is impossible to solve uniquely for any of these parameters other than the observed $(X_1 Y_1)$ by manipulating these equations, unless constraints are imposed on the solutions.

Several options for imposing such constraints are available. The most commonly employed of these is to assume that one of the coefficients in each pair (b_2, b_3) and (d_2, d_3) is zero or some other known value. A second option is to fix the ratios of two sets of parameters, such as b_2/b_3 and d_2/d_3 or b_2/d_2 and b_3/d_3. When appropriate control variables are available, a third option is to use instrumental variable techniques to estimate the seven coefficients (three b_i, three d_i, and uv). This method requires that one make the assumptions described above about the effects of at least one of the instruments on each of the endogenous variables X_2 and Y_2.

There are times when none of these approaches can be taken. Substantive considerations may dictate that all lagged and instantaneous cross-effects be kept free in the estimation, precluding the first and second options. Yet it might be impossible to find a theoretically defensible instrument, excluding the third option as well.

In this chapter, we review and examine critically a fourth option for achieving identification proposed by Greenberg and Logan (1979).[1] The method differs from more conventional strategies in two ways. First, it requires observations for at least three time points. Second, it achieves identification by making assumptions (1) about the consistency of parameter values rather than about the fixed values of any individual coefficients or else (2) about the ratios of different coefficients. Since this consistency assumption is usually plausible and is in some ways a weaker assumption than those required in the other methods, identification by means of this approach is quite attractive.

IDENTIFICATION BY MEANS OF CONSISTENCY CONSTRAINTS

To illustrate the consistency approach, we consider a three-wave generalization of the model defined by Eqs. (12.1a) and (12.1b). In this generaliza-

---

[1] Land and Felson (1978) have described a method for "partial identification" that is not reviewed here. In this approach, bounds are placed on the parameter estimates by imposing theoretically generated inequality constraints on the parameters.

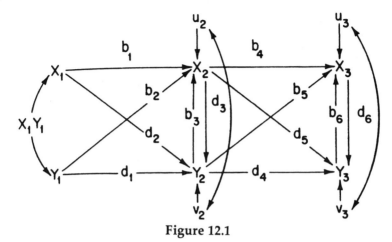

Figure 12.1

tion, shown diagramatically in Fig. 12.1, X_1 and Y_1 are assumed to influence time 3 variables only through the intervening variables X_2 and Y_2.[2] With this assumption, the structural equations are

$$X_2 = b_1X_1 + b_2Y_1 + b_3Y_2 + u_2 \qquad (12.2a)$$

$$X_3 = b_4X_2 + b_5Y_2 + b_6Y_3 + u_3 \qquad (12.2b)$$

$$Y_2 = d_1Y_1 + d_2X_1 + d_3X_2 + v_2 \qquad (12.2c)$$

$$Y_3 = d_4Y_2 + d_5X_2 + d_6X_3 + v_3 \qquad (12.2d)$$

The correlation between time 1 variables is taken into account but not subjected to causal analysis. The error terms u and v are permitted to be correlated cross-sectionally but not serially.

Concentrating on the equations for X_2 and X_3, we note that there are six regression coefficients to be estimated. By taking covariances of Eq. (12.2a) with X_1 and then with Y_1, we obtain two normal equations that can be used in the estimation of these parameters. By repeating the procedure for Eq. (12.2b) using X_2 and Y_2, we obtain two additional normal equations.

---

[2] When this assumption cannot be made, two other approaches are possible: First, if X_1 is assumed to influence both X_3 and Y_3, the consistency assumptions obviously will not hold over the two time intervals 1–2 and 2–3. However, they would still hold over the intervals 2–3 and 3–4, controlling X_1 and X_2 in the respective prediction equations. Therefore, the same approach can be used in a case of this sort, but more than three waves of data are required. Second, if X_1 influences X_3 or Y_3, but not both, the model can be identified by using X_1 as an instrumental variable.

We cannot similarly use Y_3 to identify Eq. (12.2b) because the reciprocal influence between X_3 and Y_3 implies that Y_3 cannot have a vanishing correlation with u_3.[3] For the same reason, neither Y_2 nor Y_3 can be used to help identify Eq. (12.2a).

Seemingly, we should be able to derive an additional two normal equations by taking the covariances of Eq. (12.2b) with X_1 and Y_1, as these variables are not correlated with u_3. Indeed, one can do this, and the equations so obtained are valid. The trouble is that they contain no new information beyond what is already contained in the other four normal equations. To see why this is so, note that Eqs. (12.2a) and (12.2c) can be solved to yield "reduced-form" equations that express X_2 and Y_2 in terms of X_1, Y_1, and the disturbance terms u_2 and v_2. It follows that the normal equations derived by using X_1 and Y_1 as instruments will be linear combinations of those derived by using X_2 and Y_2.

With six parameters and four normal equations that can be used to estimate them, two additional pieces of information are needed if a unique solution is to be found. In this respect, we are in the same position as when we considered the two-wave, two-variable model. However, we now have an option for identifying the model that we did not have in the two-wave case. Instead of assuming that certain parameters have known numerical values, we can assume that certain effects remain *constant* over the period between the first and third waves, a fairly weak assumption.[4] In the notation of the model, any two of the following three consistency conditions

$$b_1 = b_4 \qquad b_2 = b_5 \qquad b_3 = b_6 \qquad (12.3)$$

will reduce the number of independent parameters to be estimated sufficiently to allow the remaining parameters to be identified. If all three conditions are imposed simultaneously, the model will be overidentified.

To see that the imposition of two of these constraints does indeed enable one to obtain unique solutions for the coefficients, suppose that $b_2 = b_5$ and $b_3 = b_6$. The four normal equations become

$$(X_1 X_2) = b_1 \qquad + b_2(X_1 Y_1) + b_3(X_1 Y_2) \qquad (12.4a)$$

---

[3] Note that in Eq. (12.2d), Y_3 contains a term in X_3. If the expression for X_3 given in Eq. (12.2b) is substituted into Eq. (12.2d), it will be found that Y_3 is proportional to u_3. Hence, it cannot be uncorrelated with u_3.

[4] In fact, any relationship that determined some parameters in terms of others would reduce the number of parameters to be estimated. Our discussion will be limited to this case, which is the simplest and easiest for purposes of computation given the limitations of existing computer programs; however, the generalization poses no conceptual difficulties.

$$(Y_1X_2) = b_1(X_1Y_1) + b_2 \quad\quad + b_3(Y_1Y_2) \quad\quad (12.4b)$$

$$(X_2X_3) = \quad\quad b_2(X_2Y_2) + b_3(X_2Y_3) + b_4 \quad\quad (12.4c)$$

$$(Y_2X_3) = \quad\quad b_2 \quad\quad + b_3(Y_2Y_3) + b_4(X_2Y_2). \quad\quad (12.4d)$$

Solutions for the parameters b_1, b_2, b_3, and b_4 take the form

$$b_j = \det(B_j)/\det(B) \quad\quad (12.5)$$

where B is the coefficient matrix of the four normal equations (12.4a–4d), B_j is the matrix derived from B by replacing the jth column of B with the column of moments $[(X_1X_2), (Y_1X_2), (X_2X_3), (Y_2X_3)]$, and det symbolizes the determinant. The solutions given by Eq. (12.5) are unique as long as det(B) is non-zero.

IDENTIFICATION PROBLEMS OF THE CONSISTENCY APPROACH

By direct computation of the determinants in Eq. (12.5), we find for the model under consideration,

$$\begin{aligned}
\det(B) = &[(X_2X_3) - (X_1X_2)] + [(X_1Y_1)(X_2Y_1) \\
&- (X_2Y_2)(X_3Y_2)] + [(X_1X_2)(X_2Y_2)^2 \\
&- (X_2X_3)(X_1Y_1)^2] + [(X_2Y_2)(X_3Y_2)(X_1Y_1)^2 \\
&- (X_1Y_1)(X_2Y_1)(X_2Y_2)^2]
\end{aligned} \quad (12.6)$$

and

$$\begin{aligned}
\det(B_1) = &[(Y_1Y_2)(Y_2X_3) - (Y_2Y_3)(Y_1X_2)] \\
&+ (X_1X_2)[(X_1Y_1)(Y_2Y_3) - (X_2Y_2)(Y_1Y_2)] \\
&+ (X_1Y_2)[(Y_1X_2)(X_2Y_2) - (Y_2X_3)(X_1Y_1)] \\
&+ (Y_1Y_2)[(X_2X_3) - (X_1X_2)] \\
&+ (X_1Y_1)[(X_1X_2)(X_2Y_3) - (X_2X_3)(X_1Y_2)] \\
&+ (Y_1X_2)[(X_1Y_2) - (X_2Y_3)].
\end{aligned} \quad (12.7)$$

The other three det(B_j) have the same general form as Eq. (12.7).

These five determinants are made up of sums of terms, each of which is a difference of covariances or products of covariances that vary in time but not in time lag. It follows that all the determinants will vanish when the system described by these equations is in equilibrium. By equilibrium, we mean that the observed moments do not depend on time, only on the lag between variables. At equilibrium then, $(X_1X_2) = (X_2X_3) = (X_tX_{t+1})$, $(X_1Y_2) = (X_2Y_3) = (X_tY_{t+1})$, and so on.[5] Systems of causal relations are not always in equilibrium, but when they are, Eq. (12.5) is not defined, and the consistency approach breaks down. Unique solutions for Eqs. (12.4a)–(12.4d) cannot be obtained, and as a result, Eqs. (12.2a)–(12.2d) are underidentified.

Since the consistency approach depends critically on whether the system is in equilibrium, it is important to know two things: first, under what conditions equilibrium will be reached; and, second, how the parameter estimates behave as the system approaches equilibrium.

APPROACH TO EQUILIBRIUM

The likelihood of finding a system that meets these requirements is a function of two factors: (1) the frequency with which new sets of structural relations are known to take hold of this system in the real world, shifting it from an old equilibrium or an old pattern of change to a new pattern (which may or may not be approaching equilibrium); and (2) the speed with which this new set of structural relations approaches equilibrium.

The first of these influences will, of course, vary from one substantive situation to another. It is possible to make some general statements, though, about the speed with which equilibrium is approached for systems that *do* approach equilibrium. Consider the structural equations

$$X_t = b_1X_{t-1} + b_2Y_{t-1} + b_3Y_t + u_t$$

$$Y_t = d_tY_{t-1} + d_2X_{t-1} + d_3X_t + v_t$$

and for the sake of simplicity, assume that u_t and v_t are uncorrelated. It is a tedious but straightforward exercise in algebra to show that[6]

$$(X_tY_t) = [(b_3 + d_3 + b_1d_2 + b_2d_1) \\ + (b_1d_1 + b_2d_2)(X_{t-1}Y_{t-1})]/(1 + b_3d_3)$$

[5] In some of the literature, a system is defined to be in equilibrium only if each *variable* remains at a constant value or is stable under small displacements. This is a more stringent definition: Some systems that are in equilibrium under our definition will not be stable under this second definition. For further discussion, see Goldberg (1958: 169–184).

[6] The derivation of this equation is given in a technical appendix available from the authors on request. A more general discussion of equilibrium time can be found in Heise (1975: 227–231).

This equation has the general form

$$P_t = h + gP_{t-1} \qquad (12.8)$$

The most general solution of this recursion formula is (Goldberg, 1958: 63–67):

$$
\begin{aligned}
P_t &= h/(1-g) + [P_o - h/(1-g)]g^t & (g \neq 1) \\
&= P_o + ht & (g = 1)
\end{aligned}
$$

When the parameter

$$g = (b_1d_1 + b_2d_2)/(1 + b_3d_3) \qquad (12.9)$$

is greater than one in magnitude, or equal to one, the solution does not approach equilibrium but explodes as t increases without limit.[7] Thus, the solution converges toward the equilibrium value

$$(X_\infty Y_\infty) = (b_3 + d_3 + b_1d_2 + b_2d_1)/(1 + b_3d_3 - b_1d_1 - b_2d_2)$$

only if the absolute value of g is strictly less than 1.

It follows directly from the recursion relation from $P_t = (X_tY_t)$ that

$$\Delta(X_tY_t) = g\Delta(X_{t-1}Y_{t-1}) \qquad (12.10)$$

We can see from this expression just how g affects the approach to equilibrium. When g is small, each increment will be much smaller than the preced-

---

[7] Some structural systems have parameters such that covariances do not eventually stabilize at finite equilibrium values. Instead, they oscillate without any damping or explode. Oscillation without damping occurs when $g = -1$. Here, each increment ΔX_t is followed by an increment ΔX_{t+1} of equal magnitude but opposite sign. Explosion, corresponding to values of g that are greater than or equal to 1, or strictly less than -1, implies values of ΔX_t that increase in magnitude without any finite limit. A situation of this kind cannot prevail indefinitely. When it is encountered, one may infer that the equations are being extrapolated beyond their range of validity. Either the correct equation contains nonlinear terms that prevent covariances from growing geometrically, or the parameters themselves do not remain constant over time. Rather, the system responds to a variable or a relationship that has increased beyond a certain point by changing the structural parameters in a manner that reduces the magnitude of the variable or relationship.

ing increment, and the system will approach equilibrium rapidly, while if g is close to but less than 1, the system will approach equilibrium slowly. It follows from Eq. (12.9) that the approach to equilibrium will be slow when the product of the stability coefficients $b_1 d_1$ is large, when the cross-lagged effects of b_2 and d_2 are the same sign and large, and when the cross-instantaneous effects b_3 and d_3 are the opposite sign and large. Approach to equilibrium will be fastest when the product of the stability coefficients is small, when the cross-lagged effects are the opposite sign and large, and when the cross-instantaneous effects are the same sign and large.

By iterating Eq. (12.10), we see that $\Delta(X_t Y_t) = g^t \Delta(X_1 Y_1)$. To get an idea of what this means for the approach to equilibrium, we consider two models. In the first, the parameters are $b_1 = .3$, $b_2 = .2$, $b_3 = -.2$, $d_1 = .3$, $d_2 = -.2$, and $d_3 = .2$; we assume that the initial cross-sectional correlation is $(X_1 X_1) = -.9$. For this model, g is approximately .05, and it is apparent that after one time unit, $(X_t Y_t)$ will be very close to its equilibrium value of 0. In the second model, $b_1 = .9$, $b_2 = .1$, $b_3 = -.1$, $d_1 = .9$, $d_2 = .1$, and $d_3 = .1$, and we again assume the initial cross-sectional correlation to be $-.9$. Here, g is approximately .81, and the approach to equilibrium will be slow; after 10 time units have elapsed, the cross-sectional correlation will be .717, still some distance from the equilibrium correlation .947. More generally, the time T in which the time-dependent term in the expression for P_t in Eq. (12.8) is reduced in magnitude to a given fraction of its value at time 0 is proportional to the reciprocal of the natural logarithm of g.

It can be shown without difficulty that the parameter g, which governs the approach of the correlation $(X_t Y_t)$ to equilibrium, also governs the approach to equilibrium of the correlations $(X_t X_{t-1})$, $(Y_t Y_{t-1})$, $(X_t Y_{t-1})$, and $(Y_t X_{t-1})$; thus, the results summarized above for the correlation $(X_t Y_{t-1})$ hold equally well for the entire system of equations.

BEHAVIOR OF THE PARAMETER ESTIMATES AS EQUILIBRIUM IS APPROACHED

We have demonstrated so far that Eq. (12.5) yields unbiased estimates of b_i and d_j when the matrix B is not in equilibrium. When equilibrium is reached, though, the model parameters are not identified. But what about the transition? Intuitively, we know that the difference terms making up the estimator approach zero as the system approaches equilibrium. Yet this does not occur abruptly. As the system comes closer and closer to equilibrium, the parameter estimates become more and more inefficient.

To ground this intuitive reasoning, we carried out a series of simulations. In each simulation, we began with a "true" structural model, generated the observed correlation matrix among the variables in the model over a very

Table 12.1. Values of the stability and cross-effect coefficients used in the thirty-six (four stabilities by nine cross-effects) simulations

Stabilities	b_1	d_1		
1	.3	.3		
2	.5	.5		
3	.7	.7		
4	.3	.7		
Cross-effects	b_2	b_3	d_2	d_3
1	.1	.1	.1	.1
2	.1	−.1	−.1	.1
3	.1	.1	.1	−.1
4	.2	.2	.2	.2
5	.2	−.2	−.2	.2
6	.2	.2	.2	−.2
7	.4	.4	.4	.4
8	.4	−.4	−.4	.4
9	.4	.4	.4	−.4

long period of time,[8] and then attempted to recover the underlying structure from this matrix at different points as the system approached equilibrium.

Table 12.1 shows the parameters for 36 simulated systems. Four sets of stability coefficients (b_1, d_1) were used. For each of these, nine sets of cross-coefficients (b_2, b_3, d_2, d_3) were used. Together, these cover a range of stabilities from .3 to .7 and a range of cross-coefficients from −.4 to .4.

Beginning with the arbitrary assumption that $(X_1 Y_1) = -.9$, three-wave correlation matrices for times 1−3, 2−4, 3−5, 4−6, and 5−7 were analyzed for each of the 36 models. The LISREL IV program (Jöreskog and Sörbom, 1977) was used to impose the consistency conditions given in Eq. (12.3) and to obtain maximum-likelihood estimates of the underlying model parameters and their standard errors.

The LISREL solutions clearly demonstrated two results anticipated from

[8] The recursion relations given in the technical appendix (see footnote 6) were used to generate sets of three-wave correlation matrices for the variables X_t, Y_t, X_{t+1}, Y_{t+1}, X_{t+2}, Y_{t+2} ($t = 1, 2, 3, \ldots$). We continued generating matrices for a particular model until correlations in the 4×4 submatrix X_t, Y_t, X_{t+1}, Y_{t+1} were identical to three decimal places to the corresponding elements in the 4×4 submatrix X_{t+1}, Y_{t+1}, X_{t+2}, Y_{t+2}. If more than five three-wave matrices were generated by this procedure for a particular model, we submitted only the first five and the final matrices to analysis.

analytic investigation: (1) that the estimator will reproduce the underlying parameters without bias as long as the system is not extremely close to equilibrium; and (2) that the standard errors of the parameter estimates increase dramatically as we move from the times 1–3 matrix to the equilibrium matrix.

Table 12.2 illustrates these features with a detailed example from one of the simulated models. The value of g in this model is approximately .11. The first row presents the parameters of the underlying model. The remaining rows display the parameter estimates and their standard errors for each successive three-wave correlation matrix. (Standard errors were computed on the assumption that $N = 1000$.) The final column contains the value of the exogenous correlation $(X_t Y_t)$, with $t = 1, 2, 3, 4, 5$.

We see that the true score parameters are reproduced exactly for this model in the times 1–3 and 2–4 matrices. However, in subsequent iterations, as the correlation $(X_t Y_t)$ gets close to its equilibrium value, the estimates become wildly discrepant from the true values. This happens even though the model is formally identified in all five iterations.

We also see that the standard errors increase substantially from the first to second iteration, even though the parameter estimates themselves remain constant. The increase is particularly dramatic for the cross-coefficients, where standard errors change from between .057 and .092 in the first iteration to between .400 and .735 in the second. While all standard errors are less than one-half their associated parameters in the first iteration, they all exceed their parameters by the second iteration. By the third iteration, all standard errors exceed 1.0.

The results for the other 35 models considered are very much like those for this illustrative case. In most cases, the parameter estimates perfectly

Table 12.2. Detailed results of applying the consistency approach to the first five iterations of a simulated matrix[a]

	b_1	b_2	b_3	d_1	d_2	d_3	$X_t Y_t$
True-score parameters	.5	.4	−.4	.5	−.4	.4	
Parameter estimates times 1–3	.500	.400	−.400	.500	−.400	.400	.900
Standard errors	.028	.057	.092	.023	.040	.059	.004
Parameter estimates times 2–4	.500	.400	−.400	.500	−.400	.400	−.096
Standard errors	.128	.419	.735	.123	.400	.703	.037
Parameter estimates times 3–5	.520	.335	−.287	.519	−.336	.287	−.010
Standard errors	x[b]	x	x	x	x	x	x
Parameter estimates times 4–6	.620	.004	.296	.620	−.004	−.296	.007
Standard errors	x	x	x	x	x	x	x
Parameter estimates times 5–7	.620	.004	.296	.620	−.004	−.296	.000
Standard errors	x	x	x	x	x	x	x

[a] The model is $(X_1 Y_1) = -.9$, $b_1 = .5$, $b_2 = .4$, $b_3 = -.4$, $d_1 = .5$, $d_2 = -.4$, $d_3 = .4$.
[b] x indicates that standard error exceeds 1.0.

Table 12.3. Number of iterations (from a maximum of five) for which all model parameters are at least twice their standard errors[a]

Cross-effects	Stabilities $b_1 = .3$ $d_1 = .3$	$b_1 = .5$ $d_1 = .5$	$b_1 = .7$ $d_1 = .7$	$b_1 = .3$ $d_1 = .7$
Magnitude $= .1$				
$b_2 b_3 d_2 d_3$				
$++++$	0	0	0	0
$+--+$	0	0	0	0
$+++-$	0	0	0	0
Magnitude $= .2$				
$b_2 b_3 d_2 d_3$				
$++++$	0	0	0[b]	2[b]
$+--+$	0	0	0	0
$+++-$	0	0	2	0
Magnitude $= .4$				
$b_2 b_3 d_2 d_3$				
$++++$	0[b]	0[b]	0[b]	0[b]
$+--+$	1	1	1	0
$+++-$	1	2	3	3

[a] Standard errors are based on the assumption that $N = 1000$.
[b] Indicates that the model exploded (i.e., it was not approaching equilibrium) during the interactive calculation of the correlation matrix.

reproduce the true parameter values initially but deteriorate as equilibrium is approached. Variations among the models appear primarily in the speed with which the deterioration occurs.

Table 12.3 presents summary results for all 36 models, recording the number of iterations for which standard errors of all parameters are less than one-half the parameter values.[9] These results are discouraging. They suggest that except for systems that approach equilibrium only very slowly and that have moderately large cross-effects, parameter estimates will be too imprecise for the consistency approach to be of practical value. This will be true even when observations are collected immediately after an external shock has placed the system very far from equilibrium. In less optimal conditions, the situation would be even worse.[10]

Only where the stability coefficients are quite high, then, will the consistency approach be practically useful. And even here its usefulness will be limited to times that are fairly close to the time when the new set of struc-

[9] Detailed results of these simulations are available from the authors on request.
[10] Even more discouraging is the fact that these results ignore measurement error. In more realistic applications, the difference terms in Eq. (12.5) will become dominated by error as the true-score covariances approach equilibrium.

tural equations first took hold. For most problems, it will not be possible to obtain observations that meet this criterion, and identification via this approach will not be possible.

CONCLUSION

In practice, we have no way short of estimating the consistency model to determine if the observed data are too close to equilibrium, or moving too rapidly toward equilibrium, for the approach to be used.[11] The simulations show quite clearly, though, that the approach can be used in practice only under a very restricted set of circumstances. Consequently, the researcher who believes that it is necessary to distinguish empirically between lagged and instantaneous cross-coefficients in a panel model[12] should, whenever possible, consider the availability of theoretically justifiable instrumental variables. When these are available, it is possible to identify all three b_i's and all three d_j's even when the system is at equilibrium. Furthermore, the standard errors of these estimates will almost certainly be lower than those parameters estimated via the consistency approach, even when the latter can be used.

ACKNOWLEDGMENTS

We gratefully acknowledge the assistance of Clifford Broman, Roger Brown, and Mary Ann Caballero in carrying out the simulations. Alfred

---

[11] Lest our finding that structural equations typically reach equilibrium very rapidly be taken as an endorsement of static analyses or equilibrium models of society, we point out that the conclusion is a theoretical one, not an empirical one. It is based on the premises that (1) the system of variables under study is isolated from external shocks and (2) the system approaches equilibrium. Neither of these assumptions is necessarily valid empirically.

[12] The importance of distinguishing instantaneous from lagged cross-coefficients would seem to be greatest in situations where the signs of the two effects are opposite, for in this case the two terms will tend to sum to zero. However, it can be important to distinguish the two effects even when they are of the same sign. Suppose that an instantaneous effect is present but a lagged effect is not, and the estimation is carried out on the assumption that the cross-effect is lagged but not instantaneous. It can be shown (Greenberg and Kessler, 1981) that in this circumstance, the estimate of the cross-coefficient can have the wrong sign. One can determine quickly whether this possibility need be of concern by carrying out the estimation on the assumption that only lagged effects are present, and again on the assumption that only instantaneous effects are present. If the signs of the estimates are the same, the sign will be unbiased under either assumption, though the magnitude of the parameter may be in error in the model that is misspecified. If the signs of the estimates are opposite, one will be wrong. In the absence of *a priori* information about the correct lag, a multiwave model will have to be considered to avoid the risk of estimating a cross-coefficient with the wrong sign.

Blumstein and Robert Hauser motivated us to carry out this analysis by raising questions about the estimator. We thank them for this. Part of this work was funded by grant 80-1J-CX-0062 from the National Institute of Law Enforcement and Criminal Justice. Points of view are those of the authors and do not necessarily reflect the position of the U.S. Department of Justice.

REFERENCES

Duncan, O. D. "Some Linear Models for Two-Wave, Two-Variable Panel Analysis." *Psychological Bulletin* 72 (1969):177–182.

Duncan, O. D. *Introduction to Structural Equation Models.* New York: Academic Press, 1975.

Goldberg, S. *Introduction to Difference Equations.* New York: John Wiley, 1958.

Greenberg, D. F., and Kessler, R. C. "Panel Models in Criminology." *Mathematical Methods in Criminology,* edited by J. A. Fox. New York: Academic Press, 1981.

Greenberg, D. F., and Logan, C. H. "A Panel Model of Crime Rates and Arrest Rates." *American Sociological Review* 44 (1979):843–850.

Hanushek, E. A., and Jackson, J. E. *Statistical Methods for Social Scientists.* New York: Academic Press, 1977.

Heise, D. R. *Causal Analysis.* New York: John Wiley, 1975.

Jöreskog, K. G., and Sörbom, D. *LISREL—Analysis of Linear Structural Relationships by the Method of Maximum Likelihood.* User's Guide, Version IV. Chicago: National Educational Resources, 1978.

Kessler, R. C., and Greenberg, D. F. *Linear Panel Analysis.* New York: Academic Press, 1981.

Land, K. C., and Felson, M. "Sensitivity Analysis of Arbitrarily Identified Simultaneous-Equation Models." *Sociological Methods and Research* 6 (1978):283–307.

Namboodiri, N. K., Carter, L. F., and Blalock, H. M., Jr. *Applied Multivariate Analysis and Experimental Designs.* New York: McGraw-Hill, 1975.

13

Causal Inference in Cross-Lagged Panel Analysis*

Richard D. Shingles

Cross-lagged panel analysis (CLPA) is one of a variety of quasi-experimental forms of analysis used by an increasing number of social scientists for making causal inferences (Chaffee, Ward, and Tipton, 1970; Crano, Kenny, and Campbell, 1972; Duvall and Welfling, 1973; Shingles, 1975). Because quasi-experimental research is less rigorous than true experimentation, its results are typically subject to plausible rival interpretations. This is true of CLPA and has led to a number of attempts to refine the approach. However, the lack of consensus and the contradictory solutions stemming from these efforts discourages use of the analysis. The confusion stems partly from the fact that the contributors to the debate represent independent disciplines, characterized by different research traditions and terminologies (Goldberger, 1971) and partly from the failure of those employing the procedure to develop and articulate formal causal models or an explicit theory of CLPA.

This chapter reviews, compares, and evaluates the major approaches to CLPA. The first section presents the basic design for a two-variable, two-wave case in the context of a causal model, and the second section uses the

* Reprinted by permission of the author and publishers from *Political Methodology*, 3 (1976):95–133.

model to discuss the major cross-lagged panel derivations. The third and fourth sections present these derivations in a four-fold typology. The final section considers the relaxation of several of the principal assumptions of the model.

The chapter is intended primarily for the potential users of CLPA who find the current literature bewildering. It also serves as a warning to those who would use the design based on their familiarity with any one of the principal derivations. It will be shown that the various approaches differ in important ways from one another and that their relative value depends upon the research context in which one is working. Those who have already mastered CLPA should find the discussion useful for organizing their own thinking. I have tried to avoid an excessively mathematical discussion. A reading knowledge of basic scalar algebra suffices for a complete understanding of the topic.

THE BASIC DESIGN AND ITS DERIVATIONS

Cross-lagged panel analysis is a method of making causal inferences from temporal precedence over fixed intervals for two or more variables. Though there is no limit on either the number of the intervals or the number of variables, most published work employing the analysis has been limited to a $2v2w$ design, evaluating causal priority between two variables, each measured at two points (waves) in time. The relationships of interest between the two variables, symbolized X and Y in Fig. 13.1, are indicated by single-headed arrows representing the direction of causal influence; two-

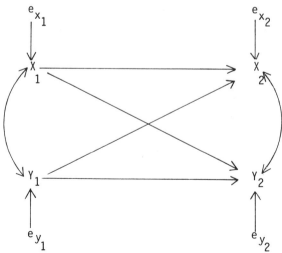

Figure 13.1. The simplified CLPA diagram.

headed, curvilinear arrows represent noncausal associations. This chapter focuses on the $2v2w$ design, though it develops rules and procedures that can be extended to more complex models.

All CLPA attempt to draw causal inferences from *cross-lagged associations*, $r_{x_1y_2}$ and $r_{y_1x_2}$. The lagged or *diachronic associations*, $r_{x_1x_2}$ and $r_{y_1y_2}$, and the cross-sectional or *synchronous associations*, $r_{x_1y_1}$ and $r_{x_2y_2}$, are of secondary interest, useful primarily as aids in interpreting cross-lagged relationships. The principal assumption upon which the inference rests is that *cause precedes effect*. It is assumed that the state of any variable at t_2 (the second observation) cannot have produced the prior state of any other variable at t_1 (the first observation). Thus, in Fig. 13.1, it would be argued that *if* there is any causal relationship between x_1 and y_2, it cannot be due to $x_1 \leftarrow y_2$. Therefore, the existence of a significant association $r_{x_1y_2}$ is taken as the basis for a proof that x is a *sufficient* cause of y. However, there remain many other interpretations of the association, $r_{x_1y_2}$, including the possibility $r_{x_1y_2}$ is the spurious product of some third variable or even that, under certain conditions, y may still be a cause of x.

The principal problem with CLPA is to take advantage of time precedence as a basis for causal analysis while avoiding erroneous inferences. The solution lies first in the use of an *explicit causal model* that specifies the assumptions that must accompany the "temporal precedence" axiom and second, in the development of an *empirical procedure* to evaluate these assumptions.

Different derivations of CLPA offer several procedures for this purpose. To date, there are four principal derivations (Table 13.1). Each derivation provides a different logic and a somewhat different set of assumptions for inferring cause from cross-lagged associations. Unfortunately, the assumptions are not always specified, and the derivations are not strictly comparable. Of the four derivatives, only the originators of the zero no-cause base technique have offered an explicit causal model based on path analysis. Yet the rules and assumptions specified (primarily by Heise) for the path analytic model are also applicable to other CLPA derivations. Thus, a common design and common problems lie behind every form of the analysis, with specific variations in assumptions required for each derivation in procedure.

Table 13.1. Major derivations of the CLPA design

General approach	Specific derivation	Originators
Asymmetry	1. Zero-order correlation	Yee and Gage (1968); Sandell (1971)
	2. Higher-order correlations and regressions	Pelz and Andrews (1964); Bohrnstedt (1969)
No-cause base line	3. Nonzero NCB	Rozelle and Campbell (1969)
	4. Zero NCB	Duncan (1969); Heise (1970)

Before proceeding with an evaluation of these derivations, a cross-lagged causal model for a 2*v*2*w* case is presented. Although not all the approaches to be discussed conform to the model, it provides a common frame of reference for the comparisons that follow.

THE BASIC MODEL

A causal model is a simplified representation of reality, focusing on a limited set of variables, the hypothetical causal relationships among them, and the specific set of assumptions necessary to test them (Blalock, 1964). Causal models may be understood in terms of what they are not as well as of what they are. They are neither causal theories nor the tests of causal theories, yet they accompany every such test and serve as representations of theory. They may be more easily understood if we maintain a distinction between conceptual and operational levels of discussion, that is, between abstract causal theory and the procedures used to test it.

The act of *testing* theory consists of the dual processes of formulating a model representing the theory, or that part of it to be tested, and the actual empirical operations (the test itself) in which the model (and thereby, indirectly, the theory) is compared to a set of observations in order to evaluate its validity. The *causal model* differs from *theory* in that the latter is a set of generalizations purporting to explain the real world, whereas the former is a set of predictions deduced from the theory that specifies both the *system of causal relations* of interest and the *working assumptions* needed to test it. The assumptions rule out other rival interpretations that offer plausible alternative explanations of the observations. Therefore, inferences derived from tests designed to evaluate the validity of the theory depend not only on the empirical observations and the methods used to obtain them but on the causal model accompanying the research. The test of a theory can only be as good as the model representing it.

The causal model differs from the actual *empirical operations (or test)* in that the latter both measures the variables and relationships of interest and determines whether the model fits the observations. The research design (itself influenced by the theory) helps determine the precise form of the model. The theory specifies the exact variables and general relationships of the model; the empirical procedures influence the operational predictions (i.e., structural equations) and the assumptions that are required for causal inference. Thus, the same theory does not have one identifiable model but several, depending upon the type of research used (e.g., whether the data are cross-sectional or longitudinal, the number of lags or waves, the degree to which the observations have been isolated from contaminating factors). In addition to influencing the precise form of the model, the test itself requires a number of working assumptions independent of the model (in that they are not necessary for the development of the structural equations) but necessary in determining whether the empirical procedures used (e.g., operational definitions and statistical procedures) adequately test the model.

Every research design for testing causal theory, no matter how rigorous, is predicated on a causal model, though the model may be developed only partially and poorly articulated, as is the case of much of the research with CLPA. The primary difference between what has come to be called causal modeling and other, looser forms of *causal analysis* is the practice of those engaged in modeling to thoroughly develop and explicitly state the exact causal relationships being tested and their underlying assumptions.

The variable set, operational predictions, and assumptions of the general CLPA model and test follow. Additional assumptions peculiar to the different variations in the test procedure are discussed later.

THE VARIABLE SET

The basic CLPA design of two variables observed at two points in time is treated as a special case of a four-variable model. Each variable, measured at two different times, is treated as two distinct variables. Two variables measured at two different times are treated as four variables. Variables are identified in terms of their causal priorities within the set (Heise, 1970; Land, 1969). The variables x_1 and y_1 are treated as *exogenous*, that is, predetermined or causally prior to other variables within the set. Variables x_2 and y_2 are considered to be *endogenous*, that is, determined by the other variables (either x_1 or y_1 or both) within the set. Those extraneous variables outside the system that affect the variables internal to it and account for the variance left unexplained by the model may be referred to as *residual variables*. The residuals associated with each system variable are known as *error terms* (indicated e_{x_1}, e_{x_2}, e_{y_1}, and e_{y_2} in Fig. 13.1).

OPERATIONAL PREDICTIONS

Though the substantive literature may suggest competing recursive causal theories ($x \rightarrow y$ versus $x \leftarrow y$) or a nonrecursive theory ($x \leftrightarrows y$), the operational predictions must be recursive in order to be identified and tested, unless one is willing to make fairly restrictive assumptions (Fisher, 1969, 1970). It is therefore more difficult to test nonrecursive or feedback theories using solely cross-sectional data. Longitudinal analysis requires less rigorous assumptions to specify distinct causal lags. Given certain common assumptions (below), all derivations of the basic 2v2w CLPA design provide the same operational predictions or structural equations (Table 13.2) in which each of the endogenous variables at t_2 is postulated to be dependent upon the two exogenous variables (the prior state of the dependent variable and the prior state of the other variable in the set) at t_1.

Table 13.2. The standard hypotheses of CLPA

	Operational predictions	
Theory	Diagrammed path	Structural equations
$X \rightarrow Y$	$X_1 \rightarrow Y_2$	$X_1 = e_{x_1}$
		$Y_1 = e_{y_1}$
		$Y_2 = b_{y_2x_1}X_1 + b_{y_2y_1}Y_1 + e_{y_2}$
$Y \rightarrow X$	$Y_1 \rightarrow X_2$	$Y_1 = e_{y_1}$
		$X_1 = e_{x_1}$
		$X_2 = b_{x_2y_1}Y_1 + b_{x_2x_1}X_1 + e_{x_2}$

The difficulty lies in the evaluation or test of the predictions, that is, in determining whether the true relationship is $x \rightarrow y$, $y \rightarrow x$, both, or neither. The several derivatives of CLPA differ substantially in their ability to do this.

COMMON ASSUMPTIONS

All CLPA, being of the same basic design, share a common set of assumptions for both the formulation and the testing of causal predictions.

1. *Generality.* It is assumed that the real world is ordered; that actual patterns do exist; that true causal laws, which are generalizable over space and time, govern these relationships; and that the laws are discernable.

2. *Continuity.* It is assumed that the causal processes are continuous or ongoing as opposed to unique or abrupt, and that therefore they may be observed (at least in part) during any temporal interval.

3. *Finite Causal Lag.* Cause is assumed to *precede* effect. The causal process is not instantaneous but occurs with some finite lag. The lag assumption replaces the often arbitrary assumptions, typical of cross-sectional analyses, about which variables are independent and which dependent, facilitating the empirical study of reciprocal causation.

4. *Congruence of Causal and Measurement Lags.* The key to valid CLPA is the accurate observation of finite causal lags. It is normally assumed that the interval between observations must be of approximately the same length as the true causal lag. The greater the discrepancy the greater the likelihood that the analysis will fail to discern the true causal process. The practical consequences are: (a) The time necessary for the first set of observations must be shorter than the true causal lag; and (b) the second observation must not be made until *after* the causal process has had time to take effect; but (c) before the effect has had time to attenuate appreciably.

5. *Equality of Causal Lags.* In cases of reciprocal causality, it is assumed that the causal lags necessary for x to affect y and for y to affect x are equal. If

this assumption is invalid, then the fourth assumption (above) is not likely to be true for at least one of the causal lags (i.e., in a $2v2w$ model). Some leeway is permissible in the congruence assumption, but only if the equality assumption is met. This is particularly essential for the asymmetry method.

6. *Closure.* One of the most essential and yet troublesome assumptions of causal modeling is that the system of variables is closed, that is, that the residual variables for any dependent variable are uncorrelated with any predictor variable within the model and have a mean value of zero. All causal models must at some point be assumed to be closed, otherwise causal relationships cannot be decisively differentiated from spurious relationships attributable to disturbances not explicitly incorporated into the analysis. In CLPA, this assumes that the error terms (in Fig. 13.1) of t_2 variables are uncorrelated with either of the t_1 variables or their error terms. Though the assumption refers principally to the cross-lagged and not the diachronic relationships, autocorrelated disturbances are almost certain to occur for the latter (the correlation of a variable with itself over time), resulting in problems of parameter estimation for higher-order partials (Hibbs, 1974:256, 293–294; Namboodiri, Carter, and Blalock, 1975:519–526).

ASSUMPTIONS OF THE TEST

1. *Minimal Measurement Error.* The operational indicators of each variable are assumed to be accurate and reliable measures of the true concepts of the theory.[1]

2. *Linearity.* It is assumed that relationships between the variables are additive as opposed to interactive.

3. *Homoscedasticity.* The standard deviations of the dependent variable are assumed to be the same for each value of the independent variable.

4. *Equal Intervals.* Continuous variables with equal intervals are required for the higher-level measures of association (Pearson product–moment correlation and regression coefficients) typically used in CLPA. The assumptions of equal intervals, linearity, and homoscedasticity allow for the generalization of an observed relationship over all possible values of the variables.

---

[1] This assumption need not be so serious as once thought. Recent research with CLPA indicates that considerable measurement error may be tolerated without seriously impairing the analysis *if* it can be assumed that the errors are uncorrelated and there is not concomitant sampling error (Heise, 1970:12–20). In addition, CLPA has an advantage over cross-sectional analysis in its ability to estimate and correct for internal inconsistencies in measurement. The procedure involves the adjustment of lagged correlations using split-half reliability coefficients (Bohrnstedt, 1969). If the Bohrnstedt correction is used, both the diachronic and cross-lagged correlation should be adjusted, each in terms of the split-half reliability of its t_1, or independent, variable.

5. *Noncolinearity.* It is assumed that the variables in either the synchronous or diachronic correlations are not so highly correlated as to impair efforts to adjust for their influence on cross-lagged correlations.[2]

Collectively, the assumptions of the model are highly restrictive, perhaps untenable. However, restrictions can be relaxed and untenable assumptions replaced by more plausible ones. A sizable proportion of the CLPA literature has been directed to this end. Similarly, most advanced textbooks on statistics provide means for both relaxing and evaluating the assumptions accompanying measurement and testing (see, for example, Blalock, 1971, 1972; Lieberman, 1971). Here, I proceed on the basis of these restrictive assumptions when discussing the main derivatives of CLPA, but at the conclusion, I address the question of relaxing or replacing key assumptions and note some of the techniques available for accomplishing this.

ASYMMETRY

Inferences about the source of a causal relationship in CLPA are based on the *relative* magnitude of cross-lagged coefficients. In the asymmetry approach, the basis for comparison is the *opposite* cross-lag.[3] In a recursive system, both cross-lags may have significant relationships, one because it reflects the true causal process, the other because it is an attenuated relationship of an earlier cause–effect process. For example, if x causes y and y does not cause x, and if both correlations are positive, we may expect $r_{x_1y_2} > r_{y_1x_2}$, since effect should correlate more strongly with prior cause than with subsequent "cause" (Campbell and Stanley, 1963:69), the latter association being a spurious product of the earlier influence of x on y. Thus, in the asymmetry approach, the test of the rival hypotheses that $x \rightarrow y$ and $y \rightarrow x$ is a decision as to whether one cross-lagged correlation is, statistically,

[2] This becomes a problem when partialing (Blalock, 1963; Darlington, 1968; Gordon, 1968). In particular, CLPA should not be used when the t_1 synchronous correlation is very high, approaching unity. The residuals resulting from the partialing process will be so small, relative to measurement or sampling error, that highly unreliable coefficients will result.

[3] The usual test of statistical significance for the difference between two correlation coefficients is

$$t = \frac{z_{12} - z_{34}}{\sigma(z_{12} - z_{34})}$$

Because all four arrays in the CLPA variable set are considered dependent, the calculation of the standard error of the difference between $r_{x_1y_2}$ and $r_{y_1x_2}$ requires several additional steps (see Peters and Van Voohris, 1940:185).

significantly larger than the other. If $r_{x_1y_2} > r_{y_1x_2}$, the likely conclusion is that x is a more *probable* cause of y than y is of x. The test does not rule out the possibility that y may also influence x in a reciprocal exchange, it only indicates the greater or the more likely cause. Symmetrical relationships, in which $r_{x_1y_2} = r_{y_1x_2}$, indicate there is no causal primacy between the two variables, meaning either that they mutually influence each other with about the same impact or that the assumption of closure is invalid and both cross-lags are the spurious products of some extraneous influence.

Without further modification, the method is severely limited in its ability to specify cause. When symmetry exists, the asymmetry method cannot distinguish between a balanced, nonrecursive system and a totally spurious relationship. More troublesome, the interpretation of asymmetry is equivocal. As Rozelle and Campbell (1969) indicate, asymmetrical, positive correlations may be interpreted to mean either that the first variable has a *positive* effect on the second (thereby increasing the size of the cross-lagged coefficient) or that the second has a *negative* impact on the first (thereby decreasing the coefficient). Thus, the relationship $r_{x_1y_2} > r_{y_1x_2}$, where both cross-lagged correlations are positive actually means that:

$$\text{The joint effect of} \left. \begin{array}{c} x_1 \xrightarrow{(+)} y_2 \\ \text{and} \\ y_1 \xrightarrow{(-)} x_2 \end{array} \right\} \text{ is greater than } \left\{ \begin{array}{c} \text{The joint effect of} \\ y_1 \xrightarrow{(+)} x_2 \\ \text{and} \\ x_1 \xrightarrow{(-)} y_2 \end{array} \right.$$

Correct interpretation is most precarious in a nonrecursive system in which a causal influence of one sign (positive or negative) is concealed by a stronger causal influence of the opposite sign. For example, if

$$x \xrightarrow{(+)} y \quad \text{and} \quad y \xrightarrow{(-)} x$$

and if the positive effect is substantially stronger, $r_{y_1x_2}$ will likely be spuriously positive, though lower in magnitude than $r_{x_1y_2}$. Unless further information is provided, the analyst is likely to interpret such a relationship to mean that the system is solely recursive with x increasing the likelihood of y.

Without further modification of the basic design, the only instances in which this problem is avoided are either (1) when there is no theoretical reason for suspecting a hidden cause of a sign other than that observed (e.g., only positive cross-lags are detected and there is no basis for expecting a negative feedback) or (2) when the prior synchronous correlation is zero. A t_1 zero synchronous correlation indicates either no causal relationship between x and y or a mixed one in which

$$x \underset{(-)}{\overset{(+)}{\rightleftharpoons}} y$$

are of approximately equal force, thereby canceling each other out at any point in time. In the latter instance, both causal processes will be accurately indicated in the separate cross-lags, one being negative, the other positive.

Several modifications of the basic asymmetry method have been developed to cope with the problem of unequivocal interpretation. I have divided these into two general categories: (1) those retaining the *simple correlation*, which rely on additional comparisons within the model and (2) those introducing *higher-order correlations and regressions* (Table 13.1).

SIMPLE-ORDER CORRELATIONS

CHANGES IN SYNCHRONOUS CORRELATIONS (CSC). The least adequate of the CLPA derivations is the "Frequency-of-Change-in-Product-Moment" technique developed by Yee and Gage. They supplement the analysis of cross-lags with a comparison of synchronous correlations. Increases and decreases in the synchronous correlations over the period t_1-t_2 are used to specify the source and the sign of the causal process, the procedure of which follows.

The *sign* of the causal process is estimated from a comparison of the synchronous correlations alone. The *source* is determined from specific combinations of synchronous and cross-lagged associations. If a positive synchronous association increases over time or a negative one decreases (*congruent* change), the causal process is inferred to be positive. If a positive synchronous association decreases or a negative one increases (*incongruent* change), cause is said to be negative. When the direction of change is congruent, the t_1 variable, which is part of the more *positive* cross-lagged correlation, is considered to be the source of influence. When the direction of influence is *incongruent*, the t_1 variable, which is part of the more *negative* (or less positive) cross-lagged correlation, is inferred to be the source. In short, the *test* for the rival hypotheses $x \rightarrow y$ and $y \rightarrow x$ (assuming all positive coefficients) is:

If $r_{x_1y_1} < r_{x_2y_2}$ and if $r_{x_1y_2} > r_{y_1x_2}$ then x is a positive cause of y.
If $r_{x_1y_1} < r_{x_2y_2}$ and if $r_{x_1y_2} < r_{y_1x_2}$ then y is a positive cause of x.
If $r_{x_1y_1} > r_{x_2y_2}$ and if $r_{x_1y_2} > r_{y_1x_2}$ then y is a negative cause of x.
If $r_{x_1y_1} > r_{x_2y_2}$ and if $r_{x_1y_2} < r_{y_1x_2}$ then x is a negative cause of y.

EVALUATION. The Yee and Gage technique has a number of difficulties, some of which are discussed elsewhere (Howard and Krause, 1970). I focus here on several additional weaknesses that are most pertinent to a comparison with other CLPA derivations. The logic that positive cause leads to increasing and negative cause to decreasing positive synchronous correlations is based on implicit assumptions about whether causal systems are in equilibrium or disequilibrium. A system is in *equilibrium* when the correlations among the variables within it reflect only the causal processes of that system. Everything else equal, the correlations will remain *stable* from one observation to the next. A system is in *disequilibrium* when the pattern of relationships among the variables of the set is disturbed by some extraneous influence. In such an event, the continued operation of the system may under certain conditions, restore equilibrium (Pelz and Lew, 1970). Yee and Gage assume a situation in which everything else is equal and in which the system studied is in disequilibrium at t_1, but restored to equilibrium by t_2.

The assumption that a system is only in equilibrium at t_2 is, of course, arbitrary unless one has some independent means of verification. The system could just as well have changed from equilibrium to disequilibrium or from one state of disequilibrium to another. The implications are devastating to the analysis. For example, a change from equilibrium to disequilibrium during $t_1 - t_2$ in a *positive* causal system, in which the true relationship stemming from internal causality is temporally distorted or concealed by t_2, leads to the same type of change in synchronous correlations ($r_{x_1 y_1} > r_{x_2 y_2}$) from which Yee and Gage (assuming a disequilibrium to equilibrium situation) infer a *negative* cause.

Leaving aside the question of equilibrium, everything else is usually *not* equal. There are too many other reasons why synchronous correlations might change over time to permit a credible inference as to the source of cause from an observation of $r_{x_1 y_1}$ and $r_{x_2 y_2}$. For example, change in synchronous correlations may be attributed to testing, attenuation, totally spurious relationships associated with external causes, or to the internal inconsistency of the measurements. While it is true that conditions of this sort threaten other forms of analysis as well, derivations of CLPA that do not rely on synchronous correlations are better able to handle them. Finally, unlike the other derivations, the CSC technique is limited to recursive systems. Reciprocal causation goes undetected.

EXTENDED CROSS-LAGGED OBSERVATIONS (ECL). Sandell's (1971) solution to the equivocality of CLPA is to extend the analysis to a third observation in time (Fig. 13.2). The procedure is based on the presumed attenuation of effect over time. Cross-lagged associations stemming from the causal processes occurring during the interval from t_1 to t_2 are expected to deteriorate over the longer period from t_1 to t_3. The source and sign of cause is inferred from a comparison of simple and extended cross-lagged correla-

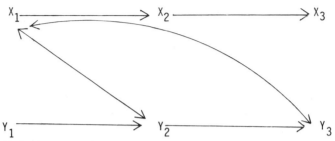

Figure 13.2. An extended CLPA diagram. (Residual and other spurious relationships are omitted to simplify the illustration.)

tions. Increasingly larger positive cross-lags indicate the deterioration of a negative effect; increasingly smaller positive cross-lags reflect the deterioration of a positive effect.

Sandell's *test* for making causal inferences, replicated here, is presented only for a situation where the researcher wishes to determine whether two positive cross-lagged correlations conceal negative feedback. A similar procedure can be worked out for tests involving negative correlations.[4]

Recursive or Unidirectional Causal Systems
  1. A positive effect

$$x \xrightarrow{(+)} y$$

is indicated when $r_{x_1y_3} < r_{x_1y_2}$, because of the attenuation of a positive effect, and $r_{y_1x_3} = r_{y_1x_2}$, reflecting a stable spurious relationship.
  2. A negative effect

$$y \xrightarrow{(-)} x$$

is indicated when $r_{y_1x_3} > r_{y_1x_2}$, because of the attenuation of a negative effect, and $r_{x_1y_3} = r_{x_1y_2}$, reflecting a stable spurious relationship.

Nonrecursive or Bidirectional Causal System
  3. A positive–positive feedback system

---

[4] For example, for a bidirectional negative–negative relationship in which the correlation coefficients are *negative*, the interpretation of $r_{x_1y_2} > r_{y_1x_2}$ is just the *opposite* of that made for positive coefficients. The comparison would mean that x decreases y, or y increases x, or both. Therefore, the test is also reversed: a bidirectional, negative–negative causal process in which x is the predominant force is indicated by $r_{x_1y_2} > r_{y_1x_2}$, $r_{y_1x_3} < r_{y_1x_2}$, and $r_{x_1y_3} < r_{x_1y_2}$.

$$x \underset{(+)}{\overset{(+)}{\rightleftarrows}} y$$

in which $x \xrightarrow{(+)} y$ is the stronger of the two, is indicated when $r_{x_1 y_2} > r_{y_1 x_2}$, $r_{x_1 y_3} < r_{x_1 y_2}$, because of the attenuation of a positive effect, and $r_{y_1 x_3} < r_{y_1 x_2}$ because of the attenuation of a positive effect.

4. A positive–negative feedback system

$$x \underset{(-)}{\overset{(+)}{\rightleftarrows}} y$$

in which $y \xrightarrow{(-)} x$ is concealed by the stronger positive process, $x \xrightarrow{(+)} y$, is indicated when $r_{x_1 y_2} > r_{y_1 x_2}$, $r_{x_1 y_3} < r_{x_1 y_2}$, because of the attenuation of a positive effect, and $r_{y_1 x_3} > r_{y_1 x_2}$, because of the attenuation of a negative effect.

5. An open negative–negative feedback system

$$x \underset{(-)}{\overset{(-)}{\rightleftarrows}} y$$

in which $x \xrightarrow{(-)} y$ is the stronger of the two processes but in which both are concealed by a spurious positive association stemming from extraneous influences, is indicated when $r_{x_1 y_2} < r_{y_1 x_2}$,[5] because of the greater ability of the stronger negative effect to wash out the spurious positive association, $r_{y_1 x_3} > r_{y_1 x_2}$, because of the attenuation of a negative effect, and $r_{x_1 y_3} > r_{x_1 y_2}$, because of the attenuation of a negative effect.

EVALUATION. The Sandell ECL derivation is more useful than the CSC technique because it is based on the attenuation of effect reflected in cross-lagged correlations rather than the production of effect in synchronous correlations. It thereby avoids the ambiguity of cross-sectional data. It has the further advantage of being able to identify nonrecursive systems. Provided that the other assumptions of the model are met, it can also operate on the assumption that cross-lagged correlations may be, in part or entirely, the spurious products of extraneous influences. The procedure would provide a firmer guarantee against misinterpretation, however, if it were continued over several more than the three observations recommended by Sandell.

The primary difficulties of the ECL technique are that it is a tedious process, heavily reliant upon the assumptions of the model, and plagued by ambiguity. The ambiguity derives from an inability to differentiate between the attenuation of *causal* relationships and the attenuation of *spurious* relationships. For example, consider item 4 of the test, which specifies the set of

---

[5] A correction is made here from Sandell's presentation (1971) which inaccurately uses the notation $>$.

cross-lagged correlations that indicate negative feedback concealed by a predominant positive causal process. The comparison $r_{y_1 x_3} > r_{y_1 x_2}$ is the basis for inferring the attenuation of a negative effect in which

$$y \xrightarrow{(-)} x$$

However, the positive effect of

$$x \xrightarrow{(+)} y$$

will also attenuate during $t_1 - t_3$. So, too, should the spurious positive relationship it has created in $r_{y_1 x_2}$. Therefore, while the attenuation of the negative effect will tend to make $r_{y_1 x_3}$ larger, the attenuation of the spurious positive relationship will tend to make it smaller. It is not at all clear just how $r_{y_1 x_3}$ should compare to the other relationships. A similar difficulty exists with item 5. The attenuation of negative influences could well be offset by the attenuation of spurious positive correlations.

The assumptions of the model are crucial to ECL analysis. Exact knowledge of the causal lags is necessary to avoid erroneous conclusions. For example, in item 3, if one underestimates the true causal lag, it actually being from t_1 to t_3, one will observe $r_{x_1 y_3} > r_{x_1 y_2}$ and not vice versa, as expected. All CLPA relies upon the *congruency* assumption, but an analysis that infers cause from assumed attenuation in successive cross-lags is particularly vulnerable to erroneous conclusions unless one has *a priori* knowledge about the length of causal lags as well as about the rate of attenuation.

Similar problems associated with *closure and measurement error* exist. With respect to the former, all one may be observing in an ECL analysis is the attenuation of spurious relationships in a noncausal system. Because of the latter, it is unlikely that spurious cross-lagged associations stemming from causal processes internal to recursive models (items 1 and 2) will produce identical correlations over extended lags. The variable x_3 is not likely to equal x_2; and y_3 is not likely to equal y_2. Therefore, $r_{y_1 x_3} \neq r_{y_1 x_2}$ and $r_{x_1 y_3} \neq r_{x_1 y_2}$.

HIGHER-ORDER CORRELATIONS AND REGRESSIONS

Some of the rival sources of asymmetry that confound the straightforward causal inference sought by users of CLPA may be controlled by replacing the simple correlation coefficient with more elaborate and powerful measures of association. The model and the test remain essentially the same as in the original 2v2w design: a comparison solely of the cross-lagged relationships between $x_1 y_2$ and $y_1 x_2$ for the purpose of detecting causal asymmetry. Only the coefficients differ. They include the partial and part correlations and standardized and unstandardized regressions. The relative advantages and disadvantages of each of these measures are discussed in the appropriate literature (Blalock, 1964, 1972; Darlington, 1968; Gordon, 1968; Kerlinger and Pedhazur, 1973). My comments are limited to the relative utility of replacing the simple correlation in CLPA with one or the other of the higher-order coefficients.

THE PARTIAL CORRELATION. The use of the first-order partial correlation to correct for confounding influences when comparing changes in one variable over time with the prior state of another for the purpose of making causal inferences is well established in the literature on experimentation and change measurement (Bereiter, 1963; Dubois and Manning, 1957; Lord, 1958, 1963). The technique, therefore, proves ideally suited for CLPA and has been adopted for the purpose by Pelz and Andrews (1964). It has several distinct advantages over the use of zero-order correlations.

Its principal advantage for correctly interpreting asymmetry is the ability of the partial correlation to control for confounding influences contributing to asymmetry. Cross-lagged associations are not independent of either the diachronic or the prior synchronous relationships. Unless adequately controlled, $r_{x_1y_2}$ and $r_{y_1x_2}$ will reflect, totally or in part, the relationship $r_{x_1y_1}$. How much they do so depends upon the stability of the *dependent* variable over the period of the study. For example, in the case where x_1 is the hypothesized predictor variable, the greater the value of $r_{x_1y_1}$ and $r_{y_1y_2}$, the greater the spuriousness of $r_{x_1y_2}$. The less y changes, the more the analysis will be confounded by the persistence of prior synchronous relations.

Spuriousness may derive from internal feedback or from external influence. Assuming closure, I will focus on the spuriousness generated from within the model, which is most likely to lead to erroneous conclusions in a nonrecursive system in which the variables have opposite or incongruent effects upon one another. Consider, for example, the system

$$x \underset{(+)}{\overset{(-)}{\rightleftarrows}} y$$

in which the impact of $x \xrightarrow{(-)} y$ is smaller than the impact $y \xrightarrow{(+)} x$. Under these circumstances, the stronger process will manifest itself in synchronous correlations. If, in addition, the variables are fairly stable, the same relationship will persist over time in the cross-lagged correlations, thereby concealing the weaker causal process. The immediate cause of the problem is the *prior* state of the variable being explained. In the case of

$$x \xrightarrow{(-)} y$$

it is y_1. If y_2 can be freed of the influence of y_1, the adjusted cross-lagged correlation can be attributed solely to the impact of x on y.

The partial correlation (Eq. 13.1) provides this adjustment. It is the correlation of the *residuals* of x_1 and y_2, that is, the correlation of the variances of the independent and dependent variables left unexplained by their mutual association with the confounding influence, y_1 (Blalock, 1972:433–440).

$$r_{x_1 y_2 \cdot y_1} = \frac{r_{x_1 y_2} - (r_{x_1 y_1})(r_{y_1 y_2})}{\sqrt{1 - r_{x_1 y_1}^2}\sqrt{1 - r_{y_1 y_2}^2}} \tag{13.1}$$

Within the framework of the model, the association $r_{x_1 y_2 \cdot y_1}$ can be considered free of confounding influences and, in the example given, will take a negative value. The partial correlation for the opposite cross-lag, $r_{y_1 x_2 \cdot x_1}$, will be positive. In a recursive system, the partial opposite the cross-lag reflecting the true causal relationship would be reduced to zero.

THE PART CORRELATION. In adjusting for the variance that y_2 shares with y_1, the partial correlation, $r_{x_1 y_2 \cdot y_1}$, controls for the association of y_1 with *both* variables. There are times, however, when this is neither desirable nor necessary, when the researcher believes that the variation shared with the confounding influence should remain as part of one of the variables (Kerlinger and Pedhazur, 1973:92–93). Such is the case with CLPA. The statistic providing this type of information is the *semi-partial* or *part correlation*.[6]

The formula for the part correlation is given in Eq. 13.2. The use of the parentheses in $r_{(y_2 \cdot y_1)x_1}$ indicates that the influence (i.e., shared variance) of y_1 has been removed from y_2 but not from the independent variable x_1. The part correlation is, therefore, the correlation between the independent variable and the residual of the dependent variable after the latter has been adjusted for the variances it shares with its prior state. The part correlation is generally smaller than the partial, since the product of the two variances left unexplained in the denominator is always less than either of the two variances left unexplained when taken separately.

$$r_{(y_2 \cdot y_1)x_1} = \frac{r_{x_1 y_2} - (r_{x_1 y_1})(r_{y_1 y_2})}{\sqrt{1 - r_{y_1 y_2}^2}} \tag{13.2}$$

[6] This position disagrees with Bohrnstedt (1969), who prefers the partial to part correlation. He believes that the part correlation fails to control for indirect effect of x_1 on y_2, particularly the path through y_1. I argue that, first, there is no need in CLPA to separate indirect from direct effect of x_1 on y_2 or y_1 on x_2 (the purpose of the analysis being to determine *relative* impact over time, regardless of the directness of the impact); and second, that the part correlation nevertheless does eliminate the path via the prior state of the dependent variable by residualizing the dependent variable in terms of its prior state.

The appeal of the part correlation is largely theoretical. First, there is no need to adjust *both* the independent and dependent variables in terms of the control variable when the *direction of cause* is known. With respect to the example $x \rightarrow y$, the model rules out the paths $y_2 \rightarrow x_1$ and $y_1 \rightarrow x_1$. The only concern is with the impact of $y_1 \rightarrow y_2$ and the persistence of the t_1 synchronous association as a confounding influence. Second, there is a special appeal in residualizing only the *dependent* variable when working with cross-lagged relationships.[7] The simple and partial correlations do not actually measure *change*; they measure associations among variables measured at different points in time that we assume result from change. The part correlation provides a more readily interpretable coefficient. The residual $(y_2 \cdot y_1)$ indicates the *change* (in terms of ranking) that has occurred in y during the period from t_1 to t_2. The larger the residual, the greater the change. The part correlation, $r_{(y_2 \cdot y_1)x_1}$ indicates the correlation between x_1 and that change. The squared part correlation represents what proportion of that change can be explained by x_1. This is, after all, exactly what CLPA is after: an indication of how much change x can independently explain in y *over time* compared to how much change y can explain in x during the same period.

STANDARDIZED AND UNSTANDARDIZED REGRESSION COEFFICIENTS. Though the partial and part correlations overcome the problem of equivocality peculiar to simple correlations, *all* correlations suffer from a common drawback that severely limits their utility for CLPA. The correlation between any two variables (with or without controls) is subject to variation from one sample to another as a function of the amount of variance in the independent variable relative to the variance in other, extraneous influences impinging upon the dependent variable (Blalock, 1964:114ff). The greater the heterogeneity or the variance of the independent variable, the larger is the correlation. The more homogeneous the independent variable, the smaller the correlation. This potential instability across samples provides a serious threat to the *asymmetry* method of CLPA. In any *2v2w* analysis, the

---

[7] This is a break with the conventional procedure common to multiple regression analysis of residualizing the independent variable in part correlations and the partial regression coefficients. In the more standard equation, the denominator is

$$\sqrt{1 - r^2_{x_1 y_1}}$$

rather than

$$\sqrt{1 - r^2_{y_1 y_2}}$$

observed asymmetry upon which causal inference is based may be due in part, or even solely, to the difference in the variances of x_1 and y_1.[8]

The regression coefficient, b, offers a limited solution to this problem. It has a general advantage over correlations particularly relevant for CLPA. Whereas r indicates only the degree of association, or "goodness of fit," of the data to the regression line between any two variables, b provides additional information as to the *slope* of the line. The difference between the formula for the regression coefficient (Eq. 13.3) and the part correlation is the introduction of the *ratio* of the standard deviations of the independent and dependent variables and the absence of the radical sign from the denominator (Darlington, 1968; Kerlinger and Pedhauzer, 1973:81–100). The ratio indicates how much change in y_2 during t_1–t_2 can be explained, or accounted for, by a unit change in x_1.

$$b_{y_2x_1 \cdot y_1} = \frac{r_{x_1y_2} - (r_{x_1y_1})(r_{y_1y_2})}{1 - r_{y_1y_2}^2} \frac{S(y_2 \cdot y_1)}{S_{x_1}} \qquad (13.3)$$

Therefore, while $r_{(y_2 \cdot y_1)x_1}$ describes the sign and degree of the association between x_1 and y_2, controlling for prior effects, $b_{y_2x_1 \cdot y_1}$ provides additional information as to how well x_1 can *produce* the observed change in y.

Assuming that the source of influence is known (and herein lies the value of CLPA), that the ratio of the variances reflects a true causal law, and that the other assumptions of the test are accurate, the slope will remain relatively stable from one sample to another. If x is a cause of y, the ability of x to produce unit changes in y, being indicative of that causal process, will remain the same from one $2v2w$ replication to another (Blalock, 1964:94ff). In short, $b_{y_2x_1 \cdot y_1}$, which is a part correlation qualified in terms of the slope, will serve as a relatively more stable measure of the relationship, and therefore of asymmetry, than $r_{x_1y_2}$, $r_{x_1y_2 \cdot y_1}$, or $r_{(y_2 \cdot y_1)x_1}$.

The regression coefficient itself, however, is subject to a specific problem that limits its utility for the *asymmetrical* method of CLPA. The ratio of the variances of the independent and dependent variables is in part contingent upon their scales of measurement. To the extent the scales differ, they will confound the analysis. The regression coefficient will reflect that inequality, confusing it with any causal relationship that may exist (Blalock, 1972:450–454). When the units of measurement of the independent variable are larger than the units of measurement of the dependent variable, the size of b increases because fewer units of change in the former produce a given

[8] This is not totally restrictive of course. An analysis in which $r(x_2 \cdot x_1)y_1 > r(y_2 \cdot y_1)x_1$ may be accepted as evidence that y causes x (1) if $S_{x_1} = S_{y_1}$, or $S_{x_1} > S_{y_1}$, or (2) if several observations over successive replications of the study demonstrate the reliability of the cross-lagged coefficients.

amount of change in the latter. Conversely, smaller units of measurement in the independent variable lead to a smaller b since a larger number of units produce the same amount of change.

The assumption of equivalency of scales is ignored (often justifiably) in most social research involving regressions; but it cannot be dismissed in CLPA where one is studying *relative* influence between two variables. Highly dissimilar scales of measurement, by themselves, are quite capable of producing an artificial asymmetry (or of concealing "true" asymmetry) leading to faulty inferences of cause.

There is *no* simple solution to this problem. The variables may be standardized, thus eliminating the inequality, but the resulting *standardized* regression coefficient, B (indicated in Eq. 13.4), is subject to the same difficulties associated with inequalities of variance found for the part correlation, the two statistics being identical except for the absence of the radical sign:

$$B_{y_2 x_1 \cdot y_1} = \frac{r_{x_1 y_2} - (r_{x_1 y_1})(r_{y_1 y_2})}{1 - r_{y_1 y_2}^2} \qquad (13.4)$$

The solution suggested for the part correlation, successive replications of the analysis over time, is of no value here since b's will consistently reflect the inequalities of scales from one observation to the next. Inferences about the source of cause are justified with b only when (1) the assumption of equivalency of scales is verified or (2) the asymmetry takes a form the opposite of that predicted from one's knowledge of the difference in scales.

CONCLUSION

The *asymmetry* method of CLPA is plagued by a series of alternative hypotheses stemming from the nature of the design and the limitations of the various measures of association that may be used with it. Though not insurmountable, these difficulties threaten causal inference and must be dealt with in research using this form of analysis. Each measure of association that may be adapted to CLPA is restricted in its utility and, unless employed under clearly specified conditions, subjects observed asymmetry to equivocal interpretation.

Causal inference relying on simple correlations requires additional information from synchronous correlations or extended cross-lags in order to specify the source and sign of causal processes. Such tactics are clumsy, subject to the deficiencies of cross-sectional data, and rely more than necessary on the assumptions of the model. Though partial and part correlations and standardized regression coefficients largely overcome or avoid these difficulties, they are potentially confounded by inequalities in the variances of the independent variables x_1 and y_1. The regression coefficient circumvents this problem but in turn must rest upon the often tenuous assumption that x and y are based on comparable scales of measurement. The difficulties of interpreting asymmetry are sufficiently bothersome to suggest the need for an alternative method for making causal inference from panel data using the CLPA design. The other major alternative is the *no-cause-base* approach.

NO-CAUSE BASE

Like the *asymmetry* approach, the other major method of CLPA also concentrates on the relative magnitude of cross-lagged coefficients. Unlike the asymmetry approach, the basis for causal inference is not the opposite cross-lagged relationship but an estimate of what an ideal cross-lagged association *would* be if there were no causal process operating between x and y. This estimate, to which cross-lags are compared, is the *no-cause base line* (NCB). Unfortunately, one cannot normally assume that, in the absence of cause, the NCB will be zero. It has been demonstrated that, given the assumptions of the model and test, spurious cross-lagged relationships will result from the persistence through time of prior synchronous associations. The only situation in which one may expect to find insignificant cross-lagged coefficients under conditions of no-cause is when $r_{x_1 y_1} = 0$. The central aim of the NCB approach, therefore, is to estimate the NCB when $r_{x_1 y_1} \neq 0$.

Rozelle and Campbell (1969) were the first to suggest the NCB approach as a means of overcoming the problem of asymmetry as well as the first to offer recommendations for estimating the NCB. Their procedure is an attempt to live with spuriousness. Cross-lagged correlations are assumed to result from both the persistence of prior associations and the potential causal processes operating between t_1 and t_2. The authors first estimate the spuriousness that would occur without the effect of x_1 on y_2 or y_1 on x_2 (the NCB) and then infer the existence and nature of cause as a deviation from the estimate. This estimate is typically a non-zero NCB. The second derivation of the NCB approach, developed principally by Heise (1970), is an effort to use higher-order statistics, path coefficients, to create the conditions necessary for a zero NCB.

NON-ZERO NCB

Since spurious cross-lagged associations stem from the persistence of durable synchronous relationships, Rozelle and Campbell estimate the NCB from observed synchronous correlations. The estimate is an attenuated, average synchronous correlation, symbolized here as r_0, in which

$$r_0 = \bar{r}_s \sqrt{\hat{r}_{x_1 x_2} \hat{r}_{y_1 y_2}} \qquad (13.5a)$$

where

$$\bar{r}_s = \frac{r_{x_1 y_1} + r_{x_2 y_2}}{2}$$
(13.5b)

and where

$$\sqrt{\hat{r}_{x_1 x_2} \hat{r}_{y_1 y_2}}$$

is the *attenuation coefficient* used to adjust average synchronous correlation at a rate equal to the average rate of attenuation found for x and y. This is calculated as the geometric mean of the diachronic correlations, $r_{x_1 x_2}$ and $r_{y_1 y_2}$, after each coefficient has been adjusted for the attenuation associated with unreliable measurement:

$$\hat{r}_{x_1 x_2} = \frac{r_{x_1 x_2}}{\bar{r}_{xx}} \quad \text{and} \quad \hat{r}_{y_1 y_2} = \frac{r_{y_1 y_2}}{\bar{r}_{yy}}$$
(13.5c)

where

$$\bar{r}_{xx} = \sqrt{(r_{x_1 x_1})(r_{x_2 x_2})} \quad \text{and} \quad \bar{r}_{yy} = \sqrt{(r_{y_1 y_1})(r_{y_2 y_2})}$$
(13.5d)

in which $r_{x_1 x_1}$, $r_{x_2 x_2}$, $r_{y_1 y_1}$, and $r_{y_2 y_2}$ are the split-half reliability coefficients with the Spearman–Brown Correction.

Once calculated, the estimate is used to evaluate the source and direction of causal relationships. All inferences about cause are dependent upon whether $r_{x_1 y_2}$, $r_{y_1 x_2}$, or both are significantly different from r_0. Whatever its actual sign, a cross-lagged correlation that is significantly less than the NCB is assumed to reflect a negative cause; one which is significantly larger indicates a positive cause. For example, if $r_0 = .55$, $r_{x_1 y_2} = .85$, and $r_{y_1 x_2} = .35$, it is inferred that

$$x \underset{(-)}{\overset{(+)}{\rightleftarrows}} y$$

Inferences are also made about the existence of simultaneous, bidirectional causality. If both $r_{x_1 y_2}$ and $r_{y_1 x_2}$ are greater than r_0, the relationship is assumed to be a nonrecursive, positive–positive feedback system. If both are smaller than r_0, negative cause with negative feedback is inferred.

EVALUATION. The Rozelle and Campbell technique has some advantages over previously discussed derivations of the CLPA model. It avoids the difficulty of interpreting asymmetry. It also increases the power of the analysis to include the detection of nonrecursive positive–positive and negative–negative causal systems. (It will be recalled that the most advanced forms of the asymmetry method are limited to recursive systems and to nonrecursive systems in which the influences are of the opposite sign.) Nevertheless, the advantages of the non-zero NCB do not outweigh the considerable disadvantages of the Rozelle and Campbell technique.

The problem is not with NCB which, if adequately treated, can offer a useful alternative, or at least a supplement, to asymmetry as a method for making causal inference. The principal difficulty is the authors' reliance on synchronous correlations as the basis for making causal inference and their abandonment of the "finite causal lag" assumption in favor of instantaneous cause.

The authors assume that cause is instantaneous and that cross-lags represent the attenuated effects of prior causal processes that have been partially "stored" or preserved through time. This is the reason for attenuating $\bar{r}_s$. They attenuate the average cross-sectional association at a rate equal to that of x and y over the period of the study, presumably to provide a more equitable standard with which to compare cross-lagged correlations. It would appear, however, that the abandonment of the finite causal lag assumption defeats the purpose of working with cross-lagged data. (Recall that the logic of CLPA is that if cause precedes effect, prior cause will have a greater relationship with subsequent effect than effect will have with a later and presumably unrelated cause.) This leaves no basis for causal inference. If cause is instantaneous, how can cross-lagged correlations ever be larger than $r_{x_1y_1}$, the point of actual causation? Even if $r_{x_1y_1}$ or an average of $r_{x_1y_1}$ and $r_{x_2y_2}$ is attenuated at the average rate of x and y, the strongest cross-lagged correlation will logically never be *larger* than the relationship closest in time to the actual point of causation, the NCB. Once one abandons the notion of finite causal lag, it is no longer clear why $r_{x_1y_2}$ and $r_{y_1x_2}$ should differ as a result of any causal process operating between x and y. Certainly, cause and effect may *both* attenuate over time. Which cross-lagged correlation is more distant from the NCB will depend not upon cause internal to the set but upon such things as the temporal stability of x and y or the relative magnitude of S_{x_1}, and S_{y_1}.

Additional problems stem from the reliance upon synchronous correlations as the primary basis for causal inference. It will be recalled that Yee and Gage relied upon the assumption of steadily increasing and decreasing synchronous correlations. In using the same relationships as the basis for the NCB estimate, Rozelle and Campbell (1969:77) find it necessary to make the opposite assumption of equal or stable synchronous correlations. It is difficult to contemplate a NCB that varies from one observation to the next as a result of changes in cross-correlations. It is not advisable to average the synchronous correlations, as the authors originally suggested, since there is no reason to believe that the factor responsible for the different synchronous correlations can be averaged (Cook and Campbell, 1974; Kenny, 1973).

The non-zero NCB derivation promises to be much more useful if used within the basic model referred to throughout this analysis, in which the true causal lag is assumed to be equal to the interval t_1-t_2 and the synchronous correlations are considered to be spurious products of prior causal processes. In those cases when synchronous correlations are stable over time, this allows either correlation to serve as a crude estimate of the amount of spuriousness that can be expected in $r_{x_1 y_2}$ and $r_{y_1 x_2}$ when there is no causal process operating within the set. Any such analysis should serve to supplement the asymmetry approach, not as an alternative.

ZERO NCB

The zero NCB procedure applies what is popularly referred to as "causal modeling": the Simon–Blalock and Path Analytical techniques (Blalock, 1964; Heise, 1969; Land, 1969). As other applications in this chapter have demonstrated, these are actually only two forms, though admittedly predominant forms, of causal modeling. As applied to CLPA, there is little difference between the Simon–Blalock procedure and path analysis, except for their respective reliances upon partial correlation and regression coefficients. Nor is there a substantial difference between either technique and the asymmetry method when used with the identical higher-order coefficient. The differences are essentially those between trying to live with spuriousness and trying to eliminate it altogether and between inferring cause on the basis of asymmetry among cross-lags and relying instead on an NCB.

Assuming the system is closed, the zero NCB procedure eliminates spuriousness by adjusting each cross-lagged coefficient for the confounding influences *within* the model. It is assumed that if one variable has no influence upon the state of another variable at a later point in time, the adjusted coefficient will be zero. Assuming positive cross-lagged correlations, it is expected that if x has no effect on y during the interval t_1-t_2, $r_{x_1 y_2} = (r_{x_1 y_1})(r_{y_1 y_2})$. Therefore, a control for y_1 will reduce $r_{x_1 y_2}$ to zero, the appropriate conclusion being that x does not influence y. If x_1 has a positive impact, $r_{x_1 y_2} > (r_{x_1 y_1})(r_{y_1 y_2})$; that is, the relationship will be greater than that which would be expected from a purely spurious association. The adjusted coefficient will therefore be larger than zero. Similarly, if

$$x \xrightarrow{(-)} y$$

$r_{x_1 y_2} < (r_{x_1 y_1})(r_{y_1 y_2})$. The procedure is applicable to any form of recursive or nonrecursive causal system for a $2v2w$ panel. The statistics used in these procedures may be any one of the higher-order coefficients previously discussed. For the reasons already stated, it is preferable to use the unstandardized regression coefficient with the prior state of the dependent variable residualized. If one cannot assume equivalency of scales, either $B_{y_2 x_1 \cdot y_1}$ or $r_{(y_2 \cdot y_1) x_1}$ is appropriate, though a lack of equivalency is not serious when coefficients are expected to adjust to zero.

EVALUATION. The most useful and powerful of the CLPS derivations is the zero NCB. It avoids the problems of asymmetry and the equivocality characteristic of other forms of CLPA. Like the non-zero NCB, it can handle the full range of causal systems possible for $2v2w$ panel data while avoiding the difficulties of relying upon synchronous correlations as the primary basis for causal inference.

A method is only as good as its assumptions, however, and in causal modeling, the assumption of *closure* needs attention. Both the asymmetry and NCB methods can be adapted to incorporate weaker versions of this assumption, but neither can escape it in full. When closure cannot be assumed and the extraneous influences are *unknown*, the *asymmetry* method using higher-order coefficients is the more practical procedure (since controls internal to the model will not reduce spurious associations to zero). The same is true when measurement error is assumed. Even then, one may proceed with *asymmetry* only under very specific conditions.

Since this and other assumptions are so essential to the validity of either method, the closing section of this chapter addresses some of the more serious issues in this area and available means of handling them.

RELAXING SOME CRITICAL ASSUMPTIONS

The relatively weak nature of CLPA (in terms of control and manipulation) makes the assumptions of the model much more suspect and therefore more important than is the case for more rigorous experimental and quasi-experimental designs (Campbell and Stanley, 1963). Given the exploratory nature of much political science, some assumptions — such as closure, congruency, or equality of causal lags — are unknown or unknowable to the researcher wishing to make causal inferences. There is consequently a need to replace, relax, or find alternative means of support for the less tenable axioms. This section explores some of these possibilities.

THE NATURE OF CAUSAL LAGS

It will be recalled that there are six assumptions to the basic CLPA model: generality, continuity, finite causal lags, congruency, equality, and closure. The assumptions of *generality, continuity,* and *finite causal lags* are indispensable to CLPA. Unless *both* diachronic relationships approach unity, suggesting the absence of any causal process during the period of study and therefore the violation of one or more of these assumptions, one may usually proceed with CLPA while relaxing the remaining assumptions of *congruency*, *equality*, and *closure*.

CONGRUENCY AND EQUALITY

The problem of *congruency* is to fit the appropriate measurement interval to the true causal lag. It may take one of two forms: (1) choosing the appropriate interval *between observations* congruent with the true causal lag; or (2) setting the length of the interval *comprising a single observation*. The latter involves the working assumption "that the time required to measure one sample unit on all variables is less than the causal lag" (Heise, 1970:11). As Heise points out, this is most likely to become a serious problem in aggregate data analysis in which the units of analysis are based on extended time periods (encompassing a month, a year, or more). Whether this provides a handicap to the use of CLPA depends upon the nature of the change studied. Aggregate data analyses often focus upon processes (such as economic stability or development, political institutionalization or decay, domestic or international conflict, or trends in public policy) that involve long-term change ranging over years, even decades, where a measurement unit of a month or a year is comparably small. In such instances, CLPA is quite applicable.

The problem of choosing the proper interval between observations is more serious. One is in danger of missing the causal process altogether. It would, nevertheless, be misleading to think of this as a problem of fitting a measurement interval to a single causal lag. The assumption of perfect congruency is both untenable and unnecessary. It is untenable because one rarely knows what is the period required for one full causal lag. Presumably, the purpose of the study is to discover whether causation even exists. The assumption is unnecessary because, assuming generality and continuity, the analysis is applied not to a single, unique event that must be precisely fitted or else go unobserved but to an on-going, continuous process that may be measured at any period of time.

It is for this reason much safer to err in the direction of a measurement interval that is *too long* rather than to risk a shorter interval that ceases before a causal process has had time to operate and its effect to become manifest. In the event one overshoots the true causal lag, causation does not necessarily go unobserved. Rather than capture a single causal lag, the period of measurement encompasses a *subset* of causal lags, the exact number or length of which is of little significance. Cross-lagged coefficients calculated for an extended period represent the *average* association produced by the series of causal operations occurring during the length of the study. Thus, in the recursive system

$$x \xrightarrow{(+)} y$$

in which the measurement interval extends well beyond the period required for x to produce a change in y, $b_{y_2 x_1 \cdot y_1}$ reflects the average change produced in y by x during the period $t_1 - t_2$. It indicates the long-term influence of continuous and repeated effect of x (which itself might have fluctuated moderately around some mean value) during the length of the study.

Difficulties remain, of course. Existing research (Pelz and Lew, 1970) has demonstrated that CLPA with 2v2w data is risky when (1) the *causal agent is highly unstable*[9] or (2) the system is *nonrecursive with mutually contradictory influences* (e.g., positive cause, negative feedback). When the independent variable is highly unstable, the cross-lagged associations resulting from causes internal to the model may attenuate very rapidly. With respect to the example

$$x \xrightarrow{(+)} y$$

there is a real danger that x_1 will have little relationship with y_2, the latter being primarily the product of some later and radically different value of x (e.g., $x_{1.2}, x_{1.4}, \ldots x_{1.9}$). In mutually contradictory, nonrecursive systems, research indicates marked oscillation in path coeffiients when the length of the lags,

$$x \xrightarrow{(+)} y \text{ and } y \xrightarrow{(-)} x$$

are unequal (Pelz and Lew, 1970). On the other hand, in stable recursive systems or nonrecursive systems in which cause and feedback are of the same sign, valid and reliable coefficients are obtained with measurement intervals substantially longer (indicated up to five times as long or more) than the true causal lag.

The problem of *equal causal lag* is an extension of the congruency problem to nonrecursive systems. In systems involving short-term stability and causal influences of the same sign, the safest procedure is to err in the direction of overestimating the true causal lag. Where instability or negative feedback is suspected, three waves or more are advisable.

---

[9] One of the problems in deciding to proceed with CLPA is in developing an *independent* measure of stability. Weak diachronic relationships are of little value, since they will reflect causal processes internal to the model and since one normally does not know which variable, whether x or y, neither or both, is a true causal agent. Information about the internal consistency of the variables is advantageous for making this determination, but the optimal solution involves repetition of the study beyond two waves to see if the alleged independent variable remains stable and if the results can be successfully replicated.

CLOSURE

The problem of any causal analysis is to delimit the system so that one can logically specify cause. As long as the system remains open, any two variables internal to the set may be related, because of their shared relationship to one or more variables not explicitly considered, thus confounding the analysis. This does not require that x and y exist in a vacuum. Either may be affected by any number of variables without threatening the analysis; and if b is used, the results are generalizable (Blalock, 1964:50–51, 83–84, 126). The assumptions that are generally necessary are that the error terms of t_2 variables are uncorrelated with either (1) t_1 variables or (2) the error terms of t_1 variables.

These assumptions must be somewhat modified for CLPA. The normal assumption that the error terms of the dependent variables may be correlated is unacceptable. Since the four-variable causal model in CLPA is really a two-variable set with measurement at two points in time, if the dependent variables x_2 and y_2 share a common relationship with a third variable or variables, so will the independent and dependent variables, x_1 with y_2 and y_1 with x_2 (unless, of course, either one or both the variables are highly unstable over time).

When considered alone, the assumption about separate and uncorrelated error terms involving the cross-lagged relationships may be relaxed if the extraneous influences can be assumed to be *stable*. This is true of both the *asymmetry* and *NCB* approaches. The *asymmetry* method assumes that cross-lagged associations are, at least in part, spurious. The source of the spuriousness does not matter, whether the result of prior interaction between x and y or of shared relationships with additional variables. As long as the extraneous influences producing a spurious association between x and y are stable throughout the analysis, they will be reflected *equally* in both the cross-lags and therefore will not alter the symmetry of the model. Any asymmetry that does occur results from influences operating within the set during the period of observation.

The presence of autocorrelated error involving the diachronic relationships complicates the problem, however. The error terms for the variables in each diachronic correlation will normally be correlated, since they are actually disturbances for the same variable measured at different points in time. Unless the disturbances are highly unstable, ordinary least-squares partialing procedures will provide biased estimates of the cross-lagged relationships. Techniques are available for estimating and correcting for autocorrelated error (Hibbs, 1974:293ff; Namboodiri *et al.*, 1975:519–526); but they require information about disturbances associated with prior operations of the system. In the social sciences, where time-series data involving multiple temporal observations are still fairly rare, such corrections are often impractical, if not impossible.

Thus CLPA may only proceed under a narrow range of conditions: (1) when the system is closed; (2) when it is open but the extraneous influences on either x or y alone are highly unstable over time or when the extraneous influences are stable but have an equal impact on both $r_{x_1y_2}$ and $r_{y_1x_2}$. If autocorrelated error cannot be assumed to be absent or, if present, cannot be assumed to be equal for both diachronic relationships, then the extent of the bias must be estimated and used to adjust the cross-lagged coefficients. If the assumptions are untenable and the corrections not possible, the disturbances must be identified, incorporated directly into the model, and controlled. The path-estimate equations of CLPA models that have been expanded in this manner are the same as those of an ordinary multiple-regression equation, with each t_2 variable being regressed off all t_1 variables specified in the model. For example, in the case where a third variable, z_1, is identified as a disturbance and brought into the model, the cross-lagged coefficients are: $b_{y_2x_1 \cdot y_1z_1}$ and $b_{x_2y_1 \cdot x_1z_1}$.

What is the procedure when one has no *a priori* basis for specifying disturbances? The expansion of the $2v2w$ model to incorporate known disturbances is the safest and most practical procedure for CLPA, but this requires that researchers know or suspect confounding influences and pinpoint and measure the variables in question. Is there any way of knowing when the assumption of closure has been violated? How does one locate the disturbance that must be incorporated into the analysis? Unfortunately, there are no satisfactory answers to either question. Several indicators have been suggested for detecting violation of closure (Campbell and Clayton, 1961; Pelz and Andrews, 1964), but they are inconclusive. To the potential user of CLPA, the best advice for avoiding these kinds of problems is to know the data and to think through the relevant theory *before* proceeding with the analysis.

CONCLUSION

All causal analysis is based on some causal model, no matter how implicit, inconsistent, or underdeveloped it may appear. The confidence that can be placed in substantive conclusions depends, in large part, on the faith one has in the assumptions of the model and in the empirical procedures used to substantiate them. For these reasons, when used with an explicit formal model, CLPA provides a more convincing and more powerful basis for causal inference than cross-sectional analysis. It is able to replace or relax some of the key assumptions normally taken as axioms when working with the latter. First, the notion of temporal priority of cause provides an *empirical* basis for inferring the direction of causal relationships. Second, research is not limited to the study of recursive or unidirectional systems. The analysis can consider the possibility of simultaneous feedback and mutual interaction. It is less likely to overlook feedback that, at any one point in time, may be concealed by stronger but opposite influences either from within or without the model. Third, some assumptions, such as the absence of measurement error, are more easily relaxed. Others that appear particularly troublesome, such as congruence and equality of causal lags, are not unique to longitudinal studies, and when made explicit in cross-sectional analyses, also provide cause for consternation.

However, compared to more rigorous experimental and quasi-experimental designs (in terms of the ability to manipulate and control), CLPA is a relatively weak procedure, limited in its ability *empirically* to narrow down, unravel, and specify causal relationships. Given these limitations, the specification and clarification of the model are, therefore, very important. The choice of a model, from the large number available, will influence the substantive conclusions derived from the analysis (Duncan, 1969).

There is much in common among the major derivations of CLPA. Amid the diversity and confusion, there is a fair amount of agreement about the basic assumptions of the analysis and about the problems encountered. Nevertheless, there are important disagreements too, principally about the empirical procedures for overcoming the limitations of the basic design and about the specific assumptions the corrections entail. The primary purpose of this chapter has been to explicate these similarities and differences and, in so doing, to provide a basis for evaluating the relative utility of the CLPA derivations.

Which derivation is most adequate for any given study depends upon the nature of the observations and the credibility of basic assumptions for the particular problem under investigation. If the model can be confidently delimited at some point, the most powerful analysis is provided by the zero NCB approach. If not, and if one is forced to work with an unknown amount of spuriousness, it is better to employ *asymmetry* as a basis for inferring *most probable cause*. In either case, statistical adjustments, in the form of higher-order coefficients, remain necessary as the most practical and efficient means of controlling for prior operations of the system. Which statistic is used depends upon what kinds of assumptions the researcher is willing to make about the nature of the data. Finally, the safest procedure, where possible, is to expand the model to include those disturbances most likely to confound the analysis and to extend the observations to at least a third wave to provide a check on the validity and reliability of the 2v2w findings.

REFERENCES

Bereiter, Carl. "Some Persisting Dilemmas in the Measurement of Change." In *Problems of Measuring Change,* edited by Chester Harris. Madison: University of Wisconsin Press, 1963.

Blalock, Hubert M. "Four-Variable Causal Models and Partial Correlation." *American Journal of Sociology* 68 (1962):182–194.

Blalock, Hubert M. "Correlated Independent Variables: The Problem of Multicolinearity." *Social Forces* 42 (1963):233–237.

Blalock, Hubert M. *Causal Inferences in Nonexperimental Research.* Chapel Hill: University of North Carolina Press, 1964.

Blalock, Hubert M. "Causal Inferences, Closed Populations, and Measurement of Association." *American Political Science Review* 61 (1967):130–136.

Blalock, Hubert M. *Causal Models in the Social Sciences.* Chicago: Aldine Publishing Co., 1971.

Blalock, Hubert M. *Social Statistics.* New York: McGraw-Hill, 1972.

Bohrnstedt, G. W. "Some Observations on the Measurement of Change." In *Sociological Methodology 1969,* edited by E. F. Borgatta and G. W. Bohrnstedt. San Francisco: Jossey-Bass, 1969.

Campbell, Donald T. "From Description to Experimentation: Interpreting Trends as Quasi-Experiments." In *Problems in Measuring Change,* edited by C. W. Harris. Madison: University of Wisconsin Press, 1963.

Campbell, Donald T., and Clayton, K. N. "Avoiding Regression Effects in Panel Studies of Communication Impact." *Studies in Public Communication.* Chicago: University of Chicago Department of Sociology 3 (1961):99–118.

Campbell, Donald T., and Stanley, J. C. *Experimental and Quasi-Experimental Designs for Research.* Chicago: Rand McNally, 1963.

Caporaso, James A. "Quasi-Experimental Approaches to Social Science: Perspectives and Problems." In *Quasi-Experimental Approaches,* edited by James A. Caporaso and Leslie L. Roos, Jr. Evanston, Ill.: Northwestern University Press, 1973.

Chaffee, Steven H., Ward, L. Scott, and Tipton, Leonard P. "Mass Communication and Political Socialization." *Journalism Quarterly* 47 (1970):647–659, 666.

Cook, Thomas D., and Campbell, Donald T. "Correlational Design." In *Handbook of Industrial and Organizational Research,* edited by M. D. Dunnette. Chicago: Rand McNally, 1974.

Crano, William D., Kenny, David A., and Campbell, Donald T. "Does Intelligence Cause Achievement, A Cross-Lagged Panel Analysis." *Educational Psychology* 63 (1972):258–275.

Darlington, Richard B. "Multiple Regression in Psychological Research and Practice." *Psychological Bulletin* 69 (1968):161–182.

DuBois, P. H., and Manning, W. H. "Methods of Research in Technical Training." Technical Report No. 3, ONR Contract No. NONR-816(02). St. Louis: Washington University, 1957.

Duncan, Otis Dudley. "Some Linear Models for Two-Wave, Two-Variable Panel Analysis." *Psychological Bulletin* 72 (1969):177–182.

DuVall, Raymond, and Welfling, Mary. "Determinants of Political Institutionalization in Black Africa." In *Quasi-Experimental Approaches,* edited by James A. Caporaso and Leslie L. Roos, Jr. Evanston, Ill.: Northwestern University Press, 1973.

Fisher, Franklin M. "Causation and Specification in Economic Theory and Econometrics." *Syntheses* 20 (1969):489–500.

Fisher, Franklin M. "A Correspondence Principle for Simultaneous Equation Models." *Econometrica* 38 (1970):73–92.

Goldberger, Arthur S. "Econometrics and Psychometrics: A Survey of Communalities." *Psychometrika* 36 (1971):83–107.

Gordon, Robert A. "Issues in Multiple Regression." *American Journal of Sociology* 73 (1968):592–616.

Heise, David R. "Problems in Path Analysis and Causal Inference." In *Sociological Methodology 1969,* edited by E. F. Borgatta and G. W. Bohrnstedt. San Francisco: Jossey-Bass, 1969.

Heise, David R. "Causal Inference From Panel Data." In *Sociological Methodology 1970*, edited by E.F. Borgatta and G.W. Bohrnstedt. San Francisco: Jossey-Bass, 1970.

Hibbs, Douglas A., Jr. "Problems of Statistical Estimation and Causal Inference in Time-Series Regression Models." *Sociological Methodology 1973-1974*, edited by Herbert Costner. San Francisco: Jossey-Bass, 1974.

Howard, Kenneth J., and Krause, Merton S. "Some Comments on Techniques for Estimating the Source and Direction of Influence in Panel Data." *Psychological Bulletin* 74 (1970):219-224.

Kemeny, John G. *A Philosopher Looks at Science.* New York: Van Nostrand Reinhold Co., 1959.

Kenny, David A. "Cross-lagged and Common Forms in Panel Data." In *Structural Equation Models in the Social Sciences*, edited by A. E. Goldberger and O. D. Duncan. New York: Seminar Press, 1973.

Kerlinger, Fred N., and Pedhazur, Elazar. *Multiple Regression in Behavioral Research.* New York: Holt, Rinehart and Winston, Inc., 1973.

Land, Kenneth C. "Principles of Path Analysis." In *Sociological Methodology 1969*, edited by E. F. Borgatta and G. W. Bohrnstedt. San Francisco: Jossey-Bass, 1969.

Lieberman, Bernhart, ed. *Contemporary Problems in Statistics.* New York: Oxford University Press, 1971.

Lord, Frederic M. "Further Problems in the Measuring of Growth." *Educational and Psychological Measurement* 18 (1958):437-451.

Lord, Frederic M. "Elementary Models for Measuring Change." In *Problems of Measuring Change*, edited by Chester Harris. Madison: University of Wisconsin Press, 1963.

Namboodiri, N. Krishnan, Carter, Lewis F., and Blalock, Hubert. *Applied Multivariate Analysis and Experimental Designs.* New York: McGraw-Hill, 1975.

Pelz, Donald C., and Andrews, F. M. "Detecting Causal Priorities in Panel Study Data." *American Sociological Review* 29 (1964):836-848.

Pelz, Donald C., and Lew, Robert A. "Heise's Causal Model Applied." In *Sociological Methodology 1970*, edited by E. F. Borgatta and G. W. Bohrnstedt. San Francisco: Jossey-Bass, 1970.

Peters, Charles C., and Van Voohris, Walter F. *Statistical Procedures and Their Mathematical Bases.* Westport, Conn.: Greenwood Press, 1940.

Rozelle, Richard M. "An Exploration of Two Quasi-Experimental Designs: The Cross-Lagged Panel Correlation and the Multiple Time Series." Masters thesis, Northwestern University, 1965.

Rozelle, Richard M., and Campbell, D.T. "More Plausible Rival Hypotheses in the Cross-lagged Panel Correlation Technique." *Psychological Bulletin* 71 (1969):74-80.

Sandell, Rolf Gunnar. "Note on Choosing between Competing Interpretations of Cross-Lagged Panel Correlations." *Psychological Bulletin* 75 (1971):367-368.

Shingles, Richard D. "Community Action and Attitude Change: A Case of Adult Political Socialization." *Experimental Study of Politics* 4 (1975):38-81.

Simon, Herbert. "Spurious Correlation: A Causal Interpretation." *Journal of American Statistical Association* 49 (1954):467-479.

Yee, A. H., and N. L. Gage. "Techniques for Estimating the Source and Direction of Causal Influence in Panel Data." *Psychological Bulletin* 70 (1968):115-126.

14

The Reciprocal Effects of the Substantive Complexity of Work and Intellectual Flexibility: A Longitudinal Assessment*

Melvin L. Kohn

Carmi Schooler

From early Marx to "Work in America" (HEW, 1973), it has been argued that work affects such facets of personality as values, orientation, and intellectual functioning. From early Taylor to the most recent personnel-selection manuals, it has been argued — or at any rate assumed — that personality is formed before occupational careers begin, with people fitting into and perhaps molding their jobs, but not being affected by them. The issue of whether jobs affect or only reflect personality is obviously crucial to occupational social psychology. More than that, the issue of the nature and direction of causal effects in the relationship between occupational conditions and psychological functioning provides a critical test of a theoretical question central to the entire field of social structure and personality — whether social structure affects personality only through its influence on childhood socialization processes or also through a continuing influence during the entire life span.

Our own interpretation of the processes by which social class affects values and orientation, for example, is premised on the assumption that people's positions in the stratificational system are systematically linked to

* Reprinted by permission of the authors from the *American Journal of Sociology* 84:24–52 (1978).

differences in the immediately impinging conditions of their lives which in turn affect their values, self-conception, and social orientation (see Kohn, 1969; Kohn and Schooler, 1969). In our analyses, we have found occupational conditions to be especially important in explaining the impact of social class on values and orientation. Our interpretation assumes that occupational conditions actually affect psychological functioning. But if the interrelationship of social class, occupational conditions, and psychological function were the result solely of selective recruitment and job-molding processes, our interpretation would be invalid.

In this chapter, we address the issue of the nature and direction of effects in the relationship between occupational conditions and psychological functioning by attempting to assess the reciprocal relationship between one pivotal dimension of occupational structure, the substantive complexity of work, and one pivotal dimension of psychological functioning, intellectual flexibility. We choose the substantive complexity of work as the occupational condition to be assessed in this analysis for three reasons. Our previous analyses have shown substantive complexity to be a central element of occupational structure—an important determinant of occupational self-direction and an important "structural imperative" of the job (Kohn and Schooler (1973, pp. 102–5). Moreover, substantive complexity is as strongly correlated with psychological functioning as any other dimension of occupation we have examined (ibid, p. 104). Finally, we have excellent descriptive information about the substantive complexity of work, which we have been able to validate by comparison with the objective job assessments of trained occupational analysts (ibid, p. 106).

Our choice of intellectual flexibility as the aspect of psychological functioning assessed in this analysis is made in part because it offers us the greatest challenge—intellectual flexibility obviously affects recruitment into substantively complex jobs, and there is every reason to expect it to be one of the most resistant to change of all facets of psychological functioning we have measured. Moreover, intellectual flexibility—though not much studied by sociologists—is a part of psychological functioning so important that we must not unthinkingly assume it to be entirely the product of genetics and early life experience. Rather, we should empirically test the possibility that intellectual flexibility may be responsive to the experiences of adult life.

In earlier analyses based on the data of a cross-sectional survey carried out in 1964, we made provisional assessments of the reciprocal relationship between the substantive complexity of work and many facets of psychological functioning, including intellectual flexibility (Kohn, 1973; Kohn and Schooler, 1976). In those analyses, we used a method called "two-stage least squares," a relatively simple technique for estimating reciprocal causal models. Our findings constitute prima facie evidence that the substantive complexity of men's work does affect their psychological functioning, independently of the selection processes that draw men into particular fields of work and independently of men's efforts to mold their jobs to fit their needs, values, and capacities. But cross-sectional data cannot provide definitive evidence of causality; only analysis of longitudinal data, measuring real change in real people, can be definitive.

Moreover, while the cross-sectional data provided retrospective information about the substantive complexity of past jobs, it could not provide information about men's psychological functioning at the times they held those jobs. Thus, we had no way of statistically controlling earlier levels of intellectual flexibility in assessing the effect of substantive complexity (or anything else) on intellectual flexibility. Nor could we examine lagged effects: For example, we could not assess the effects of earlier levels of intellectual flexibility on the substantive complexity of later jobs. Our analyses were necessarily limited to assessing the contemporaneous reciprocal effects, as of 1964, of the men's then current levels of substantive complexity and psychological functioning.[1]

Now we are able to assess the reciprocal effects of substantive complexity and intellectual flexibility much more adequately, for we have conducted a 10-year follow-up survey of a representative portion of our original sample. In this chapter, we first describe and evaluate the data of the follow-up study. Then we explain the concepts *substantive complexity* and *intellectual flexibility* and develop "measurement models" for both of them. These models are designed to deal with the most perplexing problem of longitudinal analysis — separating errors in measurement from real change in the

[1] Robert M. Hauser subsequently suggested an intriguing method of stretching our cross-sectional data to meet some of the requirements of a longitudinal model — synthetic-cohort analysis. The essence of the method, as applied here, is to use data provided by the men who have had the median number of jobs (four) to provide estimates of the correlations involving intellectual flexibility as of 1964 and data provided by the men who have had one fewer than the median number of jobs to provide estimates of the correlations involving intellectual flexibility as of the time of the "immediately prior" job. The synthetic-cohort method enables us to answer this important question: What does the model we have constructed from the cross-sectional data imply about the relationship between earlier and later intellectual flexibility? If the model implies an improbably low correlation between earlier and later intellectual flexibility, this would cast doubt on its plausibility. If, on the other hand, the model implies an expectedly high correlation between earlier and later intellectual flexibility, this would increase the plausibility of the model. Using the basic theorem of path analysis (Duncan, 1966) and following procedures similar to those used by Duncan, Haller, and Portes (1968), we find the implied correlation between earlier and later intellectual flexibility to be .78. Given some degree of unreliability of measurement (an issue we shall presently address more precisely), this strikes us as being about as high a correlation as should be expected. In fact, the longitudinal data that we shall soon present show this estimate of the stability of intellectual flexibility to be reasonable, perhaps even too high, for an estimate that does not take measurement error into account.

phenomena studied. Finally, we utilize the data provided by the measurement models to do a causal analysis of the reciprocal effects of substantive complexity and intellectual flexibility.

THE LONGITUDINAL DATA

The earlier, cross-sectional analyses were based on interviews conducted in 1964 with a sample of 3101 men, representative of all men employed in civilian occupations in the United States. (For a general description of the sampling methods, see Sudman and Feldman (1965); for more specific information on sample and research design, see Kohn (1969, pp. 235 – 64.)

In 1974, the National Opinion Research Center (NORC) carried out a follow-up survey for us, interviewing a representative sample of approximately one-fourth of those men who were less than 65 years old. The age limitation was imposed to increase the probability that the men in the follow-up study would still be in the labor force.

In this study, as in all longitudinal studies, the question of the representativeness of the follow-up sample is crucial for assessing the accuracy of any analyses.[2] Of the 883 men randomly selected for the follow-up study, NORC succeeded in locating 820 (i.e., 93%) 10 years after the original survey — in itself an interesting social fact. Apparently, men who live their lives in the ordinary institutions of the society, although they may change residences a great many times, can be traced, given a modicum of cooperation from the post office, telephone company, past employers, and unions.

Of the 820 men located, 35 had died. Of the remaining 785 men, NORC actually reinterviewed 687, that is, 78% of those originally selected and 88% of those located and found to be alive. In terms of current experience in survey research, these are certainly acceptable figures. But we must nevertheless ask, Are the men who were reinterviewed representative of all those men whom we meant to interview? Can we generalize safely to the larger universe? We attempt to answer these questions by two types of analysis.

The first type of analysis involves systematic comparison of the social and psychological characteristics of the men who were reinterviewed with those of a truly representative sample of the male working population under the age of 65. We are in an optimum position to do this, for the men who were randomly excepted from the follow-up study constitute a representative subsample of the overall sample and thus are an appropriate comparison group. The differences between the two subsamples are few and small: The men reinterviewed were, as of the time of the original interviews, a little more intellectually flexible, somewhat more trustful, slightly less self-confident, and somewhat more "liberal" in their religious backgrounds than were those in the comparison group. But the two groups do not differ

---

[2] For an assessment of the representativeness of the original sample, see Kohn (1969) appendix C.

significantly in most of the characteristics important to our analyses — for example, education, social class, major occupational characteristics, age, and even urbanicity.

Our second method of assessing the representativeness of the follow-up sample is to repeat the major substantive analyses, again using the 1964 data but this time limiting the analyses to those men reinterviewed in 1974. The rationale is that, insofar as we get the same results from analyses of the follow-up subsample as from the total sample, we can be confident that the subsample provides a good base from which to generalize to the larger population. We have repeated all the principal analyses of the relationships among social class, occupational conditions, and psychological functioning. The smaller size of the subsample means that several secondary avenues cannot be explored and that some findings are no longer statistically significant. But the main findings hold up uniformly well. Thus, we can proceed to analyze the longitudinal data with confidence that whatever we find can be generalized to the larger population of men employed in the United States.

UNRELIABILITY AND CHANGE

We now face the core technical problem in longitudinal analysis — how to separate unreliability of measurement from real change in the phenomena studied. In principle, unreliability in the measurement of the independent variables is especially likely to confound causal analysis (Duncan, 1975, p. 117). In the present analysis, both substantive complexity and intellectual flexibility serve as principal independent variables vis-à-vis each other; it is the relative magnitude of their effects that is centrally at issue. Therefore, we need to assess how much of any apparent change in substantive complexity represents real change in men's job conditions over the 10-year interval between the two surveys and how much is a function of unreliability in the measuring instruments. Similarly, we need to assess how much of any apparent change in intellectual flexibility represents real change in the men's cognitive functioning and how much is a result of measurement error.

Recently, Jöreskog and his associates have introduced powerful new procedures for using maximum-likelihood confirmatory factor analysis to separate unreliability from change (see Jöreskog, 1969, 1970, 1973a,b; Jöreskog et al., 1970; Jöreskog and van Thillo, 1972; Jöreskog and Sörbom, 1976a,b; Werts et al., 1973, 1971).[3] The essence of these methods is the use

---

[3] Other instructive discussions of the issues involved in separating unreliability from change are found in Alwin (1973, 1976); Blalock (1969); Burt (1973); Hauser and Goldberger (1971); Heise (1969, 1970, 1975); Heise and Bohrnstedt (1970); Lord and Novick (1968); and Wheaton et al. (1977). Informative applications of the technique are provided in Alwin (1973); Bielby et al. (1977); Mason et al. (1976); and Otto and Featherman (1975).

of multiple indicators for each principal concept, inferring from the covariation of the indicators the degree to which each reflects the underlying concept that they all are hypothesized to reflect and the degree to which each reflects anything else, which for measurement purposes is considered to be error. The test of our success in differentiating "true scores" on the underlying concept from errors in the indicators is how well the hypothesized model reproduces the original variance–covariance matrix of the indicators.

The first step in the use of these procedures is to develop measurement models for the principal concepts — models that will later form the basis for a causal analysis. The measurement models must specify the relationships of indicators to concepts, take account of unreliability (or measurement error) in all the items that measure a concept, and allow for the possibility that measurement errors are correlated in repeated measurements of the same phenomena. For example, any errors in the information obtained in 1964 about the complexity of men's work with "things" or in our coding of this information might well be correlated with errors in the same type of information in 1974. Such correlated error in any constituent item might make our index of substantive complexity seem more or less stable than it really is (see Bohrnstedt, 1969). Before assessing changes and the reasons for such changes in the substantive complexity of work, we must remove the effects of correlated errors in measurement of the indicators of this concept.

A MEASUREMENT MODEL FOR SUBSTANTIVE COMPLEXITY

By the "substantive complexity of work," we mean the degree to which the work in its very substance requires thought and independent judgment. Substantively complex work by its very nature requires making many decisions that must take into account ill-defined or apparently conflicting contingencies. Although, in general, work with data or people is likely to be more complex than work with things, this is not always the case, and an index of the overall complexity of the work should reflect its degree of complexity in each of these three types of activity. Work with things can vary in complexity from ditch digging to sculpting; similarly, work with people can vary in complexity from receiving simple directions or orders to giving legal advice; and work with data can vary from reading instructions to synthesizing abstract conceptual systems.

Our information about the substantive complexity of men's work is derived from detailed questioning of each respondent about his work with things, with data or ideas, and with people. Early in the 1964 interview — immediately after learning the title of the respondent's principal occupation and its institutional locus — the interviewer asked these questions:

One thing we would like to be able to pin down particularly accurately is how much of your working time is spent reading and writing, how much working with your hands, and how much dealing with people. We realize, of course, that you can be doing two or even all three of these at the same time.

1. First—reading or writing. Here we should like to include any type of written materials—letters, files, memos, books, or blueprints. About how many hours a week do you spend reading, writing, dictating, or dealing with any kind of written materials on your job? (If any time at all.)

(a) What do you do?

(b) What are they [the materials] about?

2. Second—working with your hands, using tools, using or repairing machines. We should like to include everything that involves working with your hands—operating a lathe or a dentist's drill, moving furniture, playing the piano. About how many hours a week do you spend working with your hands on your job? (if any time at all.)

(a) What do you do? [Probe: What operations do you perform?]

(b) What materials do you work on?

(c) What tools or equipment do you use?

(d) [If relevant.] What do you do to set up and maintain your equipment?

3. Third—dealing with people. Here we do not mean to include passing the time of day but only conversations necessary for the job: for example, talking to your boss, teaching, supervising, selling, advising clients. About how many hours a week does your job require you to spend dealing with people? (if any time at all.)

What kinds of things do you do—do you teach students, supervise subordinates, receive instructions from the boss, sell to customers, advise clients, discuss the work with co-workers, or what? [Be sure to ascertain what he does and to whom.]

[If more than one such activity.] At which one of these do you spend the most time?

The foregoing questions provided the basis for seven ratings: appraisals of the complexity of each man's work with things, with data, and with people; an appraisal of the overall complexity of his work, regardless of whether he works primarily with data, people, or things; and estimates of the amount of time he spends working at each type of activity. In earlier analyses, we subjected these seven ratings to a one-dimensional exploratory factor analysis, which we then used as the basis for creating factor scores.

Now, instead of using exploratory factor analysis to create a single composite score, we treat all seven ratings of the 1964 job as "indicators" of the underlying but not directly measured concept, the substantive complexity of that job (see Fig. 14.1).[4] Each indicator is understood to reflect the underlying concept, which it measures only imperfectly, and some degree of error

---

[4] In Fig. 14.1, as in all subsequent figures and in the text, we present standardized values. These are more easily comprehended than metric values, and using them makes it possible to compare indicators in the measurement models and causal paths in the structural equation models (see Blalock, 1967). But all computations have been based on unstandardized variance–covariance matrices.

in measurement (see Alwin, 1973, p. 259 and n. 2; Lord and Novick, 1968, p. 72). The follow-up survey asks the same questions and makes the same seven ratings. Again, we treat these ratings as indicators of the underlying concept, in this instance the substantive complexity of the job held at the time of the 1974 interview. Again, we conceive of each indicator as reflecting the underlying concept, together with some degree of measurement error. We also allow for the possibility that errors of measurement are correlated over time — that whatever errors there may be in the measurement of complexity of work with things in the 1964 job, for example, may be correlated with errors in the measurement of complexity of work with things in the 1974 job.

We also have information about the complexity of each man's work in two of his earlier jobs, the first job he held for 6 months or longer and the job held immediately before his 1964 job. Both of these measures are approximate scores, based on extrapolations from limited job-history information (see Kohn and Schooler, 1973, pp. 111–112 and n. 21). In our earlier analyses, we treated these as two separate variables. In the present analysis, we have no real need for measures of substantive complexity at two separate times before 1964. But the logic of our measurement model calls for using multiple indicators of important concepts whenever it is possible to do so; it is the multiplicity of indicators that enables us to differentiate unreliability of measurement from change in true scores. We therefore treat these two measures as indicators of a single concept, *"earlier" substantive complexity.*

The overall fit of this model to the data, based on a χ^2 goodness-of-fit test, is fairly good: the total χ^2 is 644.42, with 94 degrees of freedom, for a ratio of 6.86 per degree of freedom. (In this test, χ^2 is a function of the discrepancies between the actual variance–covariance matrix and the variance–covariance matrix implied by the measurement model. Therefore, the better the fit, the smaller the χ^2 per degree of freedom.) But an examination of the first-order partial derivatives of the maximum-likelihood function (see Costner and Schoenberg, 1973; Sörbom, 1975) indicates that the fit of model to data could be improved by taking into account other correlated errors of measurement — notably correlations between errors in our overall rating of the complexity of each man's work and errors in our specific ratings of the complexity of his work with things, with data, and with people. Allowing these errors to correlate reduces the χ^2 to 439.34, with 88 degrees of freedom, for a ratio of 4.99. (The difference between the initial χ^2 and that in this modified model is 205.08. At 6 degrees of freedom, which is the difference between the degrees of freedom of the two models, this is clearly a statistically significant improvement.) All the parameters of this model are consistent with our earlier analyses. In particular, the complexity of work with data and with people and the overall complexity of the work are shown to bear a strong positive relationship to the underlying concept, while the

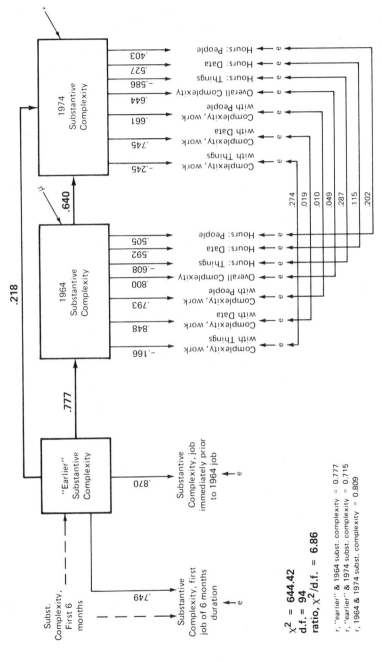

Figure 14.1. Measurement model for substantive complexity (preliminary); figures shown are standardized.

$\chi^2 = 644.42$
d.f. = 94
ratio, χ^2/d.f. = 6.86

r, "earlier" & 1964 subst. complexity = 0.777
r, "earlier" & 1974 subst. complexity = 0.715
r, 1964 & 1974 subst. complexity = 0.809

259

amount of time spent working with things is shown to be strongly negatively related to the concept in both 1964 and 1974. In these respects, the
model accurately reflects both our theoretical intent (see Kohn, 1969, pp.
139 – 140) and the factor loadings of the earlier exploratory factor analysis
(see Kohn and Schooler, 1973, n. 15).

There is, however, one flaw in this model, as well as in the earlier exploratory factor analysis: The complexity of men's work with things is depicted
as being negatively related to the substantive complexity of their work. In
principle, complexity of work in any realm — with things as well as data or
people — should contribute to the overall substantive complexity of the job.
What our model actually reflects is that we had classified men who do not
work with things into the lowest category of complexity of work with things;
thus, men who work entirely with data or with people are classified together
with ditch diggers in the lowest category and contrasted with men who do
complex work with things.

To achieve a model fully congruent with our theoretical intent, we exclude all men who do not work with things from the computation of correlations involving this indicator, on the rationale that not working with
things is qualitatively different from working with things at a low level of
complexity.[5] (Concretely, we treat not working with things as "missing
data" and use pairwise deletion in computing the correlations.) Again, we
allow errors in each indicator to correlate with errors in that same indicator
10 years later. As with the earlier model, the fit of model to data is improved
by taking into account other correlated errors. In this model, the error
correlations that best improve the fit of model to data are those between the
complexity of work with things and the amount of time spent working with
things, data, and people, both intratime and over time.[6] With these errors

---

[5] It is neither necessary nor desirable to follow a similar procedure for men who
do not work with data or people, because the logical implications for the measurement of substantive complexity of not working with things are different from those
of not working with data or people. Not working with things does not necessarily
imply anything about the substantive complexity of the job; certainly it is possible to
do substantively complex work that does not involve the direct manipulation of
physical objects. On the other hand, not working with written materials or people
does imply a low level of substantive complexity; it is hard to imagine a substantively complex job that does not require some reading (e.g., of blueprints or specifi-
cations) and some discussion with supervisors, co-workers, or others. Moreover, it is
rare for a job to require complex work with written materials and not even minimal
interaction with people or complex work with people and no reading or writing.

[6] It seems reasonable that these errors might be correlated, because descriptions
or evaluations of men's work with things might well affect or be affected by the
estimates made of how much time the men spend working in each type of activity.
Moreover, measurement errors may be similar for both interviews.

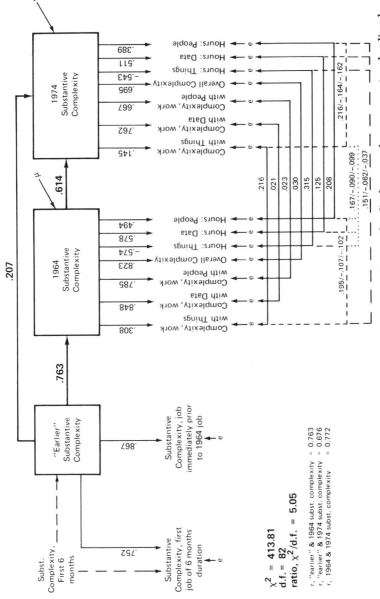

Figure 14.2. Measurement model for substantive complexity (final); figures shown are standardized.

261

allowed to correlate (Fig. 14.2), the overall χ^2 is 413.81, with 82 degrees of freedom, for a ratio of 5.05, which is nearly the same as that provided by the alternative model. What is more important, this model matches our theoretical intent exactly. The difference in the fit of model to data being minimal and the fit of model to theory much better, we shall employ the model depicted in Fig. 14.2 in our causal analyses. But to be certain that the causal inferences we draw are not somehow an artifact of the choice of measurement model, we also compute correlations for the alternative measurement model. Using this model would make no difference in the inferences we draw about the reciprocal effects of substantive complexity and intellectual flexibility.[7]

The most interesting information provided by the measurement model depicted in Figure 14.2 is the estimate of the overall stability in job complexity. The stability, as expected, is substantial; for example, the path from the substantive complexity of the 1964 job to that of the 1974 job is .61, and the correlation between the two is .77. The actual effect of earlier jobs on later jobs, as compared with the effect of other variables, can only be assessed in the causal analyses to come, when other independent variables are simultaneously considered. What the measurement model does tell us is that there has been considerable stability in the substantive complexity of the men's jobs over the course of their careers.

A MEASUREMENT MODEL FOR INTELLECTUAL FLEXIBILITY

Our index of intellectual flexibility is meant to reflect men's actual intellectual performance in the interview situation. In the 1964 interview, we

---

[7] A third approach to measuring substantive complexity, suggested by an *AJS* referee, is to split the sample into the logically possible subgroups defined in terms of whether the men work with things and also with data and people, with specified combinations of two of these three, or with a specified one of these three; then to estimate separate measurement models of substantive complexity for each subgroup for which there is an adequate number of cases; for each of the subgroups, to compute the covariances between the "true scores" for substantive complexity and for other pertinent concepts; and finally to see whether these variance–covariance matrices are essentially the same. If so, we can construct a common variance–covariance matrix for estimating the structural equation models. If not, we would have to estimate different structural equation models for the various subgroups. In fact, the only subgroup large enough to provide reliable estimates is that of the men who engage in all three activities — who work with things, data, and also people. We have reestimated the measurement models of substantive complexity and intellectual flexibility for this crucial subgroup and have carried out a structural equations causal analysis comparable to that discussed later in this chapter for the sample as a whole. This analysis fully supports the conclusions we derive from the causal analysis of the entire sample.

sampled a variety of indicators — including the men's answers to seemingly simple but highly revealing cognitive problems involving well-known issues, their handling of perceptual and projective tests, their propensity to agree when asked agree–disagree questions, and the impression they made on the interviewer during a long session that required a great deal of thought and reflection. None of these indicators is assumed to be completely valid; but we do assume that all the indicators reflect, in some substantial degree, men's flexibility in attempting to cope with the intellectual demands of a complex situation.

We claim neither that this index measures innate intellectual ability nor that intellectual flexibility evidenced in the interview situation is necessarily identical with intellectual flexibility as it might be manifested in other situations; we do not have enough information about the situational variability of intellectual functioning to be certain. We do claim that our index reflects men's actual intellectual functioning in a nonwork situation that seemed to elicit considerable intellectual effort from nearly all the respondents. That our index is not artifactual and that it measures an enduring characteristic is attested to by the evidence — to be presented shortly — of its remarkably high stability over time. Spaeth's (1976) analysis adds to the credibility of the index by showing that the correlations between an earlier variant of our index and various social phenomena are similar to those for more conventional indices of intellectual functioning.

More concretely and specifically, our index (Fig. 14.3) is based on seven indicators of each man's intellectual performance. These are (1) the Goodenough estimate of his intelligence (see Witkin et al., 1962), based on a detailed evaluation of the Draw-a-Person Test; (2) the appraisal of Witkin et al. (1962) of the sophistication of body concept in the Draw-a-Person Test; (3) a summary score for his performance on a portion of the Embedded Figures Test (see Witkin et al., 1962); (4) the interviewer's appraisal of the man's intelligence; (5) the frequency with which he agreed when asked the many agree–disagree questions included in the interview; (6) a rating of the adequacy of his answer to the apparently simple cognitive problem, "What are all the arguments you can think of for and against allowing cigarette commercials on TV?"; and (7) a rating of the adequacy of his answer to another relatively simple cognitive problem, "Suppose you wanted to open a hamburger stand and there were two locations available. What questions would you consider in deciding which of the two locations offers a better business opportunity?"

In the earlier analyses of the 1964 data, we performed an orthogonal principal components factor analysis of these various manifestations of intellectual flexibility. This analysis yielded two dimensions, one primarily perceptual, the other ideational. Since the ideational component of intellectual flexibility is of much greater theoretical interest, our analyses have focused on that dimension.

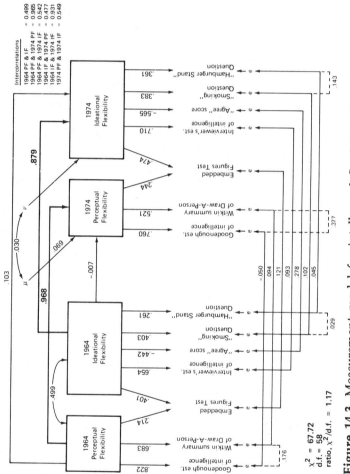

Figure 14.3. Measurement model for intellectual flexibility; figures shown are standardized.

264

In the follow-up study, we secured entirely comparable data after elaborate pretesting to be certain that the cognitive problems had the same meaning in 1974 as in 1964. The measurement model we now employ for intellectual flexibility is similar to that for substantive complexity in most respects, with the following exceptions. First, following the logic of the two-factor model derived from the earlier exploratory factor analysis, we posit two concepts underlying the seven indicators. Second, we have no assessments of intellectual flexibility prior to 1964, so there is nothing comparable to "earlier substantive complexity." Third, to take into account that two of our indicators are based on the same task, the Draw-a-Person Test, we allow those errors to be correlated. Finally, following a lead provided by the first-order partial derivatives, we also allow for the possibility of correlated error between the two cognitive problems.

We get slightly different estimates of the parameters of the measurement model, depending on whether we posit (as in the earlier analysis) that the two underlying concepts are necessarily orthogonal to each other or that they are possibly correlated with one another. The nonorthogonal model provides a significantly better fit to the data, so we shall employ it in the causal analyses that follow. (In any event, estimates of the reciprocal effects of substantive complexity and ideational flexibility prove to be virtually identical, whether based on orthogonal or on nonorthogonal measurement models of intellectual flexibility.)

Figure 14.3 depicts the measurement model for intellectual flexibility, with the two underlying concepts allowed to correlate. The model shows that some of the indicators of intellectual flexibility are not especially reliable; this is the very reason we thought it necessary to construct a measurement model that would differentiate unreliability of measurement from actual intellectual functioning. Judging by the goodness-of-fit test, the model is successful in achieving this objective: the overall χ^2 is 67.72, with 58 degrees of freedom, for a ratio of 1.17, which means that the model provides a very good approximation to the actual variances and covariances of the indicators.

From this model, we learn that the path from men's levels of ideational flexibility in 1964 to their levels in 1974, shorn of measurement error, is a very substantial .88, and that the correlation between the two is an even higher .93. We conclude that there has been great stability in men's levels of ideational flexibility over the 10-year period.[8] The question for causal analysis is whether job conditions have nevertheless had some effect.

---

[8] Parenthetically, the correlation between an index of ideational flexibility based on factor scores derived from exploratory factor analysis of the 1964 data and a similar index based on the same factor loadings for 1974 is a much lower .59. This finding dramatically illustrates the moral that methodologists have long been preaching—that correlations may be radically understated when they are not corrected for the attenuation that results from unreliability of measurement.

CAUSAL ANALYSIS: THE RECIPROCAL EFFECTS OF SUBSTANTIVE COMPLEXITY AND INTELLECTUAL FLEXIBILITY

To do structural equation causal analyses, we have computed the variances and the (unstandardized) covariances between the "true scores" for job complexity at the various stages of career, intellectual flexibility in 1964 and 1974, and all the other variables that will enter into the analyses.[9] These variances and covariances are the data on which the causal models of the reciprocal relationship between substantive complexity and intellectual flexibility are based.[10]

A reciprocal relationship can occur contemporaneously (albeit not necessarily instantaneously) or more gradually over time. Our earlier analyses, using cross-sectional data, could consider only contemporaneous effects. But there is no reason in principle why substantive complexity and intellectual flexibility might not affect each other both contemporaneously and more gradually over time. We shall therefore assess causal models that allow the possibility of both contemporaneous and lagged reciprocal effects (Fig. 14.4). Since our concern in these analyses is entirely with the ideational component of intellectual flexibility, we shall henceforth use the terms *ideational flexibility* and *intellectual flexibility* interchangeably and limit the analyses to ideational flexibility.[11]

The model depicted in Fig. 14.4 includes as potentially pertinent exogenous variables all social characteristics that prior research literature and our own earlier analyses give us any reason to believe might affect either sub-

[9] Our procedure has been to develop measurement models independently for each concept, compute the covariances among "true scores," and use these covariances as the data for causal analysis. Computing the covariances of the concepts can be done with either the ACOVS or the LISREL computer program. Using either procedure, one develops models combining the principal features of two or more measurement models. In developing these combined models, the crucial requirement is to fix, at the values derived from the measurement models, those parameters that define the relationships between concepts and their indicators (e.g., the paths from concepts to indicators, the residuals for the indicators, and the correlations among those residuals) while not inadvertently constraining the interrelationships of the concepts (e.g., when using LISREL, by fixing causal paths at zero or some other value instead of allowing them to be free or by fixing the unexplained variance of any of the concepts).

[10] In developing the causal (i.e., linear structural equation) models, we employed the LISREL computer program (Jöreskog and van Thillo, 1972), as subsequently modified by Ronald Schoenberg. Pertinent writings on the strategy of this type of causal analysis are those of Burt (1976); Duncan (1975); Heise (1970, 1975); Jöreskog (1973a,b); Jöreskog and Sörbom (1976a); and Werts *et al.* (1971, 1973).

[11] In fact, the effect of substantive complexity on perceptual flexibility is of approximately the same magnitude as its effect on ideational flexibility. But we cannot assess the reciprocal effect of perceptual flexibility on substantive complexity, because the 1964 and 1974 measures of perceptual flexibility are so highly correlated (at .96) that we encounter insuperable problems of multicollinearity.

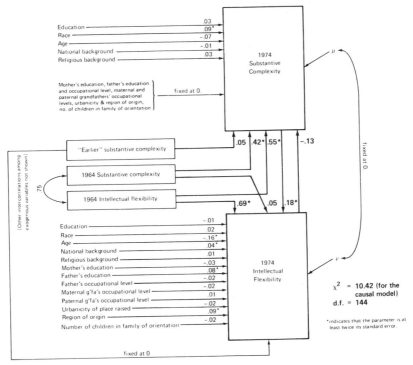

Figure 14.4. Reciprocal effects of substantive complexity and intellectual flexibility: full model; figures shown are standardized.

stantive complexity or intellectual flexibility. We thus include in the model the respondent's own age and level of education, parents' levels of education, father's occupational level, maternal and paternal grandfathers' occupational levels, race, national background and religious background, urbanicity and region of the country of the principal place where the respondent was raised, and even number of brothers and sisters.[12] We also include as exogenous variables the respondent's 1964 levels of substantive complexity and intellectual flexibility as well as the substantive complexity of his earlier (pre-1964) jobs.

[12] The indices of national background, region, and religious background are linear approximations to these nonlinear concepts. In our present use, these linearized indices represent slight underestimates of what would be shown in a more complicated dummy-variable analysis. The rationale for these linearizations is given in Schooler (1972, 1976). Essentially, all three indices are ordered in terms of environmental complexity: national background, on the basis of how long it has been since the social organization of the nation's agriculture passed beyond feudalism; region of the United States, on the basis of industrialization and expenditures for education; and religion, on the basis of fundamentalism.

For the model to be adequately identified, the direct effects of one or more exogenous variables on 1974 intellectual flexibility must be assumed to be zero; similarly, the direct effects of one or more exogenous variables on 1974 substantive complexity must also be assumed to be zero or some other specific value; otherwise there will be too little empirical information to solve the equations unequivocally.[13] Therefore, we posit that background characteristics that would not be interpreted as job credentials by employers (even by discriminatory employers) do not directly affect the substantive complexity of the 1974 job; these variables are thus used as instruments to identify the equation. The rationale is that these variables — maternal and paternal education, paternal occupational level, maternal and paternal grandfathers' occupational levels, urbanicity and region of origin, and number of children in the parental family — may very well have affected men's job placement earlier in their careers. By the time that men are at least 10 years into their careers, however, these variables should no longer have any direct effect on the substantive complexity of their jobs, certainly not when the substantive complexity of their 1964 and earlier jobs are statistically controlled. Similarly, we posit that the substantive complexity of earlier jobs should have no direct effect on the men's intellectual flexibility in 1974, when the substantive complexity of their 1964 and 1974 jos are statistically controlled.[14]

As Fig. 14.4 shows, a very important determinant of the substantive complexity of the jobs the men held in 1974 is of course the substantive complexity of the jobs they held 10 years before; an even more important determinant of their intellectual flexibility in 1974 is their intellectual flexibility at the earlier time. As we learned from the measurement models, both phenomena, particularly intellectual flexibility, are stable. Nevertheless, the

---

[13] In contemporaneous-effects models (and other "nonrecursive" models), the number of parameters to be estimated will be greater than the amount of information provided by the intercorrelations among the variables, unless some assumptions are imposed on the model, usually by setting some path(s) to zero. (Alternatively, one can impose other restrictions on the model, for example, as we have in fact done, by not allowing the residuals to be correlated.) The problem of insufficient information is generally referred to as the "identification" problem, and a variable used to help solve the identification problem is called an "instrument." For lucid discussions of this complex topic, see Duncan (1967, 1975, pp. 81–90); and Heise (1975, pp. 160–81). Still pertinent is Simon's (1957) now classic essay on the subject.

[14] These overidentifying restrictions raise a question as to whether the number of degrees of freedom computed by LISREL and presented in Figs. 14.4 and 14.5 is correct. Some contend that the correct number of degrees of freedom for an overidentified model based on a covariance matrix of "true scores" should exclude those degrees of freedom deriving from the overidentifying restrictions. We do not find this argument convincing. In any event, the number of degrees of freedom in structural equation models is important primarily for giving a comparative basis for evaluating the magnitudes of the χ^2s of alternative models. What really matters in making these comparative judgments is that the procedures be consistent.

reciprocal effects of substantive complexity and intellectual flexibility are considerable.

The effect of substantive complexity on intellectual flexibility is approximately one-fourth as great as the effect of men's 10-year earlier levels of intellectual flexibility. This effect is essentially contemporaneous:[15] The lagged path from 1964 substantive complexity to 1974 intellectual flexibility is a statistically nonsignificant .05, while the contemporaneous path from 1974 substantive complexity is a more substantial and statistically significant .18.

A path of .18 might not, in ordinary circumstances, be considered especially striking; but a continuing effect of this magnitude on so stable a phenomenon as intellectual flexibility is impressive, for the cumulative impact is much greater than the immediate effect at any one time. Continuing effects, even small-to-moderate continuing effects, on highly stable phenomena become magnified in importance. The effect of the substantive complexity of work on intellectual flexibility is especially noteworthy when we take into account that we are dealing with men no younger than 26 years of age, who are at least 10 years into their occupational careers.

The reciprocal effect of intellectual flexibility on substantive complexity is even more impressive — surpassing that of the substantive complexity of the 1964 job. This effect is entirely lagged; that is, it is the men's intellectual flexibility in 1964, not their contemporaneous flexibility, that significantly affects the substantive complexity of their 1974 jobs. The longitudinal analysis thus demonstrates something that no cross-sectional analysis could show — that over time, the relationship between substantive complexity and intellectual flexibility is truly reciprocal. The effect of substantive complexity on intellectual flexibility is more rapid: Current job demands affect current thinking processes. Intellectual flexibility, in contrast, has a delayed effect on substantive complexity: Current intellectual flexibility has scant effect on current job demands, but it will have a sizable effect on the further course of one's career. The cross-sectional analysis portrayed only part of this process, making it seem as if the relationship between the substantive complexity of work and psychological functioning were mainly unidirectional, with work affecting psychological functioning but not the reverse. The longitudinal analysis portrays a more intricate and more interesting, truly reciprocal process.

Have we somehow misspecified the equations, leaving out some impor-

[15] A cautionary note is in order here: Our analysis does not take into account the length of time the men have been in their present jobs; thus, all we mean by "contemporaneous" is that the effect results from the job currently held (for however long, short of 10 years), not from any previous job. A more exact appraisal of the timing of job effects would be exceedingly difficult to accomplish without measurements of both substantive complexity and intellectual flexibility at more frequent intervals than we have made.

tant variables that might alter the overall picture, or in some other way misconceived the true picture? Since structural models can never be "proved" (Duncan, 1975) but only compared with other plausible models, all reasonable alternatives must be considered.

One indication that the equations have not been seriously misspecified is that, if we allow the residuals for 1974 substantive complexity and intellectual flexibility to be correlated, the correlation proves to be nonsignificant and the estimates of all parameters remain essentially unchanged. Thus, it seems unlikely that some important variable affecting both substantive complexity and intellectual flexibility has been left out of the model. Moreover, the results do not depend on our choice of instruments, for using a variety of other instruments does not appreciably change the results. Nor do our findings result from the presence of statistically nonsignificant background variables in the model, for deleting the nonsignificant background variables from the predictive equations does not affect our conclusions. In particular, the effect of substantive complexity on intellectual flexibility is slightly strengthened by the deletion of background variables that do not have statistically significant effects. The model is robust, whatever reasonable modifications we try.

Finally, our findings do not result from having fixed the values of the measurement models before estimating the causal model (see Burt, 1973). We have confirmed the causal model by developing a "full-information method," in which both measurement and causal parameters are estimated simultaneously. This method confirms both the measurement models and the causal model depicted in Fig. 14.4. In particular, it shows the effect of substantive complexity on intellectual flexibility to be contemporaneous and of the same magnitude as previously shown. The effect of intellectual flexibility on substantive complexity is again shown to be lagged. The magnitude of this path, too, is exactly the same as in Fig. 14.4.

The one anomaly in the model shown in Fig. 14.4 and the corresponding full-information model is that the path from 1974 intellectual flexibility to 1974 substantive complexity is not just statistically nonsignificant; it is negative. Despite its statistical nonsignificance, the existence of such a negative path suggests a problem of multicollinearity (see Blalock, 1963; Farrar and Glauber, 1967; Gordon, 1968), probably resulting from the very high correlation ($r = .93$) between 1964 and 1974 intellectual flexibility. When we use indices of both 1964 and 1974 intellectual flexibility as independent variables vis-à-vis substantive complexity, we probably exaggerate the importance of 1964 intellectual flexibility while creating an artificially negative effect for 1974 intellectual flexibility. A proper assessment of the effect of intellectual flexibility on substantive complexity requires dropping the statistically nonsignificant contemporaneous path from the model. Similarly, a proper assessment of the effect of substantive complexity on intellectual flexibility requires dropping the statistically nonsignificant lagged path

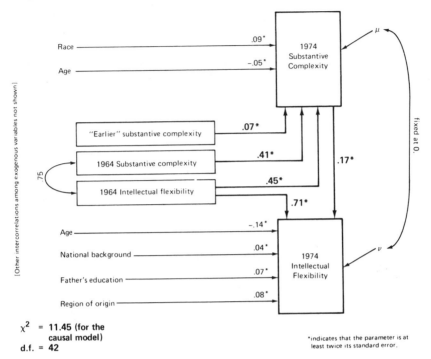

χ^2 = 11.45 (for the causal model)
d.f. = 42

*indicates that the parameter is at least twice its standard error.

Figure 14.5. Reciprocal effects of substantive complexity and intellectual flexibility: significant paths only; figures shown are standardized.

from the model. Therefore, in Fig. 14.5, we delete these (and all other) nonsignificant paths and reestimate the model. This, we believe, represents the most accurate assessment that can be made of the overall effects of substantive complexity and intellectual flexibility on each other.

This model shows the contemporaneous effect of substantive complexity on intellectual flexibility to be of virtually the same magnitude (a path of .17) as that shown in Fig. 14.4. Even with a slightly higher estimate of the stability of intellectual flexibility (at .71), the effect of substantive complexity on intellectual flexibility remains nearly one-fourth as great as that of the men's 10-year earlier levels of intellectual flexibility.

The lagged effect of intellectual flexibility on substantive complexity (a path of .45) is not quite so great as it appeared to be before we removed the nonsignificant negative contemporaneous path in Figure 14.4, but by any other standard it is very large. Intellectual flexibility surpasses even the substantive complexity of men's 1964 jobs as a determinant of the substantive complexity of their 1974 jobs.

As we did for the model depicted in Fig. 14.4, we have confirmed Figure 14.5 by developing a full-information method, in which measurement and causal parameters are simultaneously estimated.[16] All parameters of the measurement models for both substantive complexity and intellectual flexibility are very close to those shown in Figures 14.2 and 14.3, most of them nearly identical, none differing by more than .03. The causal model, too, is confirmed, the contemporaneous path from substantive complexity to intellectual flexibility being exactly as we had found it to be in Fig. 14.5 (.17), the lagged path from intellectual flexibility to substantive complexity being slightly lower (.41 versus .45). All other causal parameters are very close to those shown in Figure 14.5.

The data thus demonstrate beyond reasonable doubt what heretofore could be stated as only a plausible thesis buttressed by presumptive evidence — that the substantive complexity of men's work both considerably affects and is considerably affected by their intellectual flexibility.[17]

DISCUSSION

There are several limitations to the analyses reported in this chapter: some we hope to remedy in further analyses; the others may be beyond our ingenuity or the scope of our data.

One obvious limitation is that our analysis has been restricted thus far to

---

[16] The χ^2 for the full-information model comparable to Fig. 14.4 is 1035.23, with 546 degrees of freedom, for a ratio of 1.90, a remarkably good fit of model to data for so complex a model based on so large a number of cases. The χ^2 for the full-information model comparable to Figure 14.5 is nearly the same — 1036.68, with 548 degrees of freedom for a ratio of 1.89. Nothing is lost in the fit of model to data in simplifying the model.

[17] Although our primary interest is the reciprocal effects of substantive complexity and intellectual flexibility, the model is also instructive in telling us about the effects of social background on men's jobs and cognitive functioning in mid- and later career. By the time men are at least 10 years into their occupational careers, only race and age continue to have direct effects on the substantive complexity of their jobs; other aspects of social background have certainly affected the substantive complexity of earlier jobs, but by this career stage not even education has a statistically significant direct effect. Age is negatively related to 1974 substantive complexity when the complexity of prior jobs is statistically controlled. Since the correlation in 1964 was positive, this probably indicates that over the 10-year period, the younger men in the sample have been closing the gap. It is possible, however, that our finding reflects a curvilinear relationship between age and substantive complexity or a cohort effect. Similarly, the data suggest that blacks are catching up with whites in the substantive complexity of their jobs, probably a reflection of lessening discrimination (see Featherman and Hauser, 1976; Farley, 1977). In their effects on intellectual flexibility, age, national background, father's education, and region of origin (not education, race, size of parental family, or urbanicity) continue to be statistically significant when prior intellectual flexibility is statistically controlled. None of these variables, not even age, has so large an effect on intellectual flexibility as the substantive complexity of work.

substantive complexity and intellectual flexibility. In our further work, we intend to develop measurement models for other facets of occupational structure and other facets of psychological functioning. Our hope is ultimately to develop a causal model of the overall relationship between occupational structure and psychological functioning.

Second, the present analysis, as was true of all our previous analyses of occupational conditions, deals only with men. We are now analyzing data for women and intend in the near future to report on the relationship between women's occupational conditions and their psychological functioning.

A third limitation is that, although our measurement models take account of unreliability in indicators of the two central concepts, they have not dealt with possible unreliability of measurement for education, race, age, or any other aspect of social background. Our own data do not provide any solid basis for assessing reliability of measurement of these variables, and we are dubious about using reliability coefficients derived from other bodies of data as the basis for correcting correlations for attenuation. It would probably not make any real difference in the causal analysis. But without evidence, the issue must be left unresolved.

Fourth, conspicuously lacking in our treatment of these data is a systematic analysis of "career" patterns. We have treated prior jobs (and even the same job, held 10 years earlier) as if all series of jobs were equally continuous or discontinuous along some meaningful career line. But a more realistic conceptualization would have to take into account that some job changes represent logical progression in a meaningful sequence, while others represent shifts out of one career sequence, perhaps into another. We know of no really satisfactory way of dealing with this issue, despite early efforts by Wilensky (1961) and several more recent efforts by others (see Ladinsky, 1976) at classifying career patterns.

Fifth, both our measurement and causal models assume that relationships among variables are essentially the same for all segments of the work force. The assumption is obviously testable, and we hope to test it, although we recognize that a thorough assessment may require a much larger body of data than ours. It would be especially desirable to examine these models separately for workers at different ages and different stages of career.

Sixth, as must be apparent to the reader, changes in occupational circumstances are not the only ones that people experience in a 10-year interval: some marry, divorce, or become widowed; traumas and joyous events occur; these and other occurrences may exacerbate, mitigate, or deflect the processes our models depict. We have information about these events, but it is too early in the analytic process to tell whether the depth of the data and the size of the sample are adequate for analyzing the part they play in the ongoing process.

Despite these limitations, we believe that we have shown, more definitively than has ever been done before, that the relationship between occupational conditions and psychological functioning is reciprocal: People's occupational conditions both affect and are affected by their psychological functioning.

These findings come down solidly in support of those who see occupational conditions as affecting personality and in opposition to those who see the relationship between occupational conditions and personality as resulting solely from selective recruitment and job molding. We do not deny that personality has great importance in determining who enter what types of jobs and how they perform those jobs; in fact, our analyses underline the importance of these processes. But that has never been seriously at issue. What has been disputed is whether the reverse phenomenon — of job conditions molding personality — also occurs. The evidence of our study unequivocally supports the position that it does occur. Thus, our findings bear directly on an issue central to the field of social structure and personality — whether social-structural conditions affect personality only during childhood socialization or continue to do so throughout adulthood. Here is clear evidence that one important facet of social structure — the substantive complexity of work — directly affects adult personality.

In particular, this study adds to and helps specify the growing evidence that the structure of the environment has an important effect on cognitive development (see Rosenbaum, 1976) and that cognitive processes do not become impervious to environmental influence after adolescence or early adulthood but continue to show "plasticity" throughout the life span (see Baltes, 1968; Horn and Donaldson, 1976; Baltes and Schaie, 1976). Our findings reinforce this conclusion by showing that intellectual flexibility continues to be responsive to experience well into mid-career and probably beyond. In fact, the remarkable stability of intellectual flexibility appears to reflect, at least in part, stability in people's life circumstances. Intellectual flexibility is ever responsive to changes in the substantive complexity of people's work; for most people, though, the substantive complexity of work does not fluctuate markedly.

This study also demonstrates the importance of the impact of intellectual flexibility on substantive complexity. We think it noteworthy that this effect appears to be lagged rather than contemporaneous. The implication is that the structure of most jobs does not permit any considerable variation in the substantive complexity of the work: Job conditions are not readily modified to suit the needs or capacities of the individual worker. Over a long enough time, however — certainly over a period as long as 10 years — many men either modify their jobs or move on to others more consonant with their intellectual functioning. Thus, the long-term effects of intellectual flexibility on substantive complexity are considerable, even though the contemporaneous effects appear to be negligible.

Our models, of course, start in mid- or later career. There is every reason to believe that men's levels of intellectual flexibility in childhood, adolescence, and early adulthood might have had an important effect on their educational attainments, and our data show that educational attainment has had an extremely important effect on the substantive complexity of the early jobs in men's careers. Since such complexity is a primary determinant of the substantive complexity of later jobs, it seems safe to infer that intellectual flexibility's long-term, indirect effects on the complexity of later jobs is even greater than our analysis depicts.[18]

In the broadest sense, our findings support our general strategy for studying the relationship between social structure and personality. We have consistently argued that, in interpreting the relationship between social structure and individual psychological functioning, one should always ask how a person's position in the larger social structure affects the conditions of life that directly impinge on him (see Kohn, 1963, 1969, 1977; Kohn and Schooler, 1969, 1973; Schooler, 1972, 1976; see also Olsen, 1974). Thus, in attempting to interpret the relationship between social class and values and orientation, we saw class-correlated differences in occupational conditions as a potentially important bridge between position in the hierarchical ordering of society and conceptions of reality (Kohn, 1969; Kohn and Schooler, 1969). Substantive complexity is particularly important, for on the one hand the substantive complexity of work is closely linked to the job's location in the stratificational system, and on the other the substantive complexity of people's work is correlated with their values and orientation. Our past research demonstrated that the relationship between social class and values and orientation could reasonably be attributed, in large degree, to class-correlated differences in such occupational conditions as substantive complexity. But not even our two-stage least-squares analysis (Kohn and Schooler, 1973) demonstrated conclusively that substantive complexity has an actual causal effect on values, orientation, or any other psychological phenomenon. The present analysis buttresses our analytic strategy by showing that

---

[18] Our analysis thus has implications for that part of the process of social mobility left unanalyzed in most discussions — the paths from the occupational status of the first job to that of later jobs. The reciprocal relationship between substantive complexity and intellectual flexibility implies an internal dynamic by which relatively small differences in occupational status at early stages of a career may become magnified into larger differences later in the career. If two men of equivalent intellectual flexibility were to start their careers in jobs differing in substantive complexity, the man in the more complex job would be likely to outstrip the other in further intellectual growth. This in time would probably lead to his attainment of jobs of greater complexity, further affecting his intellectual growth. As a result, small differences in the substantive complexity of early jobs might lead to increasing differences in the substantive complexity of later jobs. Since substantive complexity is closely tied to occupational status, it is probable that differences in the status of the men's jobs wc-ld also be magnified by this process.

substantive complexity actually does have a causal impact on one pivotal aspect of psychological functioning, intellectual flexibility.

Admittedly, our research has not yet demonstrated that substantive complexity directly affects values or self-conception or social orientation — in fact, anything other than intellectual flexibility. Still, intellectual flexibility is the crucial test. Because of its remarkable stability, intellectual flexibility offers the most difficult challenge to the hypothesis that substantive complexity actually affects some important aspect of psychological functioning. Moreover, intellectual flexibility is tremendously important in its own right. Finally, we see intellectual flexibility as intimately related to values, self-conception, and social orientation. It is in fact an important link between social class and self-directed values and orientation (Kohn, 1969, pp. 186–187; Kohn and Schooler, 1969). Thus, demonstrating the causal impact of substantive complexity on intellectual flexibility gives us every reason to expect substantive complexity to have a causal impact on values and orientation, too. In our further analyses, we shall assess the hypothesized causal impact of substantive complexity — and of other structural imperatives of the job — on values, self-conception, and social orientation. For now, one crucial causal link in the relationship between social structure and psychological functioning has been conclusively demonstrated.

ACKNOWLEDGMENTS

A working draft of this chapter was reproduced and distributed in the Harvard–Yale Preprints in Mathematical Sociology series using moneys obtained under National Science Foundation grants nos. SOC76-24512 and SOC76-24394. This is a greatly revised version of a paper initially presented to the American Sociological Association at its 1976 convention in New York City. We are indebted to Frances Harris, Celia Homans, Carol Nie, and their colleagues at NORC for carrying out the surveys on which this chapter is based and coding the data of the follow-up survey; to Virginia Marbley, Margaret Renfors, Mimi Silberman, Pearl Slafkes, and Erma Jean Surman for invaluable technical and editorial assistance; to Bruce Roberts and Carrie Schoenbach for complex computer programming; to Robert M. Hauser for advice on measurement models; and to George W. Bohrnstedt, Otis Dudley Duncan, David R. Heise, Karl G. Jöreskog, William M. Mason, John Meyer, Joanne Miller, Karen Miller, Carrie Schoenbach, Ronald Schoenberg, and the AJS anonymous reviewers for constructive criticisms of earlier versions of this chapter. Most important, we are indebted to Duane F. Alwin for teaching us the concepts underlying confirmatory factor analysis, instructing us in the use of the ACOVS and LISREL computer programs, and making innumerable suggestions without which we might never have solved the intricate technical and theoretical problems encountered in developing the measurement models described in this chapter.

REFERENCES

Alwin, Duane F. "Making Inferences from Attitude-Behavior Correlations." *Sociometry* 36 (1973): 253–278.

Alwin, Duane F. "Attitude Scales as Congeneric Tests: A Re-Examination of an Attitude-Behavior Model." *Sociometry* 39 (1976): 377–383.

Baltes, Paul B. "Longitudinal and Cross-sectional Sequences in the Study of Age and Generation Effects." *Human Development* 11, no. 3 (1968): 145–171.

Baltes, Paul B., and Schaie, K. Warner. "On the Plasticity of Intelligence in Adulthood and Old Age." *American Psychologist* 31 (1976): 720–725.

Bielby, William T., Hauser, Robert M., and Featherman, David L. "Response Errors of Nonblack Males in Models of the Intergenerational Transmission of Socioeconomic Status." *American Journal of Sociology* 82 (1977): 1242–1288.

Blalock, Hubert M., Jr. "Correlated Independent Variables: The Problem of Multicollinearity." *Social Forces* 42 (1963): 233–237.

Blalock, Hubert M., Jr. "Path Coefficients versus Regression Coefficients." *American Journal of Sociology* 72 (1967): 675–676.

Blalock, Hubert, Jr. "Multiple Indicators and the Causal Approach to Measurement Error." *American Journal of Sociology* 75 (1969): 264–272.

Bohrnstedt, George W. "Observations on the Measurement of Change." In *Sociological Methodology 1969*, edited by Edgar F. Borgatta. San Francisco: Jossey-Bass, 1969.

Burt, Ronald S. "Confirmatory Factor-analytic Structures and the Theory Construction Process." *Sociological Methods and Research* 2 (1973): 131–190.

Burt, Ronald S. "Interpretational Confounding of Unobserved Variables in Structural Equation Models." *Sociological Methods and Research* 5 (1976): 3–52.

Costner, Herbert L., and Schoenberg, Ronald. "Diagnosing Indicator Ills in Multiple Indicator Models." In *Structural Equation Models in the Social Sciences*, edited by Arthur S. Goldberger and Otis Dudley Duncan. New York: Seminar, 1973.

Duncan, Otis Dudley. "Path Analysis: Sociological Examples." *American Journal of Sociology* 72 (1966): 1–16.

Duncan, Otis Dudley. "Some Linear Models for Two-Wave, Two-Variable Panel Analysis." *Psychological Bulletin* 72 (1969): 177–182.

Duncan, Otis Dudley. *Introduction to Structural Equation Models*. New York: Academic Press, 1975.

Duncan, Otis Dudley, Haller, Archibald O., and Portes, Alejandro. "Peer Influences on Aspirations: A Reinterpretation." *American Journal of Sociology* 74 (1968): 119–137.

Farley, Reynolds. "Trends in Racial Inequalities: Have the Gains of the 1960s Disappeared in the 1970s?" *American Sociological Review* 42 (1977): 189–208.

Farrar, Donald E., and Glauber, Robert R. "Multicollinearity in Regression Analysis: The Problem Revisited." *Review of Economics and Statistics* 49 (1967): 92–107.

Featherman, David L., and Hauser, Robert M. "Changes in the Socioeconomic Stratification of the Races, 1962–73." *American Journal of Sociology* 82 (1976): 621–651.

Gordon, Robert A. "Issues in Multiple Regression." *American Journal of Sociology* 73 (1968): 592–616.

Hauser, Robert M., and Goldberger, Arthur S. "The Treatment of Unobservable Variables in Path Analysis." In *Sociological Methodology 1971*, edited by Herbert L. Costner. San Francisco: Jossey-Bass, 1971.

Heise, David R. "Separating Reliability and Stability in Test-Retest Correlation." *American Sociological Review* 34 (1969): 93–101, and this volume.

Heise, David R. "Causal Inference from Panel Data." In *Sociological Methodology 1970*, edited by Edgar F. Borgatta. San Francisco: Jossey-Bass, 1970.

Heise, David R. *Causal Analysis.* New York: Wiley, 1975.

Heise, David R., and Bohrnstedt, George W. "Validity, Invalidity, and Reliability." In *Sociological Methodology 1970,* edited by Edgar F. Borgatta. San Francisco: Jossey-Bass, 1970.

HEW Task Force. *Work in America: Report of a Special Task Force to the Secretary of Health, Education, and Welfare.* Cambridge, Mass.: M.I.T. Press, 1973.

Horn, John L., and Donaldson, Gary. "On the Myth of Intellectual Decline in Adulthood." *American Psychologist* 31 (1976): 701–719.

Jöreskog, Karl G. "A General Approach to Confirmatory Maximum Likelihood Factor Analysis." *Psychometrika* 34 (1969): 183–202.

Jöreskog, Karl G. "A General Method for Analysis of Covariance Structures." *Biometrika* 57, no. 2 (1970): 239–51.

Jöreskog, Karl G. "Analysis of Covariance Structures." In *Multivariate Analysis-III,* edited by Paruchuri R. Krishnaiah. New York: Academic Press, 1973(a).

Jöreskog, Karl G. "A General Method for Estimating a Linear Structural Equation System." In *Structural Equation Models in the Social Sciences,* edited by Arthur S. Goldberger and Otis Dudley Duncan. New York: Seminar, 1973(b).

Jöreskog, Karl G. "Structural Equation Models in the Social Sciences: Specification, Estimation, and Testing." In *Proceedings of the Symposium on Applications of Statistics,* edited by Paruchuri R. Krishnaiah. New York: Academic Press, 1977.

Jöreskog, Karl G., Gruvaeus, Gunnar T., and van Thillo, Marielle. "ACOVS: A General Computer Program for Analysis of Covariance Structures." Research Bulletin 70-15. Princeton, N.J.: Educational Testing Service, 1970.

Jöreskog, Karl G., and Sörbom, D. "Statistical Models and Methods for Analysis of Longitudinal Data." In *Latent Variables in Socioeconomic Models,* edited by D. J. Aigner and A. S. Goldberger. Amsterdam: North-Holland, 1976(a).

Jöreskog, Karl G. and Sörbom, D. "Statistical Models and Methods for Test-Retest Situations." In *Advances in Psychological and Educational Measurement,* edited by D. N. M. deGruijter, L. J. Th. van der Kamp, and H. F. Crombag. New York: Wiley, 1976(b).

Jöreskog, Karl G., and van Thillo, Marielle. "LISREL: A General Computer Program for Estimating a Linear Structural Equation System Involving Multiple Indicators of Unmeasured Variables." Research Bulletin 72–56. Princeton, N.J.: Educational Testing Service, 1972.

Kohn, Melvin L. "Social Class and Parent–Child Relationships: An Interpretation." *American Journal of Sociology* 68 (1963): 471–480.

Kohn, Melvin L. *Class and Conformity: A Study in Values.* Homewood, Ill.: Dorsey, 1969.

Kohn, Melvin L. "Occupational Structure and Alienation." *American Journal of Sociology* 82 (1976): 111–130.

Kohn, Melvin L. "Reassessment, 1977." In *Class and Conformity: A Study in Values.* 2d ed. Chicago: University of Chicago Press.

Kohn, Melvin L., and Schooler, Carmi. "Class, Occupation and Orientation." *American Sociological Review* 34 (1969): 659–678.

Kohn, Melvin L., and Schooler, Carmi. "Occupational Experience and Psychological Functioning: An Assessment of Reciprocal Effects." *American Sociological Review* 38 (1973): 97–118.

Ladinsky, Jack. "Notes on the Sociological Study of Careers." Paper presented at an SSRC Conference on Occupational Careers Analysis, Greensboro. N.C., March 26–28, 1976.

Lord, F. M., and Novick, M. R. *Statistical Theories of Mental Test Scores.* Reading, Mass.: Addison-Wesley, 1968.

Mason, William M., Hauser, Robert M., Kerckhoff, Alan C., Poss, Sharon Sando-
mirsky, and Manton, Kenneth. "Models of Response Error in Student Reports of
Parental Socioeconomic Characteristics." In *Schooling and Achievement in American
Society*, edited by William H. Sewell, Robert M. Hauser, and David L. Featherman.
New York: Academic Press, 1976.

Olsen, Nancy J. "Family Structure and Socialization Patterns in Taiwan." *American Journal of Sociology* 79 (1974): 1395–1417.

Otto, Luther B., and Featherman, David L. "Social Structural and Psychological
Antecedents of Self-Estrangement and Powerlessness." *American Sociological Review* 40 (1975): 701–19.

Rosenbaum, James E. *Making Inequality: The Hidden Curriculum of High School
Tracking*. New York: Wiley, 1976.

Schooler, Carmi. "Social Antecedents of Adult Psychological Functioning."
American Journal of Sociology 78 (1972): 229–322.

Schooler, Carmi. "Serfdom's Legacy: An Ethnic Continuum." *American Journal of
Sociology* 81 (1976): 1265–1286.

Simon, Herbert A. "Causal Ordering and Identifiability." In *Models of Man: Social
and Rational*, edited by Herbert A. Simon. New York: Wiley, 1957.

Sörbom, Dag. "Detection of Correlated Errors in Longitudinal Data." *British
Journal of Mathematical and Statistical Psychology* 28 (1975): 138–151.

Spaeth, Joe L. "Characteristics of the Work Setting and the Job as Determinants
of Income." In *Schooling and Achievement in American Society*, edited by William H.
Sewell, Robert M. Hauser, and David L. Featherman. New York: Academic Press,
1976.

Sudman, Seymour, and Feldman, Jacob J. "Sample Design and Field Proce-
dures." Appendix 1 in *Volunteers for Learning: A Study of the Educational Pursuits of
American Adults*, edited by John W. C. Johnstone and Ramon J. Rivera. Chicago:
Aldine, 1965.

Werts, Charles E., Jöreskog, Karl G., and Linn, Robert L. "Identification and
Estimation in Path Analysis with Unmeasured Variables." *American Journal of Sociology* 78 (1973): 1469–1484.

Werts, Charles E., Linn, Robert L., and Jöreskog, Karl G. "Estimating the Parameters of Path Models Involving Unmeasured Variables." In *Causal Models in the Social
Sciences*, edited by Hubert M. Blalock, Jr. New York: Aldine-Atherton, 1971.

Wheaton, Blair, Muthen, Bengt, Alwin, Duane F., and Summers, Gene F. "Assessing Reliability and Stability in Panel Models." In *Sociological Methodology 1977*,
edited by David R. Heise. San Francisco: Jossey-Bass, 1977.

Wilensky, Harold L. "Orderly Careers and Social Participation: The Impact of
Work History on Social Integration in the Middle Mass." *American Sociological Review* 26 (1961): 521–539.

Witkin, H. A., Dyk, R. B., Faterson, H. F., Goodenough, D. R., and Karp,
S. A. *Psychological Differentiation: Studies of Development*. New York: Wiley, 1962.

Author Index

Subject Index